ACTING FOR SINGERS

ACTING FOR SINGERS

CREATING BELIEVABLE SINGING CHARACTERS

DAVID F. OSTWALD

UNIVERSITY PRESS

2005

OXFORD
UNIVERSITY PRESS

Oxford University Press, Inc., publishes works that further
Oxford University's objective of excellence
in research, scholarship, and education.

Oxford   New York
Auckland   Cape Town   Dar es Salaam   Hong Kong   Karachi
Kuala Lumpur   Madrid   Melbourne   Mexico City   Nairobi
New Delhi   Shanghai   Taipei   Toronto

With offices in
Argentina   Austria   Brazil   Chile   Czech Republic   France   Greece
Guatemala   Hungary   Italy   Japan   Poland   Portugal   Singapore
South Korea   Switzerland   Thailand   Turkey   Ukraine   Vietnam

Published by Oxford University Press, Inc.
198 Madison Avenue, New York, New York, 10016
www.oup.com

Oxford is a registered trademark of Oxford University Press

Library of Congress Cataloging-in-Publication Data

Ostwald, David, 1943—
  Acting for singers : creating believable singing characters /
David F. Ostwald.
      p.   cm.
  Includes bibliographical references and index.
    ISBN-13 978-019-514540-3
    ISBN 0-19-514540-2
  1. Acting—Study and teaching. 2. Singing—Instruction
and study. I. Title.
  MT956.O76 2005
  792.502′8—dc22   2004016592

9   8   7   6   5   4   3   2   1

Printed in the United States of America
on acid-free paper

"[My gestures] must always be the authentic product of the moment. Nevertheless, essential though this logical spontaneity is, the most important prerequisite of an actor (opera singers *are* actors) is to identify with the character, as created by the composer and the librettist. . . .

"The art of music is so enormous that it can envelope you and keep you in a state of almost perpetual anxiety and torture. But it is not all in vain. It is an honor and great happiness to serve music with humility and love."

Maria Callas

Quoted in *Maria Callas: Sacred Monster* by Stelios Galatopoulos

"The actor must first of all believe in everything that takes place on the stage, and most of all he must believe in what he himself is doing. And one can believe only in the truth. Therefore it is necessary to feel the truth at all times, to know how to find it, and for this it is inescapable to develop one's artistic sensitivity to the truth."

Constantin Stanislavski

My Life in Art

PREFACE

Acting for Singers was sparked by an innocent question from a colleague, Philip Bayles, some years ago. He pointed out that while directing I often gave the singers nuggets of advice about acting, each of which I handed on as "one of The First Ten Rules of Acting, All of Which Are First." When he asked whether I could give him a list of all ten, I knew immediately that I couldn't. I was neither sure how many rules there really were nor what they all might be.

Philip's question stuck with me as I continued to teach acting to singers, first at the Juilliard School and later as head of the Opera Program at the State University of New York at Purchase, and as I directed operas and plays both in regional companies and in academia. Gradually, it became clear to me that the heart of effective acting-singing is believability, and that what I now call Ten Maxims of Believable Acting all contribute to that end. These maxims, which are listed in the introduction and in appendix 1, became the launching pad of this book.

I would like to acknowledge the many people who helped bring this book into being. First of all I want to thank all the students and performers with whom it has been my pleasure to work and who taught me with their questions. I want to thank Stan Washburn for the drawings which accompany the exercises in chapter 14, the master yoga teacher Alan Bateman, who gave me permission to use them, and Rhoda Levine for her provocative thoughts and for exercise 4 in chapter 3, and to Birgitte Moyer-Vinding for her tireless proofreading. My thanks also to all my professional colleagues, especially Sylvia Anderson, Wesley Balk, Philip Bayles, Rachmael ben Avram, Ruth Bierhoff, Janet Bookspan, Anne Kish, Doris Kasloff, Matthias Kuntzsch, and Richard Woitach, who generously shared their knowledge with me. And to all those friends and colleagues—including Skye Alexander, Robert Caldwell, Angene Feeves, Judy Hubbell, Ora Lerman, Perry-Lynn Moffitt, Anne Mendelson, Ian Strasfogel, and Stan and Andrea Washburn—who gave helpful advice and support through the many years during which this book was written, may I say, "Without you this book could not have come to fruition."

CONTENTS

ACTING FOR SINGERS

Introduction

Are you a singer who would like to be a better performer? Would you like to integrate your singing with believable acting? Are you a teacher who coaches singers how to interpret roles or to become more stageworthy? *Acting for Singers* can help.

This book is the outgrowth of my several decades of hands-on experience in music-theater, both as a teacher of acting for singers and opera history and as a director of plays, musicals, and operas. It is based on the premise that good acting singing is believable acting singing, and it recognizes that singing even without acting is enormously complex. It acknowledges that the music expresses each character's feelings and controls the rate at which those feelings unfold.

At the same time, in the four-hundred-year-old controversy about whether opera is primarily a musical or a dramatic form, *Acting for Singers* sides with the dramatic. It assumes, with the Renaissance masters who developed opera as a re-creation of Greek tragedy, that opera is about telling a story by combining singing and acting. Like Monteverdi, Gluck, Mozart, Wagner, Verdi, Puccini, Britten, and Menotti, it envisions opera as a theater form in which singing, orchestral music, acting, text, and spectacle are inextricably interwoven.

The foundation of the book is the principles I call "Ten Maxims of Believable Singing Acting." These ten nuggets distill years of experience that have convinced me that the way to guarantee the members of your audience the fulfilling experience they desire—which I believe is the goal of an actor-singer—is both to gratify their aesthetic sensibilities and to touch their feelings. The first requires that—supported by the conductor, director, choreographer, designers, and fellow singers—you interpret each work beautifully to illuminate its full potential. The second requires that you arouse the audience members' empathy, which is done most effectively by creating characters who seem believable. The ten maxims also help you to meld the personality and motivations of your character with your vocal interpretations and enable you to behave *as if* you are in your character's situation.

Ten Maxims of Believable Singing Acting

• Your characters believe they're real people.

They don't think of themselves as "characters." Most often they don't know that they are singing and, even if they do, they always have their own internal dialogues running constantly in their heads.

• Your music is your characters' feelings (and vice-versa).

The composer has interpreted the characters' feelings in the music. Let the music guide you to the feelings that motivate your characters' actions and to the nuances of their responses. Look to it as the primary source of your characters' internal dialogue.

• All humans have a common reservoir of feelings.

Different people may react to the same situation differently, but each of us has the same spectrum of feelings—from hatred to love, despair to ecstasy. Therefore, you have in you the potential to portray all the feelings you need for any role. By the same token, each member of your audience has the potential to empathize with all of your characters' feelings.

• You are always you.

Each of us has our own body, voice, and personal history. Don't try to deny who you are; rather, transform yourself by selecting which traits to emphasize and which to downplay.

• If you don't let it show, the audience can't know.

Audiences read actions, not minds; so you must *allow* your characters' thoughts and feelings to be manifested physically. Remember, however, that the audience will assume that every action you make is an expression of your *characters'* thoughts and feelings.

• You are making art.

Since art is created by humans to communicate feelings and ideas, you can count on the fact that every character is created for a reason. You can figure out that reason and use your understanding to interpret your roles. In addition, since you are engaged in bringing to life the artistic creations of others, everything you do in a performance at least on some level of consciousness is an interpretation. Acknowledging that you are an interpretive artist leads you away from the destructive judgments of "right" and "wrong" that bedevil most performers and toward the constructive question "Am I being clear?"

• Believable characters engage your audiences.

When audience members believe you as your character, they identify with you. Once they identify, they extend their empathy; then they are available for you to arouse their feelings and to move them. This is equally true whether your character is a person in an opera or musical or the "I" of a song or lied.

• You make your characters believable by endowing them with convincing, apparently spontaneous, re-creations of real human behavior.

The audience knows that you have rehearsed, but they don't want to feel that your characters have.

• Play the minutiae of what is really happening.

You will seem spontaneous if you respond as your character to even the smallest things your colleagues sing or do as their characters.

• Never try to repeat results.

When you focus on the details of a past success, your mind cannot be engaged in the present; you lose the sense of spontaneity, and your performances take on a mechanical unconvincing quality. Focus instead on revivifying the sources of your characters' actions and feelings as developed in the rehearsal process; respond in the present, and you will achieve a new—and subtly different—success.

* * *

Acting for Singers equips you to solve the acting-singing problem from three different perspectives. First, it gives you a map of the realm of live performance in which acting singing takes place. This realm is a province of the world of art. It is populated by artists like yourself and the people who are your audience. Audiences enter the performance realm prepared to suspend disbelief. They are prepared to accept the stage world as an authentic one, singing as normal behavior, and characters and their circumstances as real. As suggested in the Maxims, with a little help from you in the form of a believable characterization, they will see everything you do, every thought you manifest, as an expression of your character; they will tacitly assume that by accepting each separate action as meaningful, they will ultimately be able to assemble all those bits of information into a coherent picture.

Second, this book guides you to believable interpretations and characterizations. The path can be described in nine words: "Behave *as if* you are in your character's situation." Each chapter of this book addresses some step of the process, presenting a sequence of instructions that focus on how to analyze your characters and their situations, how to step into those situations using nothing more than imagination, and how to allow your body to move intuitively "in character."

Third, this book helps you past many of the technical traps that are intrinsic to acting and singing at the same time. For instance, it shows you how to create an internal dialogue onto which you can fuse both the vocal and emotional demands of your character, so that you don't feel torn between them. It instructs you how to scale your performance believably to the appropriate size, so that you do not have to choose between being believable and filling the performing space. It also helps you skirt the borders of those personal performing quagmires that so very often form around fears and self-doubts. And, for those unhappy occasions when you find yourself trapped in one, it offers a variety of rescue techniques, including ways of improving your ability to trust yourself and your colleagues.

Using This Book

Use the book in chapter-by-chapter sequence or jump around, focusing on those chapters dealing with problems that you find vexing. Use it in a class, in a group, or by yourself. However, since listening to and interacting with your colleagues are so crucial to believable acting singing, you will benefit from at least occasionally having a working partner. Each chapter contains information from all three perspectives discussed in the previous section. Each chapter ends with exercises—some of which you can do by yourself and some you can do with a partner or group.

Part I maps out why believable characters are so crucial to the whole music-theater endeavor, and gives you the basic tools with which to create them. It addresses how most usefully to think through the circumstances in which the librettist and composer have placed your character, and how to enter those circumstances using your own imagination and improvisation.

Part II focuses on the nitty-gritty of creating a character. It helps you dissect a score to reveal the kinds of information that you need to motivate your characters. It explains how to examine the basic skeleton of music-theater pieces and investigates large structures like the dramatic theme. Then, guiding you through an examination of smaller details, it helps you develop a central line for your character, motivations for each scene, and, ultimately, motivations for each individual phrase and action.

Part III supports you in the process of bringing together all your performing skills— in auditions, rehearsals, and in performances. It focuses on the vexing questions of how to remain believable in all venues and styles.

* * *

The acting terms used in this book are in common usage in the United States, but some are not universal. The term "super-objective" (also known as a "through-line of action") describes the compelling need that drives each character through a piece. What a character really means or feels about what he says or sings is quite commonly referred to as "subtext"; I have extended the idea of subtext to those moments when a character is not singing or talking either because he has musical interludes between his singing or because he is listening, suggesting that he (like the rest of us) has a continuous internal voice that I call an "internal dialogue." To help clarify my discussion I have used "subtext" for that part of the internal dialogue that has text and "internal thoughts" for that part that does not.

No established term seems to cover not only operas, operettas, musicals (known as musical theater), and vocal recitals, but also other forms that involve singing and acting together, such as the newer forms of performance art. "Music-theater" is in increasing use, and, lacking anything better, I have adopted the term.

PART I

BELIEVABILITY: THE TERRITORY AND THE TOOLS

Part I lays out the tools you use to be believable. It shows you how to define your character's situation most usefully, how to use the "Magical *if*" to enter it, and how to improve your concentration. It explores how improvising can help you to use yourself naturally and believably in imaginary situations and how to make your singing expressive of your character.

CHAPTER 1

The Divine Marriage:
Combining Believable Acting with Expressive Singing

Being Believable as Your Character

When you perform, you want to move your audiences by communicating all the nuances of the music, ideas, and feelings of each piece. You will succeed if you are believable as your character, because believability is the magic key with which you unlock the audience's empathy. When audience members empathize with your character, they open the floodgates of their feelings; they are moved.

You are believable when you appear to be in your character's situation— when you seem to be inventing the music and words as spontaneous responses to what the character is experiencing. This requires that you understand every word that you sing and that is sung to you and that you make the connections between your thoughts, your feelings, your breathing, and your body that we do in real life.

As an actor-singer you will create this complete believability most successfully if you think of your voice as an evocative acting tool. Think of beautiful singing as an outpouring of your character's feelings.

Believability is the key to empathy, and empathy is the key to success.

Acting Actions

Audiences don't read minds, they read the physical clues that you give them— visible and audible actions. They enter your character's world by interpreting what you *do* with your voice, face, and body.

Imagine, for instance, that you are playing Alfredo in *La Traviata*. You are at the moment when you read Violetta's devastating note telling you that she has left you. Let's say you do nothing. You stand still, not moving a muscle, not uttering a sound, without a thought in your mind. Since whatever audiences can see or hear—the flicker of an eye, a barely audible sigh—they interpret as meaningful, they may take your non-action to mean you are stunned by your loss, but they are only guessing.

Now allow yourself to feel Alfredo's love for Violetta, and the wrenching loss that he experiences. Unconsciously, you will change your facial expression, shift the way you stand, and perhaps you will gesture. With these physical actions, you give the audience concrete information they will use to enter into your character's thoughts and feelings.

Go a step further. Imagine that you are so deeply involved that your feelings cause you to utter sounds. This action gives the audience still more specific clues to Alfredo's feelings. Verdi's choice of an outburst on a high A-flat accompanied by a fortissimo tremolo in the strings helps evoke both your shock and your heart-wrenching pain.

When you immerse yourself in your character's circumstances so that what he must sing and do seems not just logical but inevitable, you can let your outward bodily movements spring from your own internal impulses and feelings. Working this way, you will choose evocative and believable actions unconsciously, by intuition. You are rescued from the awkward situation of *trying* to act—placing your hands in a certain position, making a specific gesture, "putting on" a particular emotion. Instead, you have rich, complex, appropriate feelings leading to integrated gestures that create a believable character.

The more deeply you immerse yourself into your character's situation, the more expressive your choices will be—assuming that you allow your expressive impulses to be manifested, that you *allow* yourself to be transparent. Until you were about two, like all small children you allowed your thoughts and feelings to parade across your face without censorship; you were perfectly transparent. Then, like all of us, you learned to hide your feelings; you protected yourself. When you perform, ideally you temporarily drop your protective armor and reconnect with your natural expressiveness.

If you don't let it show, the audience can't know.

As the example from *La Traviata* suggests, characters' actions, like our own, very often are motivated by their feelings. This is particularly true of singing characters because music's special strength is the evocation of feelings. (This idea is explored further in chapter 6.) Even Figaro in *The Barber of Seville*, who seems like an unflappable, happy-go-lucky person and therefore might be a possible counterexample, sings almost exclusively about his feelings. In his famous entrance aria, "Largo al factotum," he sings about the pleasures of his profession. When Rosina outwits him, he sings about his astonishment. In the finale, when the Count and Rosina dally, he sings about his impatience, fear, and anger. His unruffled demeanor is merely a manifestation of his self-confidence.

Similarly, if you examine the "cool" gang members in *West Side Story*, you will discover they are brimming with feelings—including pride, hatred, fear, and even compassion. Indeed, their very need to seem "cool" is driven by the heat of very strong feelings.

In the theater, it's "cool" to be hot.

Acting Feelings

Ironically, although feelings are the main channel of communication between you and your audience, you cannot act them directly, because feelings are not actions. You cannot "do" love, hate, jealousy, or joy. You can, however, do the actions of a person who has a particular feeling. To portray love, you can play with, look at, or caress someone; you can tease, smile, laugh, cuddle, touch, or kiss. Similarly, if you want to portray happiness you can smile, laugh, tease, play, run, jump, skip, twirl, or sing.

Any single action can be ambiguous. (Notice how the list of loving actions overlaps with that of happy ones.) But if you do several actions, the audience can usually deduce what you are feeling. Since words are less ambiguous than body language, if you add the actions of speaking or singing, you help the audience understand your feelings with greater certainty.

Acting Technically; Acting Intuitively

There are essentially two different approaches to generating the actions with which you portray your character's thoughts and feelings. One is to use your imagination and empathy to enter your character's situation and allow your body to react intuitively (as just discussed in "Acting Actions"). The other is to figure out what a person with your character's mindset might appropriately do in analogous real-life situations and then intentionally re-create those actions without necessarily involving your own feelings. This is often called "technical" acting, or mimicry.

Both approaches present challenges. For the first, you have to analyze your character's situation very clearly and allow yourself to enter it. For the second, you need to develop exquisite control of your face and body and extremely good concentration. You also have to become an astute observer of human behavior to create characters who are unique individuals rather than generalized stereotypes. In spite of these difficulties, mimicry is extremely useful for those moments when you absolutely have to focus on your singing technique. With practice you can make appropriate mimicked behavior for such passages believable.

You can also blend the two approaches. You can generate your character's behavior by immersing yourself in her situation, and then use what you discover for mimicry that you produce more technically. As long as you appear to be in your character's situation and your responses appear to be spontaneously motivated from within, use whichever technique works best for you. In reality, many good American actor-singers use a shifting mix of brief moments of mimicry interspersed between longer passages of intuitive acting.

Grounding Your Acting in Hardwired Human Behavior

To be believable, you need to make your characters function the way real people do on the physical, emotional, and psychological levels. Our basic human mechanism includes six hardwired behaviors that are particularly essential to incorporate. When you successfully immerse yourself in your characters' situations, they automatically will be part of what you do without conscious effort. If, however, you are still struggling to get into a character or if you prefer to use technical acting, be sure to incorporate these behaviors:

- Your mind is always in gear.
- Every action begins with an impulse.
- Change attracts your attention.
- Consciously, you do only one thing at a time.
- You never repeat yourself exactly.
- You improvise your way through life.

• • •

Your mind is always in gear.

You may not give it much conscious attention, but at every waking second the brain is processing the input it receives from the senses, passing it through the filters of your personality and previous experiences to fit this input into understandable patterns as part of a continuous attempt to make sense of the world.

If you want to vividly experience this process, imagine yourself in a threatening situation. Think of walking in a dangerous part of town or getting caught out in the woods at night. Suddenly you are aware of how acutely you sense every noise, smell, touch, or visual clue and how urgently your brain is working to interpret them all.

One particularly human manifestation of this attempt to understand is the little voice inside your head that is always chattering away, creating an internal dialogue about you—who you are, what you are doing, and how you feel about it.

Your characters also always have their minds in gear. They, too, are trying to make sense of their worlds. As part of that process, they, too, have running internal dialogues. Indeed, one of the most potent things you can do to make your characters believable is to create internal dialogues for them.

. . .

Every action begins with an impulse.

All actions start as impulses from the brain. When something happens around you, you perceive it through your senses, which transmit messages to your brain. Then, in a series of choices that are normally unconscious, the brain processes the information. It sends a response, via the nervous system, down the spine and out to part(s) of the body, where you translate it into actions using your voluntary muscles.

To be believable as a character, you need to reproduce this process. You need to behave as if everything you do—actions, vocal utterances, even your voluntary singing or speaking breaths—is a spontaneous response by your character to something he perceives rather than something that you as a performer have rehearsed. You need to:

• See, hear, or feel any change in your surroundings *before* you react to it. It is all too easy to anticipate your character's reactions, to flinch before the sound of the gun firing. After all, you as a performer already know, at least in a general way, what is going to happen.

• Interpret all input from your character's viewpoint and choose your responses, whether verbal or physical, so they are appropriate for him.

• Reproduce the way the human behavioral brew boils in reality by starting each response with an impulse that expresses your character's intention.

You see a friend smile as you hear her say, in a warm tone of voice, "You gave a wonderful performance last night." You process that visual and aural input and are filled with good feelings that translate into the impulse to want to thank her. That impulse goes simultaneously to your breathing apparatus, where it is manifested as an in-breath, and to your mouth, tongue, lips, cheek muscles, larynx, and vocal cords, where it is manifested as a smile and the words "Thank you" on an out-breath.

Naturally, this description pertains only to breaths you take to make an intentional sound. Breaths that sustain your life processes are a function of the autonomic nervous system and are not linked to thoughts or feelings. "Catch breaths" are also an exception. When you take a quick breath in mid-phrase to sustain your singing, the motivating impulse is your need as a performer for more air. However, you can remain believable as your character if you fill your catch breath with a reinforcement of the impulse that initially inspired the phrase.

• • •

Change attracts your attention.

You can't help it. Humans go on alert when their senses detect change. The larger or the more sudden the change, the more surely it will capture your conscious attention. You can choose to filter out small changes, but large ones—like a car crash outside your window—are almost impossible to ignore.

On stage, it is the unfolding details of the other performer's behaviors that your character's antennae will be constantly sensing. Even though those changes may be brought about by the imaginary circumstances of the plot, your partners' actions are real and concrete. If one of your partners smiles, the corners of her mouth really do move upward. When in the third act of *Carmen* you hear Carmen tell you, as José, to go back to your mother, the variations in pitch, rhythm, dynamics, tempo, and vocal color in her voice and the changes in her body language and facial expression are really there for you to hear and see and to be the basis for your reactions. Of course, you react *as if* you are your character.

When you react to changes stimulated by stage effects, such as sound effects or changes in lighting, you will be believable only if you behave as your character might, and *as if* these stage effects *are* the thing they are supposed to represent.

Naturally, you should try to react only to those stimuli that are supposed to be part of your character's reality. If a stagehand accidentally drops a chair backstage, you may hear it, but your character doesn't.

Our human sensitivity to change coupled with our natural impulse to make sense of all the stimuli we receive is summed up in the famous dictum: "Acting is reacting."

• • •

Consciously, you only do one thing at a time.

In any given millisecond, you give your conscious attention to only one thing—that's all any human can. When you think you are doing two things at once, like reading and watching television, you are actually rapidly switching your conscious attention back and forth between your book and the TV.

It is this limitation that requires that you first practice your singing and acting separately. Only after you achieve some control over each can you effectively practice doing them together. Then you need to rehearse until the combined technical demands of a role become semiautomatic. Otherwise, they will still be demanding your conscious attention when you perform, and the audience will see you struggling with your technique rather than experiencing your character living her reality.

For the same reason, you will be most effective in believably evoking all the facets of a complex character if you express them one at a time. If your character is confused but defiant, don't try to evoke both at once. Rather, do actions that are evocative first of one feeling and then the other. You can, of course, move back and forth between them.

• • •

You never repeat yourself exactly.

You may think that you can say or do something exactly the same way more than once, but you can't. No one can. You may repeat yourself in a way that is *similar*, but it will not be *identical*, because variation is simply another part of our human nature.

You can observe this trait by examining your signature. No matter how similar it looks each time you write it, if you study it closely, you will see that it is never identical.

Once you are aware that every repetition is actually a unique variation, you will be on your way to animating every repeated phrase that you sing. You will wonder why your character has to say the same thing more than once; you will want to explore what your character needs to express but hasn't yet been able to fully articulate or what she wants but still has not gotten. You will also become open to receiving the subtle nuances in all you see and hear as you are performing. Knowing that each performance is different, you will sharpen your awareness of how the gesture or inflection that your partner did yesterday is different today.

.   .   .

You improvise your way through life.

When you are talking, you don't usually practice your words in your head before you say them; so how do you know what to say? You improvise!

In a process that is normally unconscious, people choose their words on the basis of a combination of the input they receive (as filtered through their individual situation and personality) and what they *want*. When we have the impulse to say something, we inhale with the feeling of our response, and then make up our actual words as we go along.

We modify the words we choose and the way we say them depending on the reactions of the people to whom we are talking. We assess their reactions by assembling many clues—including verbal responses, facial expressions, eye movements, body language, and even smell. (Naturally, our listeners are also reading our behavior, which helps shape their responses.)

For instance, you are a girl desperately eager to patch up a terrible fight you have had with your boyfriend. You decide to call up and apologize. Since it is so important, you do plan your words in advance: "I'm terribly sorry; it was all my fault." But what do you end up saying if, as soon as he answers, he says, "Oh, I'm so glad you called; the whole fight was really my fault"? What do you say if he yells, "Don't you dare try to soften me up with an apology"?

In daily life, you choose not just your words but also your gestures and actions using the same process. Whether you are talking, eating, reading, driving, or getting ready for bed, you begin with a sense of what you want and choose actions that are improvised responses to what you get. When you couple this awareness with the knowledge that you never repeat yourself exactly and incorporate these insights in your performances, you will seem to be behaving spontaneously. Of all the attributes that make characters believable, the appearance of spontaneity is probably the most important.

Singing and Acting Together—Believably

There are many steps to believable acting-singing, of which the first is surely the commitment to using your voice and body to express your character's feelings. Another is the willingness to work intensively on integrating your singing with the specific feelings suggested by the music, with the demands of the text, the conductor, the director, the staging, your colleagues, and by your character's psychology and needs.

Fortunately, you can work on each one separately as well as in conjunction with others. In addition, there are at least three different ways in which pieces with music support your work:

• Music-theater pieces are art.

Every opera, musical, song, or lied, like other art works, is an interpretation of human experience intended for communication to an audience. Each piece imitates life but is not life itself. Each has a beginning, a middle, and an end, imposing clear boundaries that distinguish it from the flow of real life and amounting to a built-in performance map. These boundaries make your task graspable by limiting the material you need to master to make a complete analysis of your character and of the work itself.

• The composer and librettist, like all artists, include in the score only material that they feel is relevant and useful to their intent.

Therefore, you can safely assume that every word, every note, every dynamic, every orchestral color, and every stage direction is there for a reason. Just as a painter carefully chooses and integrates his colors, lines, and forms to create a composition that expresses his interpretation or point of view, so the composer and librettist choose and integrate music, text, story, characters and feelings to explore theirs. But unlike the painter, the composer and librettist need you, the performer, to bring to life what is otherwise only a blueprint on paper. They design that blueprint to provide you with the information you need to create a musical, physical, and psychological portrait of your character. They intend its various elements to work together *through you.*

• Music effectively evokes the emotional life of characters and provides a persuasive channel to arouse those feelings in the audience.

In well-composed works, the music portrays both the subtle emotional colors and the complex mix of consistency and unpredictability that make characters seem real. For instance, how unexpected and yet perfectly appropriate it is that Carmen sings, "Take back your ring!" at the *bottom* of her register, rather than screaming it up high. Even for characters drawn with a broader brush like those in *Fledermaus* or *Candide,* the music captures their feelings, motivations, and attitudes so effectively that if you simply sing them with conviction and expressivity you will be well on the way to bringing them believably to life.

Jumping Your Internal Hurdles

Although the task of creating a believable singing character is enormously complex, often the biggest hurdles are those you create for yourself. Embarrassment, self-criticism and self-doubts are three such obstacles. Here are some thoughts that can help you deal with them.

    • Acting is based on skills.
    Like good singing, good acting is not just a matter of talent or inspiration; it is the result of learned skills that you can hone and control.
    • You are not expected to improve your skills during a performance.
    When you are performing—perform! Commit yourself to improving before and after.
    • The artistic boundaries of music-theater pieces protect you.
    They assure you that your audience will not confuse you with your role and the feelings you express as your character. Even more reassuring, they enable you to work out all the details of your character's feelings and actions in advance, so when you perform you can be confident that you have a plan. You are in control.

Summary

The goal of good acting singing is to communicate all the nuances of the music, text, and characters so that the audience has a fulfilling aesthetic and emotional experience. You can achieve this goal if you create believable characters whom you evoke with expressive singing. When you are believable as your character, you engage the audience's empathy. Once they empathize they respond with their feelings and are moved. The score provides the blueprint you need.

    Believable characters appear to function the way people really do. They appear to be living in the intersection where the input their senses receive crosses what they *want;* they reflect this moment-to-moment reality in their breathing, singing, and movements. They appear to be responding spontaneously.

    You will encounter various kinds of obstacles as you create believable singing characters. Some arise from the demands of singing and acting at the same time. Others you make for yourself as you struggle to meet those demands. You will be on your way to surmounting both as you learn to take advantage of the artistic boundaries that define every music-theater piece, and as you come to trust that all the elements in a score are there for a purpose.

Exercises

Exercises marked "(I)" can be done by yourself. Those marked "(G)" require a partner, or can be done by a group. A double asterisk indicates that there is a note for teachers and directors about the exercise in appendix 5.

EXERCISE 1. (G) *Facial Transparency***

Objective: to explore "acting as actions" by increasing your awareness of the expressive possibilities of your face.

Instructions:

Stand facing a partner. One of you is the "actor," the other is the "mirror." The "actor" begins.

If you are the "actor," start by choosing a feeling. (Happy feelings are as useful as sad ones.) Activate the feeling inside you. (You can use your imagination, or you can recall an actual experience.) Then express that feeling with your face. Make the expression very extreme; turn your face into an exaggerated mask. Use all of your features, including your forehead, eyebrows, eyes, cheeks, nostrils, lips, tongue, jaw, and the way you tilt your head. Once you have made your mask, freeze it. Keep your mask energized with the feeling, but do not change your expression.

If you are the "mirror," imitate the "actor's" mask as *exactly* as you can. Try to put the mask on your face in every detail. (You will need to use your eyes to examine all the nuances of the "actor's" expression, so fix all the other parts of your face before you set your eyes.)

After you have exactly imitated the "actor's" mask, switch roles. (The best way to facilitate the change of roles is to have an outside person call "Switch.") Switch back and forth at least three times. Each time make a mask of a different feeling. In order to sustain your concentration, it is best not to talk between masks.

If you allow yourself to get sidetracked into thoughts like "I feel silly" or "You look stupid" as you do the exercise, you will almost surely break your concentration. To avoid "breaking up," stop the flow of those negative judgments by focusing with fierce intensity on fulfilling a specific task. In this case, if you are the "actor," your task is to focus on having the feeling you have chosen or on keeping your mask energized without changing it; if you are the "mirror," your task is to capture the tiniest details of your partner's mask.

After the series is over, discuss your experiences. What did you find easy? What did you find difficult? What did you learn about using your face as an expressive tool? What did you learn from trying to imitate your partner's mask? What does this exercise have to do with acting?

If you had difficulty concentrating, explore why. Was it because you were self-consciously judging yourself or the other person? If so, what function did those judgments serve? How can you leave your extraneous judgments out of the exercise?

EXERCISE 2. (G) *Transparency—Face and Body*

Objective: to explore "acting as actions" by transmitting feelings without miming or speaking.

Instructions:

Choose a vivid emotional experience that you are willing to share. (An ecstatic experience such as you might have had hang gliding is as useful as a desperate one such as watching your beloved dog run out into heavy traffic.) Write the experience down, using language that captures the feelings. Keep your description short—no more than one page. You may have to write it out more than once to condense it, or to focus your feelings.

Work with a partner who has also written out a description of an experience. Sit facing each other; your knees should almost touch. One of you begins as the "reader," the other as the "listener."

1. If you are the "reader," silently read your experience to yourself, but sound the words inside your head. Have the feelings as fully as possible; let them affect you, but do not mouth the words or intentionally mime out what you are reading. When you are finished, look up and make eye contact with the "listener." Then silently read your experience a second time, with the dual intentions of getting even more deeply into the feelings and of sharing them with the "listener." Allow yourself to be facially transparent. Fully experience your feelings and let them show, but again, do not mouth the words or intentionally mime out what you are reading.

If you are the "listener," listen intently with all your senses, and extend your maximum empathy.

2. Repeat step 1 with your roles reversed.

3. Discuss your experiences. What was transmitted and how? How was the experience different for each of you? Why?

4. Take turns standing up and acting out your experience. Think your description through word by word (as you remember it) and expressively move

your body. Engage as many different parts of your body as possible. You can mime the words, events, feelings, and your reactions, or you can make it more like a dance in which you use your body to evoke the feelings. If you are the "listener," be a supportive audience.

5. Take turns repeating step 4. but add sounds. You can use any sounds that you feel are evocative, but do not use real words. You can grunt, whistle, or sing. You can use a single vowel or use nonsense syllables. If you are the "listener," be a supportive audience.

6. Take turns standing up and reading your experience aloud. Give yourself permission to express your feelings with subtle changes in your voice, face, and body. Do not try to mime the action or the words.

After you both have done steps 4, 5, and 6, discuss your experiences. What did you find easy, what did you find hard, and why? What did you learn? How did steps 4 and 5 affect step 6? How can this exercise help your acting?

EXERCISE 3. (I) *Inhaling the Idea*

Objective: to experience investing each in-breath with a feeling/idea.

Instructions:

Choose a piece of music you know well. Sing the first two phrases quietly to yourself. (For the purposes of this exercise, consider each time you inhale to be the beginning of a new phrase.)

1. Decide which feelings you want to express with each of the first two breath-phrases and warm up those feelings inside yourself. (You can do this whatever way you like. If you want help, read about the Magical *if* in chapter 2.)

2. Decide what has *just* happened to you as your character that makes it necessary for you to break into song.

3. As you focus on the feeling of the first phrase, inhale. Imbue that in-breath with the feeling you chose and the desire to communicate. ("I inhale because I *must* tell you . . . how happy I am, how confused I feel, how much my heart hurts.") Silently, release your breath. Take as much time as you need and then repeat the same process for the second phrase.

4. Inhale as you did in step 3, and then exhale, making an extended sound that expresses the feeling you want to communicate in the first phrase. You can use any kind of sound: a growl; a shriek; a gargle. Send your breath filled with the sound and the feeling across the room. Keep making the sound until you have sent out all your breath. Repeat the process for the second phrase.

5. Inhale, and again imbue your in-breath with both the desire to communicate and with the feeling of the first phrase. Then, as you exhale, sing a vowel. Choose any vowel and any pitch that expresses the feeling you want to com-

municate. You can vary the pitch making it rise or fall as feels appropriate. Send all your breath across the room. Repeat the process for the second phrase.

6. Repeat step 5, but as you breathe out, speak the words for each of the two phrases. Know why you are inhaling. Put your intention in your breath. Exhale all your breath as you say the phrases. Send the words across the room.

7. Repeat step 6; this time sing the two phrases as written (without accompaniment). You may start on whatever pitch you want. Focus on communicating the feeling with your breath.

8. Repeat step 7, with the appropriate accompaniment.

EXERCISE 4. (I) *Improvising Your Life*

Objective: to explore your daily life as a series of improvisations.
Instructions:
Choose one or two of your daily activities. Set aside time to pay conscious attention to them. For instance, observe yourself brushing your teeth, getting dressed, or cooking part of a meal. Try doing them in slow motion. Test out the idea that you improvise your behavior, making choices on the basis of what you *want* in relationship to what you *get*. For instance, you are about to go the dentist, so what you *want* is to brush your teeth really thoroughly; however, the toothpaste tube turns out to be all but empty, so what you *get* is insufficient toothpaste—How do you behave?

EXERCISE 5. (G) *Subtle Changes*

Objective: to tune into nuances of a partner's behavior and let what you receive affect what you do.
Instructions:
Work with a partner. Choose two phrases which might stimulate a strong interaction. One of you could say "I told you so," and the other "No, you didn't!" or "I don't believe you."

Create a dialogue in which each of you uses only his phrase. As you go back and forth, listen to the nuances of your partner's expression and allow what you receive to affect how you speak your phrase. Be subtle.

EXERCISE 6. (G) *Doing Feelings*

Objective: to explore the relationships between experiencing feelings and carrying out actions.

Instructions:

1. Using a partner to serve as an observer, see what you actually do if you try to act love, joy, hatred, despair, or curiosity. Your goal is to be clear and convincing to an outside observer.

If you are observing, make a detailed list of the actor's actions. Include both large movements, like a gesture using one arm raised to the sky, and subtle ones, like the lift of an eyebrow. You won't have time to write down every action, but list as many as you can. When the actor is finished, read your list aloud. How accurately did you describe what happened?

Discuss what actions the actor actually carried out. Did the actor do the feeling? What actions could she have executed to make her feelings clearer? What actions could she have executed to be more believable? If she was not believable, was it what she did, or how she did it?

2. Choose one feeling and execute some evocative actions. Try to be clear and believable but use only one part of your body. Begin with more accessible feelings such as anger, and use one of the more readily expressive parts of your body such as your face, your upper body, or your arms and hands. Then progress to feelings that you find harder to reach, either using parts of your body that are hard to control by themselves such as your eyes and mouth, or using parts of your body that you may not be accustomed to use as means of expression such as your shoulders, legs, or feet.

If you are observing, make a detailed list of everything the actor does. When the actor is finished, discuss whether she was clear and believable.

3. Repeat step 1 or step 2 and add sounds. You can choose to use either sung or spoken sounds. Do not use actual words; use gibberish, a single vowel, or a variety of grunts or other noises. Your goal is to be clear and believable. If you are watching, make a list of the actions. Pay attention to the relationship of the sounds to the actions.

When the actor is finished, discuss the effect of adding sound. What did it enhance? What did it weaken? Why? Did the sounds make the actor's intentions clearer or more believable? If they did, discuss how and why.

* * *

Exercises 7 and 8.

Objective: to help you focus your work. You are responsible for your own development. (Your teachers work for you, not vice versa.) Therefore, you need a system of self-assessment. Exercises 7 and 8 are intended to give you a personal progress scale—a way to set clear goals and to analyze how you can meet them. You will get more out of these exercises if you write out your answers.

EXERCISE 7. (I) *Self-Assessment*

Instructions:

Once a year, review the following questions. If you have been applying yourself, you should see positive growth between evaluations.

OVERVIEW

What are my goals as
> A singer?
> An actor-singer?

What are my strengths and weaknesses as
> A musician?
> A singer?
> An actor?
> An actor-singer?
> A performer expressing myself in movement?
> A self-promoter?

(If you want a professional career, don't ignore this one. Study how people develop careers in your particular area of interest, whether it is opera, musicals, oratorio, or lieder.)

Where do I want to be as an actor-singer
> In six months?
> In one year?
> In five years?

What are my realistic plans for achieving my goals?

ASSESSMENT OF SKILLS

Can I develop a continuous inner voice (subtext, internal dialogue) for my character?

How skillfully do I use my imagination to project myself into a variety of situations?

How willing am I to expose my feelings as a character?

How broad a range of feelings do I have at my disposal?

Can I leave my negative self-assessments behind as I am performing?

How reliable is my vocal technique?

How willing/able am I to color my voice according to the demands of a role?

How well do I integrate any vocal demands with my character's inner voice?

How able am I to move freely as I sing?

EXERCISE 8. (I) *Self-Assessment Videotape*

Instructions:

Every four to six months make a videotape of yourself performing. Study it closely for all aspects of your effectiveness as a performer. As you watch and listen ask yourself:

Do I seem self-conscious?

Do I stay in character?

Are my gestures expressive of my character's thoughts and feelings?

Do I gesture in a logical relationship to my breathing and to the flow of my character's ideas?

Do I make extraneous facial or body movements?

Do I have movement mannerisms?

Are there places in my body that seem rigid or tense?

Is my weight well balanced on my feet?

Do I breathe from my diaphragm, without lifting my shoulders?

Do I use my voice expressively?

The hardest part about using videotape as a constructive learning tool is setting aside irrelevant self-appraisals like "I hate my hair" and concentrating on evaluating your effectiveness. It helps to remember that just as a sound recording is not an exact reproduction of your live voice, so a videotape does not exactly reproduce what you look like. To begin with, it tends to make everyone look heavier than they are.

CHAPTER 2

To Become or Not to Become:
Using Yourself to Create a Believable Character

Entering Your Character's Reality—The Magical *If*

The most efficient way to enter your character's reality is by using the Magical *if*. Developed by the great Russian acting teacher Constantin Stanislavski, this amazing tool is no more than the provocative phrase "I'm going to behave *as if . . .*" Although these words may seem innocuous, they can powerfully stimulate your imagination. They can lift you directly into your character's world and help you generate believable actions that express your character's feelings.

For example, imagine your response *if* your mother has just been told she will die unless she has medical treatments that will cost $500,000. Imagine also that she has no insurance, and that you are the only family member who can help. Now try saying these contrasting phrases to yourself. First, "I am going to behave *as if* I have $5,000,000 in the bank," then "I am going to behave *as if* I have no money," and then "I am going to behave *as if* my mother were the cause of my three broken marriages."

As you apply the Magical *if* to each of these alternative circumstances, they will surely arouse different feelings in you, and therefore will stimulate you to take different actions. Naturally, you would be upset in all three cases. But in the first circumstance you might also feel proud and relieved that you can generously save her life, which would cause you to write a check. In the second circumstance you might also feel desperate but determined, which would cause you to search everywhere for a loan, or maybe even to sell your house to raise cash. In the last circumstance you might also feel rage and the need for revenge and refuse to help her.

If it were your character whose mother was dying, and if his circumstances and motivations were *identical* to any of these, it is likely that he would have feelings very similar to your own, and would be moved to similar actions.

You may well protest that some characters behave in ways that you never would. For instance, even as a spoiled teenager, no matter how hot your sexual desires, how great your need to have your own way, or how strong your hatred for your stepfather, and no matter how explosively that hatred might mix with your longing for revenge and with your frustration at being rejected by a man with whom you are obsessed, you would never manipulate your stepfather's lust to force him to behead the man you desire. However, that is what Salome does, and what you, as Salome, will want to make believable. The beauty of the Magical *if* is that you can achieve that believability even if your character behaves in a way that is quite outside your experience.

With the Magical *if* you create believable characters not by denying your own voice, body, and feelings but by using them. As discussed in chapter 1, the more deeply you imagine yourself into your character's circumstances, the more those circumstances arouse your feelings and lead to believable responses.

Describing Your Character's Reality

In order to behave *as if* you are your character, you need to describe her reality clearly and in detail. To develop your description, you draw on the information the composer and librettist embody in the score. Because the creators of the piece supply it, this information is commonly called your Given Circumstances. Answering the following six questions as your character and in the first person will enable you to extract the essence of those circumstances from the wealth of material in a score.

> *When* are the events taking place?
> - In history?
> - In her own life?
>
> *Where* is my character?
> - In the world?
> - In her surroundings?
>
> *Who* is my character—including her relationships to the other characters?
> *What* does my character *want?* (Your character's *want* distills the need that drives her to do what she does.)
> - For the entire piece? (This is called your character's "super-objective," and is explored in chapter 8.)

• For each scene or stanza? (These are called your character's "objectives," and are explored in chapter 9.)

Why does she want it?
   • For the entire piece?
   • For each scene or stanza?

What has just happened—literally, what has just occurred that causes her to sing?

When you are developing the Given Circumstances for your character in a song or lied, you may have to use your imagination to augment the information in the score—particularly to describe your character's *want, why,* and *what,* since often they are not well defined.

Here is an analysis of Salome's Given Circumstances in Richard Strauss's opera *Salome.*

When: The beginning of the Christian era. Evening. My stepfather, King Herod's, birthday.

Where: An outdoor terrace in my stepfather's immense palace in Judea.

Who: "I am the fourteen-year-old Princess Salome, daughter of Queen Herodias. My mother is now married to King Herod, who constantly undresses me with longing glances. My stepfather is wealthy and powerful. He has imprisoned the apostle Jokanaan (John the Baptist) in a deep cistern beneath the terrace, from which we hear him raving against the excesses of my stepfather's court. I am fascinated by this strange man, in part because it is obvious that my stepfather is afraid of him."

Want: "I, Salome, *want* anything I can't have" or "I, Salome, *must* be free" (beyond moral or sexual constraints).

Why: "I am an adult with a will and feelings of my own" or "I've got to get away from my stepfather."

What: (has to be defined for each vocal response she makes.)

Making Your Character's Given Circumstances Your Own

You can use the Magical *if* to build any aspect of your character or her Given Circumstances. As examples, let's explore how you might apply the Magical *if* to one element of the *who,* first for Carmen and then for Tony from *West Side Story*—two characters with circumstances less unusual than Salome's. Think of these explorations as models of the process.

Using the Magical If *to Explore Carmen as Gypsy*

As you create your Carmen, you will want to explore how your character and her responses might be shaped by being a gypsy living by her wits in nineteenth-century Spain. You may want to begin by reading the story *Carmen,* by Prosper Mérimée, on which the opera is based. You could also research "gypsy," "Spain," and "Bohemia"; examine historical costume books; consult with a local Roma cultural organization or gypsy fortuneteller.

Let's assume you discover that as a gypsy in nineteenth-century Spain, you are not allowed to own land or sleep within the city limits. You are not allowed to attend school or practice any profession. You live out of wagons in small groups, ready to move on whenever the authorities harass you. Neither you nor most of your clan of fellow "outcasts" can read or write. You all scrape for a living as best you can, which includes begging, smuggling, and prostitution. You wear cast-off clothes, and, as a child, you went barefoot. Even as an adult you wear shoes only in the winter.

What *if* it were you? How would you feel, what would you do *if:*

- People treat you like dirt? (As you try this out, remember you are a member of a tiny, despised minority. The established authorities always side against you.)
- You need money, but only the most menial jobs are available to you?
- You, an outsider, find yourself desired by a man from the "in" group?
- You can advance yourself by throwing over one lover for another?

Using the Magical If *to Explore Tony as Leader of a Street Gang*

Tony is a twenty-two-year-old Polish American who, until recently, was the leader of a New York City street gang. Perhaps you find that you can easily arouse the feelings of pride, responsibility, and self-confidence that might motivate you as a young man in your late teens to lead other teenagers. However, you find it hard to arouse the uniquely fierce blend of fear, anger, and hate that would compel you to lead a street gang. Your research in this case might take you to newspapers and magazines from the 1950s, to appropriate movies or videos, or to an interview with someone who has inner-city "street" experience.

Let's suppose that from your research you get a feeling for the deep prejudice against Puerto Ricans that was rife in some poorer neighborhoods in New York City during the 1950s; that you come to understand how many people viewed them as clannish foreigners who threatened their well-being, in part because they were willing to work for low wages.

Construct imaginary situations based on this research that might arouse feelings that would compel you to form a gang. For instance: You are growing up in a closely-knit urban neighborhood of apartment houses. When you are about fourteen or fifteen, your familiar life begins to change. Your favorite uncle loses his job to someone of a different ethnic group, and he and his family have to move away. The corner store where you congregate with your friends is taken over by a member of the same ethnic group, and you no longer feel at home there. The children of this ethnic group barely speak English and don't want to interact with you or your friends.

What *if:*

- One oppressively hot August evening when you're sixteen, your father comes home and announces that he, too, has lost his job to a member of this ethnic group.
- The next day you and your friends are on the school playground shooting baskets. A group of slightly older kids from this ethnic group force you out. One of them shoves your best friend; your friend hits the pavement with such force that he breaks his arm.
- That afternoon your after-school job is given to a member of this ethnic group who will work for less.
- That evening you gather with your friends in the street. Your friend's arm is in a cast. Down the block, some older boys from this ethnic group hassle your girlfriend as she comes to join you.

Is it time to take action? Is it time to form a gang?

* * *

As you develop characters, keep in mind that they are always more complicated than any single trait. Carmen, for instance, is not only gypsy but also young, female, unattached, beautiful, angry, passionate, fearless, and independent. If you try to create your Carmen solely by acting "gypsy" or your Tony solely as a street tough, you will almost inevitably use stereotypical gestures and a limited palette of feelings. One technique that can help you create multi-faceted characters is to be aware of the variety of different feelings that are aroused as you explore situations such as those suggested for Carmen and Tony. Then explore whether any of them can be useful as you build the individual qualities of your character one characteristic at a time.

No character is ever defined by a single trait.

Sharing Your Character's World

When you behave *as if* you are in your character's circumstances, you don't literally *become* your character. After all, you still are using your own body, voice, and mind. However, when you emphasize those aspects of yourself that are suitable to your character while deemphasizing those that are less so, and when you let the appropriate feelings penetrate your voice and motivate your actions, a remarkable transformation happens. You find yourself in your character and your character finds herself in you!

You can create this transformation because you and your character share the same set of feelings—human ones. Not that any particular situation will necessarily arouse identical feelings in any two people, but whatever feelings they experience will belong to the repertoire of human emotions. Even if your character prefers pain to pleasure, enjoys eating human flesh, or makes love to gold, he has human feelings. This includes characters who are part animal, like Papagano in *The Magic Flute.* When he despairs of ever finding a sweetheart and attempts suicide, he is motivated by the human feelings of loneliness, lust, and rejection. Ultimately, it is because all humans share the same set of feelings that you and your audiences can understand any character—even those that are based on stories that are centuries old or are from different cultures.

Not only do you and your character share the same kinds of feelings but you almost certainly already have had some taste of each of them, or, at the very least, have experienced kindred ones. If you haven't experienced uncontrollable rage, hatred, terror, or lust, you have felt anger, dislike, fear, or sexual attraction.

Just like muscles, you can develop your feelings so you have them available to impel you to believable actions. With exercises you can gain greater control and make your feelings more flexible. You can pump up a kindred feeling into its more extreme expression, and you can calibrate the strength of any of your feelings to the intensity suitable to support your role.

In your real life, every situation that arouses your feelings also causes you to act. Even behaving as if what has just happened makes no difference to you is an action in its own way and will affect your body. The same should be true for your character. Respond *as if* you are in your character's situation, let the appropriate feelings well up, and allow your body to express them in actions. (Potentially, you can behave *as if* a situation is real even if you choose not to put yourself inside it, so you can also apply the Magical *if* to actions or feelings you portray using impeccable mimicry.)

Putting It Together

Salome is only one of many opera characters whose passions drive her to extreme measures. To perform her and her ilk effectively, you have to expand your own empathetic abilities and your willingness to explore and share the depths of the human soul. This takes courage and lots of practice with special tools like the Magical *if.* (In chapter 11 there is a detailed discussion of how to use the Magical *if* to heighten each feeling you need to the kindling point that will believably motivate your character's actions.)

In some productions and in some late twentieth-century music-theater pieces, you may be asked to stretch yourself even farther than you must for a character like Salome. You may be required not only to be intensely histrionic but at the same time to perform difficult physical actions, do apparently absurd pantomime, or sing nonsense syllables. To perform these pieces you may need to add training in dance, martial arts, pantomime, or even circus skills to those traditionally required to be an actor-singer. However, as long as your character is intended to be believable, the techniques in this book will provide a useful basis for your work.

Summary

The gap between you and your character can be closed by a clear analysis of your character's *when, where, who, want, why,* and *what,* to which you apply the Magical *if.* You use the Magical *if* to stimulate your imagination to lift you into your character's world.

On a more fundamental level, any gap between you and your characters, as well as between you and your audience, is closed by your shared humanity. It is your shared humanity that provides the common universe of feelings that make communication possible. It enables librettists and composers to create your characters and their music, it enables you to find yourself in your characters, and it enables audiences to respond to your characters with empathy.

Exercises

EXERCISE 1. (I/G) *Changes***

Objective: to explore how different situations conjure up different feelings that in turn evoke different behavior.

The more you can use your imagination to stimulate a variety of feelings and physical behaviors in yourself, the more easily you can stimulate the feelings and behaviors you need for your characters. This exercise is intended to engage your creativity and, by imposing different "filters," to alter the way you to feel, behave, and sound.

You cannot do this exercise wrong. Feel free to make your own variations on the suggestions listed here, or even to invent new ones. Pay close attention to everything you experience. Have fun.

Instructions:

1. Choose a piece of clothing that you seldom use—perhaps something given to you by someone you no longer like. Put it on. How does wearing it make you feel?

Let the feelings affect the way you move: the way you walk, sit, comb your hair, etc. (Since you may get a variety of feelings from a single piece of clothing, you can do this exercise several times exploring a different feeling each time.) You can repeat this exercise with something you borrow. Each person in a group can bring a piece of clothing to exchange.

Make up a simple sentence that expresses the way the clothing makes you feel. Say it several times, overtly expressing the feeling. If different feelings are aroused, say the sentence different ways.

Sing a phrase from a favorite aria or song. Color your voice to express the way the clothing makes you feel.

Look in a mirror. What "kind of person" does the piece of clothing make you look like? Make gestures, say sentences, sing melodies that fit "that kind of person."

2. Put on some music. Move to it—walk, gesture, dance.

a. *Imagine* different physical circumstance and let them affect the way you move. Choose a different age: you are three years old; you are eighty. You are a twenty-one-year-old of the opposite sex.

Change your physical characteristics: your left leg is rigid; your neck is a
    rubber band; your arm is a rope.
Change locations: you are on the moon, in the Sahara desert, under water.
Move to the music *as if* you are a different personality: the czar of Russia, a
    model for *Vogue* magazine, an Australian aborigine, Carmen, Fagin, Fal-
    staff, Evita, Lulu.

Combine several of these different imaginary circumstances: you are Eliza Doolittle on Mars when she was three years old.

Move in couples or as an ensemble, if you're in a group. Create a street people's carnival, a giant's social dance, a sports team.

b. *Sing* as you move. Alter the kinds of sounds you make and the way you make them to reflect your physical circumstances or character.

3. Go through a part of your day with a restriction that will generate an altered perspective. For instance, you can only crawl; you can only use one hand; your tongue is thick and heavy so it takes up your whole mouth; or you only have one eye. (It is wonderful to practice going through part of a day with both eyes closed, but please, only try being "blind" if you use a seeing guide.) Or: you can understand English, but you can only make grunting, guttural noises in response; you can understand English, but you can't speak at all, or you can only respond in singing; you can't understand English at all. (To create the feeling that you can't understand English, listen incredibly intently to what everyone says; hear it as sounds, syllables, noises. The harder you try to understand, the less you will.)

* * *

Exercises 2–5 involve intensifying your feelings.

EXERCISE 2. (I/G) *Exploring***

Objective: to plunge yourself into different Given Circumstances using the Magical *if;* to explore how different Given Circumstances arouse different feelings and give rise to different actions.

Instructions:

Try these activities in which you change one or more elements of your Given Circumstances.

1. Eat a meal *as if:*
   - You are famished, and late for an urgent appointment.
   - You are famished, and you have three hours to waste.
   - You are a tourist eating at an outdoor restaurant in a foreign country; people begging for food surround your table.
   - You are a starving beggar at an outdoor restaurant, where you were given a meal as an act of charity; other starving beggars are watching you.

2. Brush your teeth *as if:*
   - Your dentist has warned you that if you don't brush thoroughly your teeth will fall out.

- Three other people (who are they?) are waiting for their turn at the sink. (It's the only one in the house.)
- You have never used a toothbrush before.

3. Get into bed *as if:*
   - You've been looking forward to it for hours.
   - You want to stay up, but you have to get up early tomorrow.
   - You are in an old hotel with fleas.

4. Do steps 1–3 again, but this time *as if:*
   - You are a child.
   - You are a young teenager.
   - You are an elderly person.

5. Walk into your room and see it *as if:*
   - You are an expert interior designer.
   - You are your mother, your father, a professional cleaning person or your landlord.
   - You are a burglar desperately seeking something valuable.
   - You are an FBI agent, suspecting that a smuggler occupies the room.

6. Do step 5 again with a room you imagine belongs to:
   - Your sibling
   - Your parents
   - Your dentist

If you are working in a group, you can practice steps 5 and 6 using two people. One person can play the entering character, the other the occupant.

When you are finished, analyze your experiences. Did your feelings change? What did you notice that was new? Did you find yourself moving differently? Would you say you were yourself or a character? Why? What was different?

EXERCISE 3. (I) *Private Scripts***

Objective: to allow different circumstances to arouse feelings, and to allow those feelings to be manifested in overt behavior.

Instructions:

1. Set aside free time in a quiet place where you won't be disturbed. Choose a feeling that you want to be able to use in a song you are singing or for a character you are developing. Think of an experience in your life in which you have had that feeling—even a hint of it will do. If you can't find an experience that has the feeling you want, search for one in which you had some kindred feeling—happiness for ecstasy, desire for lust, dislike for repulsion.

Once you have remembered an experience, dredge up as much about it as you can. Exclude nothing. The smallest detail—the color of the shoes you wore that day, the smell of the space—can sometimes trigger the most intense memories.

2. After you have recalled the experience and the feelings it aroused, write a description of it in the first person. Use evocative, descriptive details and include everything that might be pertinent.

3. Use what you have written as a script, and silently read your words slowly to yourself. Let your feelings come.

4. Read the script aloud with as much feeling as you can. Allow yourself to make gestures.

5. Read the script aloud with as much feeling as you can and record it. Listen to the recording. What parts are most believable? Explore the feelings underlying the parts that you find least convincing. Try recording yourself again.

EXERCISE 4. (G) *Public Scripts***

Objective: to allow different circumstances to arouse feelings in front of others.

This exercise takes "Transparency—Face and Body" (chapter 1, exercise 2) to a new level. It allows you to explore feelings that are conjured up by someone else's experience, and to share them in public—the essence of playing a role. It also helps you to develop trust in yourself and in the other members of your group. As in the previous exercise, you may use it to explore a feeling you need for a particular piece or role.

Instructions:

1. Each person in the group chooses an experience from his life that aroused strong feelings. It must be an experience that he is ready to revisit and is willing to share with the group. (Be cautious about using potent experiences that occurred in the very recent past as they may be too strong; let your intuition be your guide.) An experience that aroused feelings of joy is just as useful as one that aroused sorrow. Each person writes a brief but evocative description of his experience. A single page is plenty, but it should capture the essence of the experience, so that as another person reads it, the feeling(s) in the experience may come welling up.

2. Pair off; sit facing each other with your knees almost touching. In each pair, one person reads his own essay silently to himself, experiencing the feelings as fully as possible; the other "listens" with intense, silent empathy, using all his senses. After the first person has finished reading, switch roles. When you are the reader, do not make any attempt to mime or act out what you are reading. After both of you are finished, quietly discuss what each of you experienced.

3. Working with the same partner, one person reads his essay aloud with as much feeling as possible while the listener gives total, intense, sympathetic attention. When you are reading, concentrate on being expressive with your voice, not on acting anything out. Let your body take care of itself. Switch roles. After both of you have read, discuss your experiences with each other. What did you discover? What feelings came across when you were listening to the silent reading? Were they different from what you received from the spoken reading? How was reading silently different from reading aloud?

4. Each person reads his experience aloud to the entire group with as much feeling as he can conjure.

After everyone is finished, have an open discussion. Explore how the three kinds of readings were different and why; did the readers allow the feelings appropriate to the experience they were describing? Were some feelings harder to reach than others? How is this exercise relevant to acting?

5. Each person trades papers with his initial partner. Repeat all three steps using your partner's essay. Feel your way into your partner's experience.

After everyone is finished, have an open discussion. How was reading someone else's experience different from reading your own?

EXERCISE 5. (I/G) *The Outcast***

Objective: to arouse feelings and the impulse to action by projecting yourself into an imaginary situation.

You may do this exercise in your imagination using the Magical *if,* or you may try it out with improvisations. For either approach, make your Given Circumstances specific, and give yourself permission to enter those circumstances *as if* they are real. (If you are not already familiar with how to improvise, you may want to read chapter 3 before doing this exercise.)

This particular situation is intended to be pertinent to both *Carmen* and *West Side Story.*

Instructions:

1. You are a member of an amateur performing society, of which you have been the leading singer for several years. The society holds auditions for each production, and the casting is announced at a party a week later. The next production is a piece you have always wanted to do. It has a leading role that is perfect for you. On the evening of the auditions you have other obligations, so you can only be there long enough to sing; however, you do very well. Since there is no question in your mind that the part is yours, you begin to memorize it. What *if:*

• On the day before the casting party, a friend calls you and leaks the fact that someone else got the part. (How do you feel? What do you do?)

- The person awarded the role is someone with a magnificent voice with whom you were close in college and who went on to have the professional singing career that you wanted for yourself. You haven't been in contact for years, and you didn't know that she had moved to your city. (How do you feel? What do you do?)
- Since you aren't supposed to know that someone else was cast for the role you desired, you can't very well skip the casting party; after the cast is announced, the chosen performer comes over to you full of smiles and warmth. (How do you feel? What do you do?)

2. You are the aforementioned singer who has just come to town. (What caused you to move? Did you move to be with your spouse who got a new job? Did you move because your career is in shreds?) How do you approach your old friend?

EXERCISE 6. (I/G) *Carmen Scenario: Carmen as Outcast***

Objective: to use the Magical *if* to explore some of the feelings you might use to act Carmen.

You can imagine the following scenario using the Magical *if* or you can actually try improvising it. When you are exploring your character, don't worry about behaving like someone else's vision of her, doing what you think ought to be done, or what others have done. You do not need to be original; you need to be expressive and believable.

In this scenario you will employ some details based on your research to taste how it might feel to be a woman in an outcast group. Since it involves Given Circumstances that are probably outside your daily experience, you will have to extend your imagination farther than in the previous situations.

Instructions:

Behave *as if:*

1. You're a sixteen-year-old gypsy. All your life you have been expected to pull your own weight by cooking, sewing, baby-sitting the younger kids, and tending the goats that travel with your group. Today for the first time you are working in a cigarette factory sorting tobacco leaves. (How do you feel? Are you excited? Proud? Curious? Scared? Uncertain?)

2. You're sitting at a long table in a close, hot room. You are surrounded by women chewing tobacco and spitting as they sort the tobacco leaves. You were placed away from anyone you know by the overseer, who is a fat, dirty, foul-mouthed older man. You have heard that he is violent, cruel, and lecherous. Earlier you saw him hit a woman down the table for not working fast enough. You are aware that as he paced back and forth he has been staring at you all morn-

ing. (Try to imagine as many details as you can: feel the heat; smell the tobacco; hear the sounds of the other women talking and of the overseer's footsteps.)

3. It's time for a break. As you stand up, your back tired and arms shaky, the overseer grabs you by the arm and pulls you aside. (How do you feel? How do you react?)

CHAPTER 3

Playing in the Moment:
Using Improvisation to Be Believable

How Improvising Helps You to Act Believably

Improvising is the single most potent technique you can use to improve your believability on stage. It gives you an opportunity to arouse and share your feelings in imaginary situations, to stimulate specific feelings, and to intuitively find the actions that express those feelings. It allows you to practice spontaneously acting and reacting in situations with predetermined circumstances.

Improvising is no more than setting up a situation with clear Given Circumstances and then, assisted by the Magical *if*, using your imagination to enter the situation. You improvise with the same sense of no-risk fun you used when you played house, doctor, or space pioneers as a child.

You can either speak or sing improvisations. Singing improvisations offer a wonderful opportunity to practice singing and acting at the same time without worrying about your vocal technique. They are a great way to integrate your singing voice with a variety of feelings and to practice being spontaneous while singing. In addition, they give you a chance to explore the balance between the demands of your vocal production and those of your character.

There are really only two steps to creating an improvisation: set up a situation, and then behave *as if* you are in it.

Setting Up Successful Improvisational Situations

The situations that work best have three qualities: they have inherent conflicts; they are within the range of experiences of the participants; and they offer the possibility that each participant might conceivably fulfill his essential *want*. In this example and those that follow I will propose situations for possible improvisations to illustrate my points.

Situation

A single father has promised his teenage son that he can use the car to take his date to the senior prom. The son is in his rented tux and is preparing to leave when the father receives a call from the nursing home where his aging mother lives. The father is told that she has taken a turn for the worse. The nursing home is fifty miles away, and there is no public transportation. (Clearly you could also improvise this with a single mother and her daughter.)

The more clearly you delineate the situation the more easily you will get involved in it. (How well do the father and son get along? What are the usual arrangements about using the car? What kind of car is it? How do the father and the son feel about the "date"? How does each of them feel about the aging mother?) It is important to agree on the facts, but you do *not* need to agree on their *interpretation*. (The father loves his ten-year-old car; the son thinks it's barely okay.) In improvising, just as in real life, you should interpret reality through the filter of your characters' particular point of view.

It is perfectly possible to use situations within your range of experiences to conjure up both feelings about situations you have never experienced and feelings that you have not had a chance to explore deeply. For instance, you could explore the feeling of dying in a rocket in outer space by imagining yourself trapped in your car after it is badly damaged spinning off a deserted road. You could explore a character who lusts for her mother using a situation in which you lust for an object.

As you create the situation, all the participants should discuss in detail the *when, where,* and *who*. When you define your *who*, be sure to decide how your character feels about the other characters as the improvisation begins.

Situation

You are setting up an improvisation in which a boy is eating dinner with his fiancée and his future in-laws at their house. There is a knock on the door. Astonishingly, it is the boy's old girlfriend, who is bringing important and unexpected news about the boy's parents. The boy and the old girlfriend step out onto the porch to talk alone.

You will serve yourself well if, as you discuss your who, you agree on a lot of details that the two of you as former sweethearts would be bound to know: how long you have known each other, how you met, when, where, and how you spent most of your time together, how old you are, whether you were lovers, how long it has been since you have seen each other, and what your last meeting was like.

You will also want to agree on some details about the boy's parents: how old they are, whether they are together or divorced, where they live, what they do for a living, and what each of your relationships to them is like.

I repeat, that although you want to define and agree on the facts, you do not have to discuss or agree on how your characters feel about them.

Situation

You may decide that you broke up by mutual agreement. However, privately you could choose to have some serious regrets about it.

Naturally, your character's feelings toward the other participants may change as the improvisation proceeds.

Situation

As you converse, you may find you like your old boy/girlfriend less and less, or more and more.

• Although it is essential that you are clear about what you as your character *want* and *why* you want it, often it is better not to share this information with your partners, as it can defeat the purpose of the improvisation.

• Always make your *why* so compelling that if your *want* is not fulfilled, you, as your character, experience a crisis.

"If I can't get my old girlfriend out of here, my very jealous fiancée may cancel the wedding."

• Invent a *secret agenda*. Your secret agenda is something you want but do not wish to reveal.

As the old girlfriend, your secret agenda could be to get the boy back. As the boy, you could secretly want your fiancée's money. To that end you might find it useful to have your character represent himself as coming from a higher social stratum than he really does. (In which case, when your old girlfriend arrives, you could be worried that she will reveal the truth.)

• As you develop your Given Circumstances and your *secret agenda,* make bold choices.

"I sort-of like this person," "I kind-of have to talk to you," "I sort-of need the money" will not motivate you into action. "I am madly in love," "I desperately need to talk to you," "I've got to have the money" will drive you through the scene and greatly increase the chances that appropriate feelings will arise.

• Don't decide the ending in advance. It is usually more fruitful to let the ending evolve out of the interactions between you and your partners. Let the teacher, director, or some other designated person decide when it is over.

• Use your real name and your normal speaking voice. Fake names and vocal distortions, whether they are accents or unusual vocal colors, can easily become barriers between you and your feelings.

• Avoid going out of character by making background sounds that your character would not make. It is more useful to stamp your foot when knocking on an imaginary door than to say "Knock, knock." It is more useful to say "Do you hear the phone ringing?" than to say "Ring, ring."

Setting Up Successful Singing Improvisations

You can do singing improvisations with or without accompaniment. If you do them a capella, you need do nothing more than commit to making sung rather than spoken sounds. If you work with an accompanist, include him in your discussions of the Given Circumstances, so he can start with a sound texture that provides an appropriate jumping-off point. Then, like a jazz ensemble, play off each other; let the sound evolve and develop just as you do the situation and the characters.

* * *

When you are singing an improvisation:

• Sing as a natural expression of the way you feel. Short of singing in a way that is physically harmful, put any concerns about your vocal technique on the back burner. Give yourself permission to make "ugly" sounds. *Beauty of tone is not important.*

• Give yourself permission to sing in whatever style best expresses the feelings that arise during the improvisation. You can mix all periods of classical, pop, jazz, country, gospel, ethnic, or rock.

• Give yourself permission to sing whatever feels expressive of your character, situation, and feelings. You can't sing a "wrong" note. You're the composer!

When you improvise with an accompanist, you are composing the "score" together, but you do not have to make music in a conventional sense; you are free of any constraints of melody or harmony. Do not even give a thought to "matching" any accompaniment in pitch, rhythm, or musical style. All that matters is that you are spontaneously engaged in the situation making evocative singing sounds.

• Give yourself permission to repeat words or phrases. This allows you to focus on exploring your feelings in the situation and encourages you to sing expressively.

• Give yourself permission to sing full arias or to join with others in creating ensembles.

A terrific aria could consist of singing nothing but "I hate spinach" numerous times—exploring all the different colors of your dislike. It can become a duet with one person repeatedly singing "I hate spinach" and another singing "Eat your spinach." It can grow into a trio by adding a third voice singing "Be quiet, we're in a restaurant," or it can be a quartet with the addition of someone singing "If you don't behave, I'll send you to the car."

• Give yourself permission to use both your full dynamic and vocal range. The extremes can be particularly expressive.

• When you are setting up an improvisation with an accompanist, include in your discussion the kind of sound with which it would be most evocative to begin—Afro-Caribbean, Sondheim, Stravinsky, Sullivan, Mozart, twenties jazz, Beatles, or whatever seems appropriate. Naturally, the accompanist will let the music evolve to support whatever happens in the improvisation.

• It can be useful to have each participant talk to the accompanist privately about his *want, why,* and *secret agenda.*

Beginning an Improvisation

Always make an agreement with your colleagues that no one will hurt anyone or damage anything. If you make this conscious commitment in advance, you will remember it even in the midst of the hottest improvisation.

Set up your space. You do not need to be literal about your use of objects. You may use pantomime and your imagination to fill in for things you don't have or to convert what you have into what you need.

Once your circumstances are clear and your space is arranged, use the Magical *if* to thrust yourself into the situation. If you are doing a singing improvisation, just use your singing voice when you have the impulse to express yourself. You will be amazed to discover not only how easy it is but how liberating. If you are working with an accompanist, it is helpful to let her start playing before you start singing.

(A list of ideas for improvisations follows the exercises at the end of this chapter.)

Helpful Tips

• While you are improvising, don't try to assess how you are doing. Save your self-evaluations for before and after the improvisation; otherwise, you can't be involved in the moment.

• Keep your character's motivation—what he *wants* and *why* he wants it— firmly in mind, as you play off the other participants.

• Don't worry about the plot. Use what you actually experience or observe from moment-to-moment.

> For instance, your partner asks, "Why do you think our mother hates us?" Instead of trying to fabricate an explanation, respond to something that is actually happening:
>
> "Why is your voice quavering as you ask that?"
>
> "Why are you raising your eyebrows as you ask that?"
>
> "How can you even think that?"
>
> "Do you realize you've had your arms folded over your chest for at least ten minutes?"
>
> Your partner can then respond with how she feels about your observation:
>
> "Are you afraid to consider the question?"
>
> "I can raise my eyebrows if I like!!"
>
> "I may be raising my eyebrows, but you look really uncomfortable."
>
> "How can you avoid the truth?"

• Make choices you can believe. If you don't believe what you are doing, it is unlikely that anyone else will.

• You don't have to explain the situation to any audience; they will figure it out.

• Keep the improvisation going until the person chosen as the outside observer calls a halt. Try to incorporate any contradictions and to stay in the scene. When you have a desperate urge to stop, you are probably on the verge of breaking into important emotional territory.

> Let's say you are participating in an improvisation in which you run an isolated gas station in the Nevada desert. The phone is out of order, and you are beyond the reach of a cell phone. A car pulls up. A man jumps out; his daughter is in the car—desperately sick. It might be appendicitis.
>
> Don't avoid committing to the situation by being a recluse who is indifferent to everyone in the world, or by deciding that it is closing time so that you can lock up your station and drive away. Choose a role that will in-

ject momentum. Be hard of hearing, slightly senile, and so lonely that you won't stop talking; or be a surgeon who retired to the desert because you developed a terrible shake in your hand, or because you have never gotten over accidentally killing a child while you were operating on him.

• When you repeat an improvisatory situation, for instance, if you first speak it and then sing it, *don't try to make it the same.* The most useful approach is to view each repetition as a completely new piece that happens to have the same characters and Given Circumstances. Play off what you actually receive from your partners; expect it to be the same but different.

Discussing the Improvisation

It is very important to discuss each improvisation after it is over, so that if you were an observer you can explore with the performers what was believable, or if you were a participant you can release and integrate any feelings you experience.

If you have very intense feelings in an improvisation, the discussion alone may not be sufficient to immediately restore your usual equilibrium. You may feel shaky for several hours. Be patient and do not worry. You may also excuse yourself and walk rapidly around the building. Fresh air and a little exercise is usually very helpful. As you become more accustomed to arousing your feelings as a performer, you will get better at releasing them.

If you did an improvisation to develop a specific character, discuss where you can use any feelings you had. Approach this discussion with imagination; the richer your character's emotional palette, the more believable she will be. For instance, say that as part of your preparation for Carmen you improvise a situation in which you happen to experience jealousy. Although jealousy is clearly not one of her major personality traits, explore where you can use it. Could she have a flash of jealousy when José first says he won't spend the night in act II? Is it possible that she is jealous of Micaela? Could that come out in act III?

Handling Possible Fears about Improvising

There are no "right" or "wrong" ways to improvise, only ways that are more or less useful. In addition, even if you have never done a formal improvisation, remember that because all of us improvise throughout daily life (chapter 1), you are already completely conversant in the basic techniques.

If you are hesitant to try improvising, remember that you can always step out of an improvisation if you need to. In addition, when you improvise be assured that

- Any feelings you engage will be ones that everyone has experienced at one time or another.
- You will be choosing, consciously or unconsciously, the particular feelings that you engage.
- You will not compromise or change your personality, or lose your ability to control your feelings in your daily life.

If what makes you anxious about improvising is the idea of sharing your feelings in public, you are not alone. However just as when you perform a scripted role, everyone will understand that you are using yourself *in the service of your character.*

For most people the best way to reduce that anxiety is to risk repeatedly working in front of people, but that can be an act of bravery. It can be helpful to try to pinpoint the causes of your anxiety, and then to hold them up to the light of day. It can also be useful to literally give yourself permission to engage. Depending on your particular concerns, before you begin try saying to yourself, "I give myself permission to be passionate" or, more specifically, "to feel ecstasy (or another powerful emotion) and express it through action."

Summary

Improvisations provide the ideal playground in which to exercise feelings appropriate to specific situations and to let those feelings motivate actions. Improvisations allow you to arouse your feelings as a character, practice spontaneity, and practice sharing your feelings in public. Singing improvisations allow you to combine all these benefits with the singing process.

The basic rules are simple. Define a possible situation with clear Given Circumstances. Use the Magical *if* to plunge yourself into that imaginary reality and then react to what you actually experience. Whether you use your speaking or singing voice, it is really all the same.

Exercises

Remember that as you do the following exercises, you may use pantomime and imagination to fill in for objects you don't have or to convert objects you have into what you need.

Always clearly define your *when, where,* and *who* with your partners, and what you as your character *want* and *why* you want it for yourself.

Be sure to have a discussion after each group does each exercise.
You can do any of these setups singing or speaking.

EXERCISE 1. (I/G) *Seeing the World Through the Eyes of Another*

Objective: to taste the experience of improvising.
Instructions:

1. Behave *as if* you are a dog or cat.
  • Your owner is petting you, playing with you, feeding you. Make up
    a monologue about your experience.
  • You are observing a room, a street, a restaurant, a play, a sporting
    event. Make up a short monologue about what you see.

2. Select a picture with people in it from a magazine, newspaper, book,
postcard, or advertisement. Imagine you are one of the people in the picture.
  • Make up a monologue of your thoughts.
  • Make up a story of how you came to be there. Be as fanciful as you
    like, as long as you can believe the story.

Select a picture that includes your family or friends. Repeat the two preceding activities.

3. Approach a partner and behave *as if* you are selling something. It can be
a magazine subscription, Christmas cards, raffle tickets, one of your personal
possessions, a bicycle, a leather coat, a computer—whatever you like. Your *want*
is: "I, (your name), *need* to sell . . . " You should have a forceful reason *why* you
must make the sale. You may use this *why* as part of your sales pitch, or you may
use make-believe *why*s for each individual you approach—tailoring them to
improve your chances of making the sale.

You may set the sale in a specific situation. You might be a flood victim selling your last possession for some uncontaminated drinking water to give your
child, or you might be the most successful insurance salesman in your firm
demonstrating a sale for a teaching video. The person who is approached
should have his own Given Circumstances—including a *want,* a *why,* and a *secret agenda.*

To get the most out of this exercise, be keenly aware of each potential "customer's" reactions to your pitch. Notice her body language. Adjust your pitch
with strategic responses to what you observe. If she seems tense, perhaps you
should begin by trying to relax her. If she seems rushed, promise to be brief. You
can be extra polite, brash, forceful; whatever you think will be most effective.

* * *

Exercises 2 and 3: (G)
    Objective: to practice improvising with other performers in specific situations.

EXERCISE 2. (G) *Moving Sculptures***

Instructions:

Divide into groups of twos or threes, leaving one non-participant to be the "leader." Begin exploring the space between you and the other members of your group by moving your body slowly while they do the same. Bring as many parts of your body into play as possible. Respond to the movements of the others, but without touching. Think of yourself as part of a slowly evolving sculpture.

When the leader calls "hold," freeze in whatever position you are in. While you are frozen, notice exactly how you are holding each part of your body, from your toes and ankles to your neck and eyebrows. When the leader gives the signal, relax. Then you and your group develop an improvisation that logically leads everyone in your group to *end up* in their frozen positions. After you have developed an idea and everyone has clear Given Circumstances, try it out. Then do your improvisation for the other groups.

EXERCISE 3. (G) *Flow***

Instructions:

This exercise can be done in any size group of three or more people, although it is best if no more than five participate in a particular setup. One person begins by pantomiming an activity. When another member of the group has a clear impulse in reaction to the pantomime, as soon as he has made up clear Given Circumstances, he enters. Whatever the *entering* person establishes— whether with words or actions—becomes the situation. The person who began adopts the new *when,* the *where,* and *who,* adjusts her *want* and *why* as necessary, and begins to interact using dialogue.

Other people may enter as they have the impulse, but they do not change the *when,* the *where* or the relationships already established; they add to them. Each person who enters should be clear about the existing Given Circumstances and have a well-defined *who, want,* and *why.*

As each person enters he should clearly identify his relationship to the situation: "Hi, Mom!" "Did someone call for a TV repairman?" "What's going on here? I'm the police," and so on.

Allow at least a minute after one person enters before the next person joins in to give the participants time to adjust.

For example, the person who begins behaves *as if* she is in a park on a Saturday afternoon in June (*when* and *where*); she looks around critically, and then pantomimes laying out a blanket in anticipation of a picnic with her parents, at which she is going to announce her engagement. Her exciting news is tempered by the fact that, unbeknownst to her parents, she is already pregnant. (*Who, want,* and *why.*)

The first person to enter comes running in, saying, "I'm so sorry I'm late, but my boss wouldn't let me off until five o'clock. There was a lot of summer weekend traffic, and, stupidly, I got lost trying to find your new apartment. Well, at least I'm here, and I've already got my old clothes on. Oh, great! You've got the tarps down and everything ready, so when we paint we won't mess up the floor. I know you want it to look really great when your boyfriend sees it."

The situation becomes a friend arriving to help paint her friend's apartment on a Friday afternoon in summer. People entering later could include: the landlord, neighbors, other friends, parents, an interior decorator, the cable TV installer, moving men, the boyfriend.

EXERCISE 4. (G) *You Look Worried*

Instructions:
Divide into groups of two or threes. Each group develops an improvisation beginning with the following script:

Person 1: "You look worried."
Person 2: "I'm not worried!"
Person 1: "Well, you look worried."
Person 2: "_____ found out!"

As you develop your Given Circumstances, decide who "found out," and what they discovered. If there are three people in the group, you can have two people divide up person 1 or person 2, or you can have person 3 enter later as the person who found out. No matter how you set it up, begin this improvisation with these four lines.

EXERCISE 5. (I) *Private Singing Improvisations*

Objective: to have and share feelings appropriate to your Given Circumstances and express them through singing.

You can work on singing improvisations in the privacy in your room. For instance, you could sing parts 1 and 2 of exercise 1 of this chapter ("Seeing the World Through the Eyes of Another") by yourself, or you could try the following exercises.

Instructions:
Choose a song or aria you know well. After you define your Given Circumstances, use the Magical *if,* and imagine yourself in the situation. Now sing the piece, keeping the words the same, but improvising a new melody based on how you feel in the situation.

Choose a song or aria you know well. Change one or more elements of the original Given Circumstances. For instance:

- You can change the *when, where,* or *who.* (Set *Carmen* in the southern United States during the Civil War. Carmen is a runaway slave; José is a Confederate soldier.)
- You can change what the character *wants.* (Carmen sings the "Habanera" to discourage an admirer.)
- You can change the character's *who.* (Carmen sings the "Habanera" as: a stripper, Mickey Mouse, a country-western star.)

Sing a song or aria you know well, keeping the melody the same, but improvise new words.

Ideas for Improvisations

Sources

Possible sources for improvisations are endless. You can build them on material from television programs, newspapers, books, plays, musicals, operas, the classroom, your family, your work, social situations, other people's lives, or your own. Here are some suggestions.

Myths, Biblical Stories, or Nursery Rhymes

Use any story that is familiar to all the participants—be it Abraham and Isaac, Orpheus and Eurydice, or Jack and Jill. Feel free to fill out the story. In Jack and Jill, someone could be the bucket, another the hill. You could add a concerned parent or a doctor.

Newspaper Headlines

Pick any headline. Develop the situation so that the information in the headline personally affects the participants. Here are two examples.

"The Dollar Plunges": One person is a tourist from the United States in a foreign country. After staying at a hotel for a month, she is checking out. She has carefully calculated her vacation expenditures to have just enough left to pay the bill, but because the dollar suddenly is devalued, her money no longer suffices. She has no credit cards. (Were they stolen from her hotel room?) The last bus that will get her to the airport on time is leaving in two minutes. Other

participants might include: the hotel clerk, the hotel manager, another tourist, the bus driver.

(If members of your group speak foreign languages fluently, this is an ideal opportunity to let them use their skills; they could be the clerk, the other tourist, the bus driver, a police officer.)

"Police Officer Accused of Being Mafia Spy": You can do this with two people (the accused interviewed by his boss), or you could involve more (a courtroom scene, or a bar with the solitary "accuser" confronting the police officer surrounded by his mob pals).

Newspaper or Magazine Pictures

Choose a picture with people in it and, ignoring any caption, improvise the situation.

Specific Character Traits

Pick a trait and build a scene around it: a child who can foresee the future, a person who loves everyone, a person who is consumed by greed.

Someone's Experience

Have each member of the group recall something that has happened to him that involved at least one other person and aroused strong feelings. Other members use the experience as the basis for an improvisation, but are free to elaborate. For example:

- "I was in a bus on my way to the airport to catch a charter plane to the Caribbean and was caught in a terrible traffic jam." (The participants can all be on the bus; each with his own travel plans and needs.)
- "Last week I ate in one of the fanciest restaurants in town and broke my tooth on a piece of bone in the mashed potatoes." (Participants might include: the person who breaks her tooth; that person's husband, parents, boss, client; the waiter; the chef; the owner; a customer who is a dentist; a health inspector; a lawyer.)

A Character and an Action

Choose a character and an action: " a millionaire gives away all his money," "an old lady buys a hat," "a homeless person applies for a job."

A Sentence

Someone invents a sentence that includes or implies a feeling; other participants build a scene around it. "I can't believe you ate that entire half gallon of ice cream"; "Jon, if you don't stop that, I'll hit you"; "I just love daffodils."

A Visual Situation

Observe two people together in a restaurant, on a bus, in a museum, a park, a store. Focus on what they do, storing as many details as possible in your memory. Later develop an improvisation based on their actions (not on what they may have said).

Look at the display in a store window and improvise a conversation between the clothes dummies based on their clothes and poses.

Ideas for Improvisations Based on the Text of Your Piece

Improvisations Based on the Theme of a Piece

Invent a contemporary situation to explore the theme of a piece. (The theme of a piece is the big idea that the piece is about. It is different from the plot, which consists of the story and actions with which the theme is explored. For help on developing a theme, you may want to consult chapter 6.) For example, a possible theme for *Carmen* is that it is about differing needs in love. It could be explored as follows.

Pair up; set up a relationship in which the participants have conflicting needs for happiness: a party person with a retiring one, a person who needs to be independent with someone who needs to possess. You could be: husband/wife; parent/child; boyfriend/girlfriend; employer/employee; colleagues; two good friends. Then create situations in which your differences might create a crisis. For instance:

- The party person and the retiring person have been married for one year. It is the evening of their anniversary. They have agreed to spend it alone together. The retiring person arrives home looking forward to a quiet, intimate evening with the person whom she loves and finds the living room full of decorations (or guests). The party person announces that at the last minute he has decided to invite fifteen friends.
- After dating for months, the independent person and the possessive person get engaged; they plan to meet at an elegant restaurant the following evening to celebrate. During the intervening day the possessive person discovers that the independent person has recently been seeing someone else.

• A single father needs the companionship of his teenage son. The father, as a special surprise, has bought two tickets for a game of the son's favorite baseball team. The son already has plans to go to a rock concert with friends.

Improvisations Based on the Plot of a Piece

Strip down the plot to its essential conflicts. To see these more clearly, label the characters by their basic roles or relationships, like mother, father, husband, wife, boss, stranger. Choose one of the conflicts and set it in a contemporary or more familiar setting.

> • Use the conflict you choose as a starting point, and let the improvisation roughly parallel the plot of the piece.
> • Use the conflict you choose as a starting point, but allow the situation to develop based on the actual interactions between the participants as they improvise.

Here are examples of improvisatory set-ups you might use to explore the relationships and the feelings the characters have toward each other in the opening scenes of *Carmen.*

1a. "Old girlfriend" comes with personal news about the "boy's" family (Micaëla-José). Old girlfriend chooses what news she is bringing but does not divulge it in advance: boy's mother is dying, boy's parents just won a million dollars, boy's brother has escaped from prison where he was serving time for murder. For this last one, old girlfriend and boy should agree in advance that boy has a brother in prison.

b. Valentine's Day; a restaurant; boy has just proposed to his new girlfriend. Old girlfriend walks in.

c. Snowy evening; fiancée's house; boy is meeting her parents for the first time. Old girlfriend arrives at the front door.

2. New hire is trained for his job (José-Morales).

An office, a store, a school, a theater, a factory. The "new hire" chooses whether he is confident or fearful, whether the job seems easy or difficult, attractive or disgusting, and what he *wants* and *why.* ("I *want* to impress the person training me, because I want to keep the job"; "I *want* to get the job of the person who is training me, because I need more money to pay for an operation for my sickly child"; "I *want* to set a very low level of expectations about my abilities, because I need free time to write my novel.")

The "trainer" can choose to like or dislike the "new hire," to find him stupid, smart, attractive, threatening. He can resent the new hire, he can resent doing the training, or he can love it. He, too, has a *want* and a *why.* ("I *want* the new hire to like me, because I need an ally in my fight with the boss"; "I *want* the new hire to fear me, because I want an obedient slave to take over much of my work"; "I *want* to postpone getting back to my desk, because I have a tedious financial report to write"; "I *want* to get the new hire fired, because I want my best friend to have the job.")

3. You're new on the job and someone pressures you to break the rules (José-Carmen). (For example, your superior might lean on you to steal a letter from your boss's files or to change his time card.)

Improvisations Based on the Text of a Song or Aria

Speak or sing the words of a song or aria as if you are different people in specific settings. For example, the text of "Tonight" from *West Side Story* as delivered by:

• Seventy-year-old sweethearts in an old folks' home.
• Teenagers who meet and fall in love on the day the boy has to go off to war; they are in an airport lounge.
• A wealthy older woman who has fallen in love with her young hairdresser (or the reverse); they are in the beauty salon.

Repeat any of the situations, but rather than using the actual text of the song, improvise your version of it.

Improvisations Based on Your Character

Make a list of descriptive phrases about your character and then explore each one with an improvisation using a contemporary situation. For example:

"*Carmen* is fun-loving":
  • You (Carmen) and some friends are studying for a crucial exam. Try to convince the others to go out for pizza.
"*Carmen* is domineering":
  • You (Carmen) are the new member on a committee that has been planning a big dance for six months. (This could be a high school, college, or adult dance. It could be a social, a benefit, a showcase.) For reasons of your own (*why*), try to convince the committee to change major elements of their plan: the theme, the decor, the date. You may cajole, bully, bribe, and so on.
"*Micaëla* is a peacemaker":
  • You (Micaëla) are a reference librarian dealing with two elderly men who want the same section of a newspaper.

- You (Micaëla) are hosting a family Thanksgiving dinner. Two of your siblings, or maybe your parents, get into a terrible argument.

Improvisations Based on one of Your Character's Feelings

Choose any feeling your character has in the piece. (It is just as useful to explore a fleeting feeling that may only color one word as a feeling that is a major element of your character's personality.) Improvise a contemporary situation that you think *may* arouse that feeling in you. Once you have created the Given Circumstances of the situation, improvise the scene exactly as you experience it. Do not try to force any particular feeling. If you don't happen to arouse the feeling that you set out to capture, it doesn't matter; you will experience other feelings that may be useful.

In *West Side Story*, Maria and Tony both have moments when they feel bewildered. Here are some examples of contemporary situations that might arouse feelings of bewilderment.

- You come home from school/work; all the furniture in the living room is gone.
- You have had a terrible fight with your husband on the phone when you were at work. That evening you arrive at your house full of remorse, bringing flowers; he opens the door dressed in gorgeous evening wear, wreathed in smiles. Alternatively, you arrive full of bitter anger, ready to have it out, and he opens the door dressed in gorgeous evening wear, wreathed in smiles.

CHAPTER 4

Judgments and Trust:
Improving Your Concentration

Introduction

Since audiences read whatever you are consciously thinking as your character's thoughts, controlling the object of your concentration is an essential component of creating a believable character. Although it is difficult, you don't want to concentrate on your own personal internal dialogue or vocal technique, because that is not what is on your character's mind. (Even Cherubino nervously singing his love song to the Countess in the second act of *The Marriage of Figaro* is worrying about his voice, not yours.) Rather, you want the object of your concentration to be your character's thoughts as they unfold in his internal dialogue (or at least you need to create that impression).

This chapter will explore a number of techniques to help you improve your ability to concentrate on the object of your choice.

Improving Your Concentration by Increasing Your Ability to Trust

When you improve your ability to trust, you improve your ability to focus your concentration, because trust soothes the fears that fuel your distracting internal critics.

Trusting Yourself

If you are like most singers, your vocal technique is the issue that causes the clamor of your internal self-criticism to reach fortissimo most easily. Solidify your technique, and the din will decrescendo. You can also improve your self-trust by remembering that what you do onstage never has devastating consequences offstage. No one will die, no one will starve, no one will be divorced or orphaned as a result of your performance. Indeed, you can be quite sure that the worst that will happen is that you may make a fool of yourself.

Trusting Your Piece

It is hard to trust something you don't understand, so it is important to study and analyze the music and text of each piece until you appreciate how and why it works. Often as your understanding deepens, your love increases. Once you fall in love with a piece, you can lean not only on your understanding but on the trust that is an inextricable part of love. (When you love a work, it also adds a wondrous luster to your performances.)

Trusting Your Colleagues

You are not likely to trust someone you don't know. Seek out opportunities to interact with your colleagues through improvisations or theater games, or just go have coffee together. You can facilitate and accelerate the growth of trust if you remember that it is a two-way street. If you give trust, you get trust.

Improving Your Concentration by Putting Judgments in Perspective

One of the frustrating ironies of being a performer is that you cannot hear or see yourself as your audiences do. Therefore, you are dependent on critics, such as teachers, vocal coaches, directors, and conductors to mirror back your work to you. However, when you are actually performing it is seldom productive to be thinking about their criticisms, so it is useful to get them in perspective.

Evaluating the Judgments Others Make of You

Your critics are not gods. No matter how bright and trustworthy they are, they can only offer their informed opinions. Their power to affect you is really in your keeping.

Test the comments you receive against your own experience. If they seem accurate, use them to help you improve. If their judgments don't match your own critique of your work or are out of line with what others say, don't just dismiss them. First explore what you are doing that may contribute to your critics' impressions, and then put them in perspective. Do the same with judgments that appear in the media.

Remember that it is just as destructive to your concentration to allow positive judgments to overinflate your sense of yourself as it is to be deflated by negative ones. Most important, remember that your critics are judging your work, not you.

If you receive a negative review—and sooner or later if you perform publicly you will—bear in mind that after six months most often no one will remember what the media critic said, but only that you were mentioned. It's free publicity.

Evaluating the Judgments You Make of Yourself

If you are like most performers, you find it easier to be objective about the comments of external critics than about those of your internal ones. Try the following techniques to defang the non-constructive critical judgments of your internal critics.

- Make a dispassionate assessment of your vocal and dramatic strengths and weaknesses and then engage in a well-defined course of study. With this disciplined work underway, you can silence your disruptive nay-saying impulses by reminding yourself, "I am working on that."
- Avoid using "good" and "bad" in your self-evaluations; they are too general to be useful and can easily trap you into confusing your*self* with your work. Instead, analyze not just the underlying causes of any difficulties but also the underlying causes of those elements that are effective.
- Only accept assignments that present a reasonable level of challenge, both in terms of their dramatic and vocal demands such as range, size, and technical complexity. Nothing is more likely to start your internal critics howling than biting off more than you know you can chew.
- Before you begin to perform, promise yourself that after you are finished you will be constructively analytical. If you want to be sure that you will recall the details of what you did, install the image of an internal tape machine in your mind. Imagine yourself starting the tape before you begin. Play it back later when you have time to reflect.
- Don't criticize yourself for things that are truly out of your control.
- Ask yourself whether your unhappiness with what you are doing in a class, rehearsal, or performance is really about the quality of your work. You may discover that some of it arises from other issues that you are projecting as deficiencies in your performance. These may include your feelings about displaying emotions, having a career in the arts, making your-

self the center of attention, or becoming a success. If issues of this sort are giving you a negative view of your work, you can address them most effectively outside of the theatrical context.

• Remind yourself that allowing appropriate feelings to show in the service of your character is success!

Improving Your Concentration by Intensifying Your Engagement

When you intensify your engagement in your character's situation, you buffer your concentration both by drowning out distractions with the sound of your character's internal dialogue and by giving your mind concrete and compelling material on which to focus.

The easiest way to intensify your engagement in your character's situation is to make your *want* or *why* more compelling. Let's say you are playing the scene with Carmen in which she is trying to get you to run off with her to the mountains. As you sing, "Oh Carmen, stop," your internal critic interrupts, shouting, "That sure was fake!" Light a fire under your *want*. If you have been using "I *want* to stay out of trouble," try switching to something hotter, like "I *must* protect our love!"

It is also very useful to fill any pauses between your lines with intense listening. Tune into the tiniest subtleties of what the other characters are singing, and be hyperaware of the music and how it reflects your character's thoughts and reactions. Articulate your character's responses as active dialogue inside your head. You need not worry that by increasing the volume of your character's internal dialogue you will accidentally silence your own critical voices. They will continue their chatter—just less intrusively.

Maintaining Your Concentration in Demanding Vocal Passages

Demanding vocal passages present one of the greatest challenges to keeping your concentration on your character's internal dialogue. You can meet that challenge using a process of association. Begin by figuring out what is driving your character to sing so high, so low, so fast, or so slow. (Remember that composers write demanding passages not just to show off your vocal prowess but to express your character's most intense thoughts or feelings.) Then figure out what you must do technically to negotiate the passage successfully and condense it into commands using the fewest possible words.

Next, determine the exact note or word on which it is most effective to give yourself those commands. (Don't be surprised if the "trigger" spot is well in advance of the demanding passage.) Finally, repeat that spot and the demanding passage that follows many times. Alternate between thinking your character's internal dialogue for the trigger spot and thinking your vocal commands. Gradually the commands will become part of a reflex set in motion by the note or text and will be incorporated into your character's internal dialogue.

For example, you are singing a piece in which the words "I love you" have been set with a difficult upward vocal leap on "love." To execute the leap you need to remember to drop your larynx and raise your soft palate. Shorten the command to "drop; raise," or maybe "larynx; palate."

Two measures before the leap, you have the word "Oh," on a single note, for which your internal dialogue is "Please touch me." The most effective trigger spot for your command turns out to be as you initiate the "Oh." So you repeatedly practice that measure alternately thinking "drop; raise" and "please touch me," until it is an automatic reflex to drop your larynx and raise your palate when you start to sing "Oh." Once the association is made, your conscious mind to free to focus on expressing your character's internal dialogue—"Please touch me."

It is, of course, also possible to be an effective acting singer and to concentrate on your vocal technique rather than on your character's internal dialogue for difficult vocal passages—if you keep your character believable. You can use the same process of association to that end. Practice alternating behaving precisely as a non-singing person in your character's situation might and focusing on your technique until the two are inextricably associated; but this time weld your behavior onto your vocal technique rather than vice versa.

The advantages of maintaining your concentration on your character's internal dialogue rather than on your vocal technique are that it offers you a single continuous strand to hold onto through the entire piece, and it allows you to let your body behave appropriately by intuition.

You can use the same associative technique to help yourself concentrate in moments that are dramatically demanding. Let's say that you have a line that you must sing with ecstatic glee. You have succeeded in finding an image that successfully arouses that glee in yourself. Now explore on exactly which word or note it is most effective to stimulate that image so you have it available for the line, then alternate repeating the "trigger" spot and the line until the image is welded to your character's internal dialogue.

Recovering Your Concentration

Occasionally you will lose your concentration—everyone does. At such moments you can get right back on track by quickly asking yourself, "What do I, as my character, *want*, and what can I do to get it?"

If you break your concentration because you forget the words, try going back to your character's internal dialogue. If that doesn't fish them back, combine your internal dialogue with your character's objectives, and you will astonish yourself by the ease with which you will improvise something appropriate.

The least constructive things you can do are to focus on the break or to indulge in negative feelings about it. Remember, if you don't tell the audience you have made a mistake, most often they won't notice.

Summary

To create a believable character, you need to keep your attention concentrated on your character's thoughts and perceptions (or appear to do so). You can improve your ability to maintain concentration by putting aside judgments and increasing your trust in yourself, your piece, and your colleagues. You will also find it invaluable to develop associative reflexes with which you can link particular technical demands of your singing and acting with particular moments in your character's internal dialogue.

Exercises**

EXERCISE 1. (I) *Stopping Your Negative Internal Critics*

Objective: to learn to recognize when you are being negatively critical and undermining yourself.

Instructions:

Choose a short period of time—say five minutes—in a practice session, voice lesson, coaching or solo rehearsal and commit yourself to stopping every time you hear a negative self-criticism in your head. Repeat the criticism to yourself, evaluate it, and then go on.

For the following five minutes, every time you hear some inner carping, briefly acknowledge it with a "Thank you" or a short laugh, and then continue.

Enlist the help of your teacher, coach, or director for this exercise.

* * *

Exercises 2 and 3:

Objective: to improve your concentration by involving yourself in your material.

You can improve your concentration by focusing on a simple physical task. Let the pressure from your peers help you intensify your concentration as you participate in the following exercises.

EXERCISE 2. (G) *Signals*

Instructions:

1. Form a circle. Hold hands. One person begins by squeezing the hand of the person to her right. That person immediately squeezes the hand of the person to her right, and so the "signal" is passed as rapidly as possible around the circle.

Concentrate on passing the "signal" as soon as you receive it. Do the exercise in absolute silence.

2. Repeat the exercise. Each time you receive the signal, make some sort of noise. You can choose your own, or the group can specify categories: animal noises, city noises, expressions of joy, etc.

3. You can do this exercise with variations. The person who starts can simultaneously squeeze the hands of the people on both sides. If the circle is large, two or even three people can start signals simultaneously. In this latter case, each person should start his signal in the same direction.

EXERCISE 3. (G) *Catch*

Instructions:

1. Form a circle. One person starts by throwing an imaginary beach ball to someone across the circle, who immediately throws it to someone else. Concentrate on throwing a ball of the same size and weight as the one you catch. Do the exercise without talking.

2. Play "catch" with variations: different size balls, different weight balls, different numbers of balls, flaming hot balls, or freezing cold ones.

3. Have the person who starts imbue the ball with a feeling or a message. The person who receives the ball also tries to catch the message. When she throws the ball, she passes on the message.

EXERCISE 4. (I) *The Circle of Concentration***

Objective: to maintain your concentration in both large spaces and distracting ones.

Constantin Stanislavski designed this exercise. It allows you to practice concentrating on a specific thought or feeling without denying or being distracted by any activities around you.

Instructions:

Stand in the middle of a room. Choose a desire, image, or feeling on which to concentrate, and conjure it up inside you. (Use your imagination, use the Magical *if,* or recall a real experience.) Then imagine that you are standing in the center of a small but intense circle of light coming from a source directly overhead. Fill that circle with the object of your concentration.

Gradually expand the circle of light by letting the energy of your object of concentration push outward. Let the circle get larger and larger, allowing it to encompass any objects or other people in the space. If you lose your connection with your object of concentration, reestablish it by shrinking your circle slightly. Then let its energy expand the circle again. Continue to let the circle of light grow until it fills the entire space in which you are standing. You should feel centered and aware of radiating the desire, image, or feeling to the farthest reaches of the space.

1. Practice this exercise silently.
2. Practice it while speaking lines. You may repeat the same phrases again and again.
3. Practice it while singing. Sing softly, but with intensity. As you expand your circle of concentration, focus on letting your quiet voice fill the expanding circle.
4. Practice creating a "circle of concentration" in a place with lots of activity. Accept everything that is going on without focusing on it; include everything in your circle. As before, if you lose your connection with your object of concentration, shrink your circle slightly until you can reestablish it.

EXERCISE 5. (I/G) *Improvisations for Concentration*

Objective: to improve your concentration by intensifying your Given Circumstances.

Here are two improvisations that are specifically tailored to help you improve your concentration by setting you to work on a vital task. They are short and intense.

Instructions:

1. Choose a simple task. Set it in Given Circumstances that make completing it compellingly urgent, and give yourself a limited amount of time—two or three minutes are plenty. Set an alarm clock if you like. Make an agreement with yourself to use that time exclusively for this exercise, and to suspend extraneous judgments until you are finished.

For instance, you are in your room. You have two minutes to make it impeccably orderly. If you succeed, you will get a wonderful prize; if not, you will be subjected to an awful penalty. Choose something that really excites you: a $50,000 scholarship; a chance to perform with a major opera company. It is helpful to establish *why* you must get the prize, and what devastating thing will happen if you don't succeed.

Let yourself loose on your room for the exact length of time allotted; see how orderly you can make it. Strictly limit your internal dialogue to thoughts about getting it in order, the prize you will get, why you must get the prize, and the terrible consequences of not succeeding.

When the exercise is over evaluate how successful you were in keeping your mind focused and what you could do the next time to improve your concentration.

You can repeat the exercise with the same or different tasks for increasingly longer periods of time.

2. Work with a partner. Develop a scenario in which one of you attempts to do a simple task, which the other tries try to block without using physical contact. Set up your Given Circumstances so you are both totally committed. As when you did this exercise alone, set aside a specific period of time; agree to use the time exclusively for this exercise and to set aside all extraneous critical thoughts (about yourself, your partner, and the exercise) until you are finished. When the time is up, discuss how you did and what you could do to stay more focused.

For instance: one person's task is to sort a randomly shuffled deck of cards by suits in sixty seconds. The other person's task is to prevent it. Each person has compelling Given Circumstances: Could it be that the person sorting is a prisoner of war? If he can successfully complete the task, he will be set free; if he fails, he will be shot. The other person is the guard. She hates the prisoner and wants him to be killed. However, if she hurts or even physically touches the prisoner, or if he succeeds at the task, she herself will be tortured.

3. Ultimately, almost every exercise in this book is an exercise in concentration. Choose any one. Increase the "stakes"—both what wonderful rewards you will get if you succeed, and what bad things will happen if you don't. Apply the Magical *if* so that completing the goal of the exercise momentarily feels more important than anything else in your life, and then do the exercise.

EXERCISE 6. (I) *Thought Exercise*

Objective: to improve you concentration by transferring your skills.

If you can concentrate when you are doing one kind of activity, you can learn to concentrate when you are doing other kinds. Choose an activity in which you have good concentration whether it be playing baseball, video games or the accordion. (Think about activities you do well or love.) Analyze which factors help you to concentrate. Can you apply any of them to your acting singing?

EXERCISE 7. (I) *Taking the First Steps of Trust*

Objective: to increase your trust in yourself.

Instructions:

1. Choose a specific and not-too-challenging example of a performing element that is hard for you. Give yourself permission to try it in a class, coaching, or rehearsal. For example, "Tomorrow in rehearsal (or coaching or class) *I give myself permission* to:

- give full breath support to that high A, and let whatever sound comes out fill the entire space";
- let loose the feelings I feel as my character (on some particular word or phrase)";
- let my partner embrace me, and to receive his (character's) positive feelings when he sings, 'I love you.'"

2. As part of your plan, run through the scenarios of the worst things that could happen if you dare to take the risk you are considering. Don't edit out a thought or feeling just because it may seem irrational. Write them down. For instance: "My voice will crack," "My feelings will swamp my voice," "I'll blush," "I'll feel sexually excited," "My partner will think I love/hate him," or any of a myriad of other fears that may come to mind.

Below each of your worst possible scenarios, write down the phrases that you think would offset it most effectively. Some possible neutralizers: "It's just a class, a coaching, a rehearsal, an opera," "Nobody will confuse me with my character," "I'll never know how far 'too far' is until I try," "I'll receive applause for sharing my (character's) feelings."

3. Recall a situation in which you risked trusting yourself that turned out badly. Make a careful examination of how that may be affecting your current difficulties with self-trust. Ask yourself "What about that past experience is relevant to this present situation?" Try to separate out factors that are not relevant to an act of self-trust in the theater.

4. Recall a situation in which you had to say or do something difficult that worked out well. Recall the feelings of fear, anxiety, or insecurity that preceded that challenge; then recall the feelings that followed your success. Examine what you might usefully apply from that experience.

5. Before the rehearsal, coaching, or class actually begins, again reinforce the permission you have given yourself, and again remind yourself of your resolve. When the moment comes—risk it!

Afterwards, give yourself credit for any success—no matter how small. Use any positive feelings to bolster your self-trust and to build courage for your next attempt. Also notice any negative feelings, so you can try to lay them to rest before you try again.

If you did not go as far as you would have liked with the element you were trying to cultivate, do not punish yourself. Acknowledge what happened, do more private preparation, and try again another time.

Since you may have difficulty evaluating your success, consider asking someone to be an objective witness. Choose someone whose opinion you respect and who is not on stage with you for the moment in question. (The stage director, vocal coach, or teacher is often ideal.) Tell him what you are going to try. After the class, coaching, or rehearsal get his evaluation. Compare it with your own.

EXERCISE 8. (G) *Leaning* and *Leading the Blind*

Objective: to give your trust to others.

Trust developed in physically oriented exercises, such as the two that follow, can lay the foundation for psychological trust.

LEANING

Instructions:

Make a circle of five or six people with everyone standing shoulder-to-shoulder and facing in. Choose one person to go to the center to be "it." (By extending their arms, all the people in the circle should be able to reach the shoulders of the person who is "it"; if not, make the circle smaller.)

The person who is "it" allows herself to lean straight backward, and, keeping her body rigid, begins to fall until she is caught by members of the circle behind her.

The members of the circle are committed to preventing the leaning person from falling to the floor. After they catch her, they raise her to her feet and then gently push her off balance until she falls toward other people in the circle. The person who is "it" lets herself fall in the direction she is pushed until she is caught again—trusting that the others will protect her from harm.

Continue this process slowly and gently four or five times; then choose a new person to be "it."

LEADING THE BLIND

Instructions:

1. Pair off. One member of each pair closes his eyes or is blindfolded and allows himself to be led by the other. After the blindfold is on, other participants may rearrange the objects in the room. The leader's task is to be sure that the

"blind" person comes to no harm; the "blind" person's task is to explore his world using all his senses except sight.

2. Repeat step 1, but the leader may use only her voice to guide the "blind" person.

3. Repeat step 1, but with a dramatic premise. For instance: you two are the only survivors of a plane crash in the mountains, in a forest, or on a deserted island. You are best friends, or siblings, or husband and wife, or archenemies. One of you has been blinded in the crash. (Is the other person also injured? Perhaps she has a broken leg?) You must get help or die.

PART II

CREATING YOUR CHARACTER

Part II will help you decode the material in musical scores to build believable characters. Chapters 5 and 6 give an overview of how to make the most effective interpretive choices and how music-theater works are constructed.

Chapters 7 through 10 help you work through a piece from the big ideas to the small details. You will first learn how to fashion a theme statement that organizes your other choices, and how to fashion a super-objective that clarifies the need driving your character through the entire piece. Next, you will explore how to fashion objectives and acting beats to motivate each of your character's individual actions. Finally, you are given the techniques you need to fashion an internal dialogue for your character out of his subtext and internal thoughts.

If you are pressed for time when preparing a role, focus on the chapters on fashioning objectives and subtext as they are the most essential for creating believable characters.

CHAPTER 5

Neither "Right" nor "Wrong": Making Effective Interpretive Choices

Freeing Yourself to Make Interpretive Choices

Why would Carmen want to dump José only days after she begged him to run off with her? Is it that she cannot be faithful to one man, or is it that she feels she cannot be the person that he wants? Either answer is plausible, but each would create a different personality, so which one is right? Even Bizet and his librettists, Meilhac and Halévy, couldn't tell you. They could explain what they intended, but since what emerges out of the creative act often has subtleties, complexities, and possibilities beyond the makers' intentions, even their answers would not be the last word.

As you interpret your material, you will confront numerous questions about your character that have several possible answers. Like forks in a road, these divergent possibilities will lead your character to different ways of behaving on stage, different personalities, different vocal colors. At each junction you can only choose one fork. How do you choose?

In this part of the book you will be given many helpful questions to raise about your character and ways to plumb the score for useful answers. However, because the answers you choose are interpretive ones, they will be not "right" or "wrong" but instead more or less clear and useful.

As you search not for a single right road but rather for the clearest or most effective one, you are aided enormously by two facts I have touched on before: the territory you're exploring has distinct boundaries; and every note, word and action was included by the composer and librettist in the belief that they would effectively further their intentions. The first fact limits the possible paths you must choose among; you do not need to find your way to the riverhead-of-all-creativity or surmount the mountain-of-all-musicals. The second guarantees that you can make your choices with the certainty that everything your character does has at least one reason.

Start with the conviction that everything in a piece makes sense, and you will find sense in everything in it.

A useful way to make clear and effective choices is to ask questions about every piece of information that is either in or relevant to the score. Start with large questions about the composer and librettist. What issues preoccupied their times? What issues interested them? What socio-political changes were occurring? For instance, Mozart lived during the transition from the Age of Enlightenment to the Romantic era; this was also the time of the decline of the great absolutist monarchies in Europe and the rise of the new republican ideals. This knowledge can help you see that two themes penetrate Mozart's operas: a deep exploration into the nature of love and loving and, in all the mature works except *Cosi fan tutte*, a deep attraction to the ideals of a more democratic, just, and humanitarian society.

Ask questions about the formal construction of the work, and continue to pose ever more probing queries to work your way deeper and deeper into the details of the piece. The more questions you ask, even if you can only speculate on the answers, the more clues to viable choices you will uncover. (See exercise 4, "Questions," at the end of the chapter.)

Recognizing When Your Character Choices Will Work Well

As you sift through the many answers your questions will generate and insights your analysis will reveal, your goal is to assemble an effective and believable interpretation of your character. To this end it is very useful to add into the mix both your imagination (to re-create your character's experiences) and your empathy (to identify with his feelings and dilemmas).

You have developed an effective interpretation when:

• It clarifies every word you sing and every action you do.
• It leads to actions you can execute and believe in.

• It maintains the integrity of the piece.
• It is internally consistent.
• It meshes well with the choices of your colleagues: the other performers, the conductor, the director, the choreographer, and the designers.
• It is based on a thorough understanding of the piece—including the period, the composer's style, the dramatic theme, the music, the text, the characters, and the way these components reinforce each other.
• It is convincing and packs enough of an appropriate emotional wallop to bring the piece to life.

As you mold your character by your interpretive answers, your work as a performer becomes a creative adventure. Like the librettist and composer of your piece, you are an artist interpreting the human experience in art.

Interpreting the Music to Help Make Effective Character Choices

Music with Text

Tonight, tonight,
It all began tonight,
I saw you and the world went away.
West Side Story

If you are like millions of people around the globe, when you read these words, a melody immediately comes to mind; but these words didn't always have a tune.

When Steven Sondheim created this text, he looked for words to express the excitement and commitment of two young people in love, but he wrote them without music. Leonard Bernstein invented the melody and set the words to it. Like most composers setting text, he sought to capture the character's feelings. This process reflects the way music-theater pieces, and particularly operas, lieder, and art songs are most often created. First the librettist writes the text, often in consultation with the composer, then the composer interprets the words and the emotions they express in music and in so doing gives the words new depths of feeling.

Like the composer, you, too, can usefully start your interpretation from the text. Use it as a key to reveal what feelings the music may be exploring, then pay attention to the subtle nuances of feeling that the music is adding. What emotional colors does it suggest that you can use to give additional depth and believability to the choices you are making about your character?

Music Without Text

Just as with the music that has text, once you get a feel for the emotional colors that music that is not accompanying text suggests, you can use it to help make effective choices—naturally these would be mostly for your character's internal dialogue.

If, in a passage without text such as a prelude, interlude, or postlude, you find music that does not seem to be expressive of any characters' feelings as suggested by words that come before or after, ask these questions:

> "*Does* this music reflect an idea or dramatic theme?" (Listen to hear whether the music appears more than once, and whether it appears predictably with a recurring event or specific character.)
>
> "*Does* this music evoke a mood or place? Does it reflect text or stage directions that suggest a particular time or locale?" For example, is it dawn by a bubbling brook?
>
> "*Is* this music a comment on the action, the characters, or their feelings?" For instance, has the composer used the bassoon to help us see a character as pompous and foolish?

Since music can be astonishingly multilayered, explore whether it is functioning simultaneously both as an evocation of a character's feelings and a comment on them.

Summary

Since every music-theater piece expresses its creators' interpretation of human experience, your preparation and performance are an interpretation of an interpretation. This means you do not have to worry about whether your choices are "right" but only whether they are illuminating and sensitive to the material, and whether they help you create a believable character. You are free to exercise your judgment, intelligence, empathy, and imagination.

Most often, the music you sing directly or indirectly expresses feelings that arise from the text. Therefore, you can use the text as a window to understand the music. Once you can see the nuances of feelings the music suggests, you can use it as an aid to make effective and believable choices about your character.

Exercises

These exercises help you to experience both text and music as material you can interpret to create a character. Exercises 1 and 2 focus on the text; exercises 4–6 focus on the music; exercise 3 requires close examination of both.

EXERCISE 1. (G) *Description as Interpretation*

Objective: to experience how differently people may interpret the same event.

Instructions:

One person in a group takes a pose (it needs to be one that he can hold for three minutes). Everyone looks at the "model" as if he is in an emotional situation. Each person writes a description of the situation she imagines the model to be in. After three minutes, the writers share and compare.

EXERCISE 2. (I/G) *Reading Texts as Choice*

Objective: to experience how interpretive choices alter the meaning of a text.

Instructions:

1. Read the following paragraphs aloud several times; each time with a different motivation. For instance, "I *want* to entertain," "I *want* to do it right," "I *want* to terrify," or "I *want* to escape punishment." Exactly what do you change to make your motivations clear? How do the different motivations change the meaning of the paragraphs?

> Last Monday was not a day I would wish on anybody—not even on Richard. It was the kind of day that defies retelling, since listing the disasters would only make them seem ridiculous, but had they happened to you, I promise you, you would not have laughed.
>
> Richard might have laughed, but, of course, one of his most endearing traits is his ability to take pleasure in the sorrows of others. Yes, I know it's hard to imagine that as an endearing trait, but believe me, compared to his other twisted attributes, that one is positively charming.

Try to choose a motivation that turns these paragraphs into nonsense. Can you find one? If you can't, speculate why not. Could it be that a text can take on an infinite variety of colors? That in some sense the meaning is less in the words themselves than in what the speaker is trying to express?

2. See how many ways you can say the phrase: "It was the kind of day that defies retelling." If you are in a group, the listeners should indicate what they think the speaker felt and meant after each version.

3. Choose a short article from a magazine or newspaper. As in the previous exercise, read it several times, giving yourself a different motivation each time. What motivation would make your reading come out the way you believe the author intended? What clues to his intention can you discover? Consider the sequence of ideas and his specific word choices.

EXERCISE 3. (I) *Viewpoint*

Objective: to explore a piece for its content and viewpoint.

Instructions:

Choose an aria or song you know well. Make a list of at least six items or concepts about which it implies some judgment or interpretive comment. For each item write a brief summary. For example, Carmen's "Seguidilla":

Gypsy women: unconventional, promiscuous, dangerous

Spanish towns: volatile (need soldiers); strong class differences

The relationship between the sexes: women are temptresses, men temptable

Seduction: a contest

Life as a soldier: a conflict between duty and desire

Manipulation: people's emotions make them vulnerable

EXERCISE 4. (I) *Questions***

Objective: to learn how to use questions to make interpretive choices about your music.

As discussed earlier, you can count on the fact that the composer and librettist had a reason for each note and word that they included in their score, that if you can figure out their logic it will help you to make informed choices, and that one effective way to explore their logic is to question every piece of information in the score. Question everything from the formal construction of the piece—including the order and manner in which the characters are introduced and developed—to the orchestration for a particular word. You cannot ask too many questions.

For many of the questions you may ask there are no right or wrong answers. Research may help, but ultimately you can only make informed interpretations. Nonetheless, you will be amazed at how much you can discover about a piece by asking questions and then speculating intelligently on the answers.

Instructions:

1. Choose a music-theater piece on which you are currently working, or that you know well. Start at the top of the first page of the score. Ask questions about everything on the page: every note, word, tempo marking, or dynamic indication. Ask yourself:

"Why did the composer or librettist choose this particular title?"

Maybe he chose it to emphasize a character, a quality, or an event. Maybe he chose it to de-emphasize another obvious option. Rossini, for example, may have chosen the title *The Barber of Seville* over *Figaro* to emphasize the social role of a barber over the personality of a character. Assume the title is an arrow pointing to a central theme or issue of the piece.

"Who is the composer?"

When did he live? What other music-theater pieces did he compose? Who were his contemporaries—in music, art, architecture, politics, religion, scene design, literature?

"Who is the librettist?"

Answer the same questions about his contemporaries as you did for the composer. Ask: "What else did he write; what were the major themes of those works?"

2. Consider the score as a whole. Look at the way the piece is structured and the orchestra is used. Some of the many questions you might pose and then try to answer: How many acts are there and how does the number of acts relate to how the story and characters are developed? How many characters are there? How does each one contribute to developing the theme? How many ensembles are there? Where do they occur? Is the action developed in them? How many arias are there? Do they help move the action forward? Who sings them? What precipitates their need to sing? Consider the instrumentation: How large is the orchestra? What kinds of instruments are in it? How is the instrumentation used to develop the characters or their feelings?

3. Go to the first page you sing. Keep asking and answering questions.

"Why did the composer choose this particular tempo or mood marking at the beginning of this piece?" ("andante," "lento," "quickly," "with feeling," etc.) What does it suggest about the feeling of the piece? About the composer's intention?

"Why did the composer choose this particular form?" (For instance, in the *Magic Flute*, why did Mozart use the melody of an old Lutheran chorale with a solemn counterpoint for the duet of the two Armed Men? Why did he choose a folksong style for Papageno's first aria?)

"Why did the composer write using this particular clef?" Is there a reason that each character is set in a particular range? Does the range of each character suggest anything about his personality, age, or function? (Does it, for instance, reinforce his identity as the good guy?) Is there a reason that particular characters are male or female? Are the ideas, thoughts, or feelings of any of the main characters especially appropriate for a particular sex? (Watch out for stereotypes.) Does the choice of sex reflect a particular propensity of the composer? (Puccini preferred women as main characters; Verdi mostly used men). How does this relate to the issues that concerned them? How does it relate to the social movements of their times?

"Why did the composer choose this particular time signature?" (Different time signatures have different stress patterns, and set up different pulses.) How does the musical meter reflect the meter of the text, and what effect does that create? What does it tell us about the characters who are singing the music? What does it suggest about what they are feeling?

"Why did he choose this particular rhythmic quality (e.g., a march, a waltz, a minuet)?"

"Why did the composer choose this particular key?" (Different keys suggest different moods. Many composers consistently use particular keys for certain kinds of feelings. Mozart, for instance, uses D minor consistently in *Don Giovanni* to evoke damnation and hellfire.) What does the key tell you about the feeling of the piece?

Examine each pitch and rhythmic value in relation to its text, or to the text it precedes or follows.

"Why did the composer begin on this particular pitch?" What does it tell us about the character or the action? Ask the same question for the second note, and the third.

"Why did he choose this particular duration for the first note? The second? The third?" What sort of feelings do his choices create?

As you search for the answers to the questions about individual notes and rhythms, you may find it fruitful to think in terms of the phrase, the musical sentence of which they are a part.

Question each dynamic marking. What does it suggest about the characters' thoughts or feelings?

"Why did the composer choose this instrumentation?"

Keep asking questions.

EXERCISE 5. *Composing***

Objective: to experience music as an interpretation of words.

Even if you have never composed before, you can deepen your understanding of music as an interpretation of a text by trying your hand at setting some words to a few measures of music.

Instructions:

1. Choose two lines of sung text from an opera, musical, lied, or song; set them to your own melody. Start by exploring the text; what is your interpretation of the literal and emotional meanings of the words? Hum a tune that expresses your feelings about the words or, if you prefer, imagine yourself as the "I" of the song and try humming a melody that is expressive of his feelings. Try several melodies. Record or notate them as you make them up. After you have hummed a tune that feels right, try singing it with the words. (You will probably have to make some changes to make the words fit. You do not have to set

each syllable to a separate note, but be sure the words are stressed correctly.) Sing your tune with the words into a tape recorder.

Compare your melody to the one the composer wrote. What feelings do you hear in yours that are different from those evoked by the original composer? What elements in your composition evoke the feelings?

If you are in a group, have each person do her version of the melody and discuss what qualities she hoped to capture.

2. Choose a short spoken phrase that expresses a strong feeling: "I can't stand it when you leave me," "My parents make me crazy," "I love living in a big city." Say the phrase with three different intentions. Make up a melody for each version that reflects the different feelings.

EXERCISE 6. (I) *Taking the Long View*

Objective: to see an opera or musical as an interpretation of human experience.

It is often easier to see the relationship between a work's music and the issues it addresses in contemporary compositions, since they tend to reflect your own times. Therefore, for this exercise focus on recently composed musicals.

Instructions:

Listen to some musicals of the 1940s and 1950s (*Street Scene, Most Happy Fella, Oklahoma, West Side Story*) and compare them with recent ones.

Do you observe any changes in the issues they address? How would you describe these changes—from more romantic to more realistic, or from public to personal? Do you observe a change in their view of love? Of hope? What do you think has caused any changes? Were they written during war or peace, during economic depression or prosperity? Do you think the changes reflect a shift of interest in the audiences, or are they, perhaps, the result of a different class or age of people buying the tickets?

Look at the ways in which musical, structural, and theatrical conventions may have changed between earlier and more recent musicals. Are there more or fewer large production numbers? Do the production numbers serve the same functions? Have the musical numbers and dialogues continued to be the same length? Is the relationship between the orchestra and the action the same? Is the orchestra the same size? Does it have the same instruments in it? Is the same kind of singing expected? Speculate on the causes of any changes.

CHAPTER 6

Your Character's Universe: Analyzing the Dramatic Structure of Music-Theater Pieces

The Music-Theater Master Plan

The overwhelming majority of music-theater pieces are built from closely similar blueprints. They combine four kinds of building blocks—the first three of which they share with spoken theater pieces—to create variations of a stock dramatic structure. This common origin allows you to construct believable characters by using only a few powerful tools that are applicable to songs, art songs, lieder, musicals, and operas alike.

The Four Dramatic Building Blocks

Characters: All dramatic pieces are developed using characters. These characters always believe they are real. They inevitably engage in dialogue, either with themselves or with others.

Actions: Characters are driven to action by overwhelming needs that motivate their every thought, word, and deed.

Conflicts: As the characters take action, they come into conflict with each other. The conflicts are chosen to explore some central theme and to arouse strong feelings that motivate the music, reveal the characters, and engage the audience.

Music: Characters sing when their feelings are so strong that mere speech is insufficient. The music reveals and heightens these feelings. It deepens the engagement of the audience and lends color, nuance, and energy to the characters' lives and dilemmas.

Developing the Action in the Stock Dramatic Structure

The stock dramatic structure organizes the flow of time and action in a piece. It shapes the music and the development of the characters' encounters by giving a four-part form to a story known as the plot.

> *The exposition* is the opening section in which the characters, their personalities, relationships, conflicts, and points of view are introduced.
>
> *The development* makes up the body of a piece and consists of a sequence of situations designed to bring the characters into conflicts of increasing intensity that deepen our understanding of them and of the theme.
>
> *The climax* is the ultimate confrontation in which the main characters face off, with everything at stake.
>
> *The resolution* brings the piece to a close, resolving the conflicts and establishing a new order that illuminates the theme.

The four parts of the stock dramatic structure are the same for both comedies and tragedies. The differences between the two lie primarily in how the conflicts are resolved and how far-reaching the effects of the resolution are implied to be.

In comedies, the conflicts are resolved in favor of the "Good Guys" and often lead to their marriage. The resolution only directly affects those immediately involved—usually the lovers, their families, and the "Bad Guy." In *The Barber of Seville*, for example, the conflicts are resolved by the Good Guy and the Girl eloping and the Bad Guy being paid off. They are the only ones who are directly affected. ("Good Guy" and "Bad Guy" as used here are not terms of moral judgment but simply describe how the characters function in the plot.)

In tragedies, the stakes are elevated to matters of life and death. The Good Guys do not succeed in getting what they *want*, and often the resolution has serious social consequences. In *Macbeth*, Macbeth does not fulfill his ambitions, and the consequences of his actions are multiple deaths and a change in the ruling dynasty of Scotland. In *Lucia di Lammermoor*, Lucia does not succeed in marrying Edgardo, and her unfulfilled love for him precipitates not only her death, and that of Edgardo and Arturo, but the fall of her family from power. *Carmen* ends with the death of the Girl and the profound despair (and likely execution) of the Good Guy; in this case, however, there are no larger social consequences. In *West Side Story* the lives of two young people are squandered and the consequences are mixed. On the one hand, love has been left unfilled and two young men—their lives once full of promise—are dead. On the other hand, the surviving young people declare their belief in the future and in so doing offer us all hope.

In songs, art songs, and lieder, the stock dramatic structure is often abbreviated and may not have an overtly depicted development, climax, and resolution. In most cases the "I" of the song does have something he *wants* that causes conflicts so intense that he must sing. These conflicts may be with others, or they may be internal. Sometimes, however, the "I" of the song bursts into song simply because he is overflowing with feelings: "I *love* Spring!"

Developing the Action in a Typical Plot

By far the most common plot is the love triangle. The three essential characters are the Good Guy, the Girl, and the Bad Guy (who may be male or female and who personifies the obstacle to the successful union of the Good Guy and the Girl). Typically, the Good Guy *wants* the Girl, and the Girl *wants* the Good Guy (although sometimes she must be wooed). The Bad Guy *wants* to get rid of the Good Guy—usually because he *wants* the Girl for himself, but sometimes he has another motive such as revenge. Occasionally the Bad Guy is not an actual villain but a destructive force, as in *West Side Story.*

The love triangle plot can be used in either tragedies or comedies to explore an astonishing variety of themes. In comedies it is often employed to develop some version of the theme "True love wins out." (*The Barber of Seville, The Elixir of Love, La Cenerentola, Oklahoma,* and *Most Happy Fella* are all examples.)

To clarify the love triangle plot, I will examine a simplified imaginary model—focusing on characters, actions, and conflicts. Then I will briefly compare the use of those same elements in actual operas with love triangle plots. Later I will discuss how to add the element of music to the model.

I will use the version of the love triangle in which the Good Guy must woo the Girl, and the Bad Guy is out to get rid of the Good Guy not because he wants the Girl but because he wants to eliminate the Good Guy. I have also chosen to make it comedy, which, as you will observe, does not affect the intensity of the conflicts. The theme will be the often explored "True love wins out."

As I outline the action of each scene, I will also describe how the action functions to develop the theme and the characters, so it is clear why the scene needs to be included.

First Scene

(The locker room after a basketball game.) The Good Guy is the center on a team which has just won the championship. He has invited the Girl to come to the locker room after the game. The Good Guy is celebrated, and the Girl is admired by his teammates. (The scene functions to establish the Good Guy and the Girl as desirable—he for being a successful athlete, she for being attractive.)

Second Scene

(Outside the gym.) As the Good Guy escorts the Girl out of the gym, the Bad Guy, who is hiding on the roof, drops a concrete block on the Good Guy. The Good Guy, sensing danger, sweeps the Girl to safety and jumps aside as the block crashes harmlessly to the ground. (The scene functions to set up the conflict, to establish the Bad Guy as dangerous, to establish the Good Guy as heroic, and to give the Girl reasons to admire the Good Guy.) Obviously, the Good Guy must escape from the Bad Guy's first attempt to kill him, or the piece would be over.

Third Scene

(Restaurant.) As they enter, the Good Guy buys the Girl a beautiful corsage, and pins it on her; the Girl is pleased and flattered. (The scene functions to establish that the Good Guy is generous and that the Girl is gracious, as well as to heighten her beauty and provide a moment of physical closeness between them.)

The Good Guy orders an excellent wine and an elegant dinner with great verve. (The scene functions to show that the Good Guy is more than just a good athlete, it confirms his generosity, and suggests that as a husband he will be a good provider.)

Soup is served. Just as they are about to eat it, the Girl smells something wrong. She pushes the spoon away from the Good Guy's mouth, saving him from being poisoned. She runs to the kitchen, where the Bad Guy is seen escaping through the back door. (The scene functions to establish the Girl as intelligent and heroic and, therefore, even more desirable, and to show that the Bad Guy is dangerously cunning.)

Fourth Scene

(Outside the restaurant.) After dinner, the Good Guy and the Girl walk out of the restaurant hand in hand. As they step off the curb, the Bad Guy attempts to run the Good Guy over with his car. The Good Guy deftly jumps out of the way, pulling the Girl to safety. He picks up a rock, and throws it with such force and accuracy that it hits the Bad Guy in the head as he drives away. The car crashes, and the Bad Guy runs off on foot. (The scene functions to further confirm the Bad Guy's villainy, to confirm the Good Guy's desirability, and to reinforce the elements of gratitude and admiration in the Girl's growing attraction to the Good Guy.)

Completing the stock dramatic structure, there is a string of such scenes in which the Girl and the Good Guy fall increasingly in love, and the Bad Guy becomes increasingly cunning in his attempts to kill the Good Guy. Ultimately, the piece rises to a climax in which there is a face-to-face showdown. Since the piece is a comedy, the Good Guy, perhaps aided by the Girl, triumphs over the Bad Guy, confirming that love wins out. If the piece were a tragedy exploring a theme like "The world is too bad for love to flourish," then the Bad Guy would win—perhaps killing them both.

Here is a brief overview of how the love triangle plot is used in a number of operas. Let us first look at some comedies and then some tragedies.

In *The Marriage of Figaro,* the Good Guy, Figaro, and the Girl, Susanna, want each other from the beginning. The Bad Guy, the Count, is doubly bad in that he wants the Girl, and he is a married man. In *The Elixir of Love,* the Good Guy, Nemorino, wants the girl, and the Girl wants the Good Guy, although she is unable to acknowledge it at first. There is a Bad Guy, Belcore, who gets in the Good Guy's way, but the real obstacle is the fears of the Good Guy and the Girl. In *La Cenerentola,* the Good Guy, the Prince, wants the Girl, Cenerentola. The stepfather and stepsisters are the Bad Guy; the sisters want the Good Guy, and the stepfather wants a rich, hassle-free life, which motivates him to promote the stepsisters' designs on the Prince. In the main plot of *Falstaff,* Mrs. Ford and Mrs. Page are the Girls; it is implied that their husbands are the Good Guys. Falstaff is the Bad Guy because he abuses the very idea of love. In the subplot, Fenton is the Good Guy, Anne is the Girl, and her father is the Bad Guy who stands between them.

There are tragedies that use the love triangle plot in quite straightforward versions, such as *Otello* and *Wozzeck.* However, tragedies often employ complex variations. In *Lucia di Lammermoor,* it is the Girl's own brother who is the Bad Guy. In *Madama Butterfly,* the Good Guy becomes the Bad Guy when he abandons the Girl. In *Tristan und Isolde,* the Bad Guy may be Tristan, or the demonic power of love—depending on your interpretation. In *West Side Story,* the Bad Guy isn't really a person, but, as I already suggested, the force of hatred.

The Music as an Emotional and Dramatic Voice

Picture the drinking scene with the Toreador in *Carmen* without the music, or "Tonight" from *West Side Story* without singing and orchestration. Imagine how unmemorable and unmoving they would be. Music is used in the theater because it has an amazing ability to heighten the expression of feelings. It can create excitement and adulation for a character; it can turn simple words into a deeply moving experience. However, music, and singing in particular, requires strong motivations to justify its presence, which is why the plots of music-theater pieces are so filled with crises.

Although the details vary depending whether the piece is an opera, operetta, or musical and how exactly the composer has manipulated the form, normally when characters in music-theater pieces are not emotionally agitated, they "talk." This may take the form of speak-singing, like secco recitative in operas, or normal speech in operettas and musicals. Such sections may have a light accompaniment or no accompaniment at all. As the emotional tension heats up, the accompaniment gets richer, or provides the motivation to add musical underscoring where there was none. When the characters' feelings become so strong that they break into song, the intensity of the accompaniment also increases, although it still can vary from a light instrumental texture to full orchestration. The choice of musical accompaniment is partly a matter of style and convention. However, whether the music is for a recitative, aria, ensemble, or orchestral interlude, whether in a musical, operetta, or opera, it almost always increases in density and more forcefully illustrates emotions in synchrony with the words and action as the emotional tension rises.

Once a piece moves into full-throated musical expression, time is allowed to expand, and the full resources of music to explore feelings are given sway. This may include flights of coloratura like those Lucia uses as an expression of her madness, the evocative use of orchestral colors like Mozart's chilling use of the trombones as Don Giovanni goes to hell, or the extended use of the orchestra to add a whole emotional voice of its own as Wagner did in *Tristan und Isolde.*

With these general principals in mind, consider how you would add music to the model love triangle scenario we developed earlier. Your first decision will be to choose the musical style that is most suitable for the situations, the conflicts, and the character's feelings. Since my scenario is essentially light in content and tone; uses young people in a casual, contemporary, American setting; involves situations that are only slightly heightened from daily events and have consequences only for the people directly involved, you will probably serve the piece best by using a musical comedy style. It offers the possibility of a contemporary sound and a free-flowing mix of speaking and singing.

If you do choose an operatic sound for this scenario, you will want to keep it light, or you will almost surely appear to be making fun of the characters because their troubles will seem trivial in comparison to the weight of the music.

After you choose a musical style, select the appropriate places for orchestration and singing. These will be the moments when the emotional tension is the highest. In the first scene, you might use orchestration as the team celebrates their victory, for the entrance of the Girl, and for the walk into danger as the Good Guy and the Girl leave the gym.

You might start the orchestration as the team comes running in; you could build it to the entrance of the Good Guy, when you could have the team break into a chorus number celebrating their heroic center. Then, after some dialogue, you could start the orchestration again as the Girl is about to enter, and have it climax when the eyes of the Girl and the Good Guy meet. (Do you want it to serve as the preparation for a duet between them?) After this intense moment, everyone probably returns to nonsung-dialogue. As the Good Guy and the Girl get ready to leave, you might resume the orchestration and have it climax with a sound illustrating the crash of the cement block.

Based on the intense feelings involved, you could also justify moving into singing again right before the Bad Guy drops the cement block. He might even sing a song about his hatred of the Good Guy. Immediately after the block is dropped, you could have a trio for the Good Guy, the Girl, and the Bad Guy, or maybe just a duet for the Good Guy and the Girl.

The duet might be called "Surviving the Cement Block." Its major textual idea might be "I can't believe how lucky we are"; its central emotion would be relief.

Slightly developed, the text might go: "I can't believe how lucky we are; no, no, I can't believe it. You're not hurt, I'm not hurt, I can't believe it, we're so very lucky, Oh, how lucky we are!"

Since this is the beginning of a love story, the duet might have a middle section in which the Good Guy and the Girl sing simultaneously but independently:

> *He:* "Her skin was warm and soft as I brushed her arm. Oh how very, very lovely."
> *She:* "He moved so swiftly to save me from harm. Oh how very, very swiftly."

The duet could conclude with a repetition of the first section.

Summary

All theater pieces, comedies and tragedies alike, are developed using the same basic structure: the main characters struggle to attain something they passionately *want*, which brings them into conflict. The conflicts generate strong feelings and are designed to illuminate some central theme. As the piece proceeds, the conflicts increase in intensity. Finally, the main characters clash in an ultimate confrontation that leads to a resolution of the conflicts and to the conclusion of the piece.

In music-theater, the expression of feelings is heightened by the added element of music. Music gives the characters time and subtle means to explore many emotional colors and can add additional layers of commentary as well. Thus in Carmen's "Seguidilla," the music adds a smoldering sensuality and supports Carmen as she tries to seduce José by teasing, cajoling, enticing, rejecting, and tempting him. The density of the textures of the musical accompaniment and the degree to which it illustrates specific words or actions almost always parallels the intensity of the characters' feelings.

The consistency with which these patterns are employed enables you to use the same basic approach to analyze and to interpret songs, lieder, art songs, and your roles in operas and musicals.

Exercises: Understanding Dramatic Construction

EXERCISE 1. (I) *Break It Down*

Objective: to practice analyzing the structure of music-theater pieces to reveal the conflicts between the characters.

Instructions:

1. Choose a musical or opera you know well or are currently working on. Using stock labels like "Good Guy" or "Evil Servant," make a list of the conflicts between the major characters.

Identify the source(s) of their conflicts.
Identify what is at stake for the characters in each conflict. Is there a progression in the depth or intensity of the conflicts?
Identify the climactic conflict.
Briefly describe the resolution.

Develop Given Circumstances for the character you might perform—whether major or not. As you develop your *want* and *why,* be sure that they set in motion the appropriate conflicts with the other characters.

2. Choose a song, lied, or art song you know well. Make a list of the conflicts the "I" of the song is experiencing. Remember that his conflict may be an internal struggle—for example, between the part that loves someone and the part that is too shy to take any action. As you did in step 1, identify the source of his conflicts, what's at stake, when the climax comes, and how the piece handles the conflict at its conclusion. (Skip any step that truly doesn't apply.)

If the "I" of your song is not in any conflict, identify what he *wants.*

EXERCISE 2. (I) *No Conflict*

Objective: to explore the usefulness of conflict as a dramatic device.
Instructions:

1. Try to invent a scenario for a piece with two or three characters in which the characters don't conflict. It has to be something that would hold an audi-

ence's interest, and it has to offer opportunities for singing. You don't have to develop the dialogue or any minor characters—just sketch out the idea, and list the major scenes. For instance you might begin with "A single mother wants to give her baby to an orphanage."

2. See if you can find some exceptions to the assertion that all operas and musicals are constructed by setting some of the major characters into conflict with each other. Discuss what keeps the audiences' interest.

3. Consider how the conflicts between or within the characters is handled in the construction of several different pieces. Try comparing a serious and a comic piece, or an opera and a musical. Examine any of the following pieces for some interesting problems of construction: *Sunday in the Park with George, A Chorus Line, Suor Angelica, Hair, Amahl and the Night Visitors.*

EXERCISE 3. (I/G)   *No Emotions*

Objective: to explore the usefulness of feelings in motivating singing.
Instructions:

1. See if you can name any songs or arias that are not about, or don't include, intense feelings. What are they about? What makes them interesting?

2. Choose two songs or arias that have a lot of words and little repetition. One might be a "patter" song. How are the words set? (Do they have a complicated melody or rhythm?) What is the accompaniment like? What feelings are expressed, how intensely, and through what means?

3. Choose a song or aria that has a very brief text and a lot of repetition. (Can you find any that have fewer than three words? (How about: "Leave me" or "Love me"?) How are the words set? What is the accompaniment like? Is it the same for each repetition? If it is different, how is it different? Do the differences suggest changing emotional colors? In a song with so little text, what has the composer done to hold the audience's interest?

4. Either by yourself or with friends, try writing the text and music for a song with intense feelings.

EXERCISE 4. (I)   *Love Triangles*

Objective: to clarify the usefulness of the love triangle as a basic plot device.
Instructions:

Identify some opera or musical theater plots that do not involve a love triangle. How do these plots work? What holds our interest? What gets us emotionally involved? Some operas to consider: *Billy Budd, Das Rheingold, The Turn of the Screw.*

CHAPTER 7

Your Character's World:
Fashioning a Theme Statement

Defining the Theme

The theme is the central issue or question that a piece explores. It is the big idea that holds the music, words, and actions together. The theme may revolve around any topic of human interest, from love, hatred, and jealousy to power, family, politics, money, religion, health, homelessness, mercy killing, or aging.

A theme statement combines your distillation of the main issue of a piece and the viewpoint from which it is explored. Possible points of view are as varied as the issues themselves. If the issue is aging, a piece might explore it as the fulfill-ment of life's experiences, a process to be postponed as long as possible, the loss of possibilities, or the gateway to enlightenment. You develop a theme statement based on a comprehensive view of all the material in the score: the music in all its aspects (melody, harmony, rhythm, instrumentation, and dynamics), the text (including the characters and the conflicts of the plot), and the stage directions.

Your interpretation of the theme is one of your most important artistic choices. Once you encapsulate it in a concise theme statement it becomes the compass that guides you toward a believable character at each fork of the road.

Here are examples of possible theme statements for some well-known op-eras and musicals. Naturally, since they are interpretations, they are neither de-finitive or exclusive.

> *Carmen* decries the disaster of mismatched needs in love.
> *West Side Story* celebrates the triumph of love over hate.
> *The Marriage of Figaro* applauds the erosion of aristocratic privilege or, equally viable, it commends reconciliation as the maturation of love.

La Bohème explores how young people grow in the face of death.
The Man of La Mancha glorifies the rewards of pursuing your own vision.
Falstaff extols the integration of the outcast.
Lucia di Lammermoor confronts personal passion with political necessity.

Defining the Qualities of the Most Useful Theme Statements

The most useful theme statements define the necessity for the presence of each major character and tie together the actions and feelings of the major characters into a coherent vision. They concisely clarify what is unique about the piece. For instance, although *Carmen* and *West Side Story* both involve unfulfilled love and tragic deaths, useful theme statements, like those listed earlier, clarify how they are different.

When fashioning a theme statement for any piece that involves a love story, be careful to distinguish whether love is a thematic issue or simply a plot device, For instance, in *Rigoletto* love is used as a plot device to examine the misuse of power. The Duke's manipulation of Gilda through her love for him demonstrates how he abuses his position. In *Falstaff*, Falstaff's self-serving actions in the name of love are used as a plot device to establish how far outside the norms of society he stands and, therefore, how crucial is his reintegration.

The Marriage of Figaro is an interesting case since, depending on your interpretation, love may be central to the theme or it may be a device used to examine other issues. If you focus on the Count's philandering, his jealousy, and his desire to decide Marcellina's lawsuit against Figaro, you might say the theme revolves around questions of power and control. However, if you focus on the amazing reunion between Figaro and his parents in the third act and on the extraordinary moment of forgiveness between the Count and Countess at the end of the opera, then you might say the theme revolves around reconciliation and the maturation of love.

Fashioning a Theme Statement

As previously mentioned, your theme statement will be useful only if you base it on all the materials in the score. The very best way to begin is to play and sing through the score several times yourself. If that is not practical, an efficient process is to listen to a recording of the entire piece a number of times while following the score. Notice the orchestration, dynamic markings, and any stage directions. (Notice, too, what has been left out or changed to suit the interpretation of the performers, such as cuts in recitatives or interpolated high notes.) You may want to enrich your sense of the piece by also watching a video.

Get to know the characters, the story, and the way it is told. Notice the ideas and interactions that stand out for you. Then, as you listen to the piece and follow the score again, ask yourself "What is the entire piece about?" Take note of any ideas, conflicts, or feelings that are emphasized by the melodies, rhythms, or orchestration. Jot down your thoughts. The next time through, stop after each scene. (For these purposes, consider a new scene to begin each time one of the main characters enters or exits.) Try making a list of the most important conflicts and the major issues that are raised in the scene. Ask yourself what theme the scene may be helping to develop.

When you have thoroughly familiarized yourself with the piece, review your list of conflicts and your notes on the issues. Apply your imagination to see if there seems to be a single idea that ties all the scenes together. Include in your considerations the kind of message you, as an artist, want to put out into the world. For instance, if in *The Marriage of Figaro* you focus on the Count's need for power, you might see his reconciliation with the Countess as only a brief moment of peace in a deeply troubled relationship. Then your theme statement would emphasize how difficult it is for humans to change. If, on the other hand, you focus on the reconciliations, then your theme statement would emphasize love. Which message do you want to send? (In my mind, the joyful music in the Sextet that accompanies Figaro, Susanna, Marcellina, and Bartolo as they celebrate Figaro's reunion with his parents and the astonishing music to which the Count begs forgiveness of the Countess leaves no question of Mozart's intended message.)

How to Use the Plot to Fashion a Theme Statement

The plot is not the theme; however, an analysis of the plot and the characters in it can help you to fashion a theme statement. After all, the conflicts in the plot are chosen to explore the central issue, and each of the main characters embodies a point of view toward it.

In the following sections I will explore two somewhat different techniques you can use to fashion a theme statement from the plot. Using *Carmen*, I will analyze a list of the actions and conflicts. Using *West Side Story*, I will analyze a plot summary that describes the characters in terms of their functions in the action.

Use the Actions and Conflicts of the Plot

Here is a list of actions and conflicts in *Carmen*, focusing on the interactions between Carmen and José.

ACT I

Carmen *throws* a (magical) flower at José. ("Habanera")

José *drags* Carmen out of the factory for fighting.

Carmen *begs* José to untie her.

Carmen *seduces* José—letting him know that she is available, interested, and where he can find her. ("Seguidilla")

Carmen *convinces* José to let her go free.

ACT II

Carmen *welcomes* José after he is released from prison, and *dances* for him. (Duet)

Carmen attempts to *persuade* José not to go back to the barracks for the night.

Carmen *rescues* José from a fight with his superior officer.

Carmen *cajoles* José into *joining* her and the other gypsies in the mountains.

ACT III

José tries to *hold on* to Carmen; Carmen *rejects* him and *predicts* they will die together.

José *leaves* to see his dying mother but *threatens* to return. Carmen *urges* him to go.

ACT IV

José, determined to win Carmen back, *grovels* at her feet. Carmen *spurns* him.

José *kills* her and *confesses* (so his execution seems inevitable).

On the basis of this breakdown, you could conclude that a logical theme statement for *Carmen* is "The price of love is death." However, to be really helpful, a theme statement needs to take the actions of all the main characters into account.

Escamillo's major actions are as follows.

ACT II

Escamillo *flirts* with Carmen.

ACT III

Escamillo *seeks out* Carmen in the mountains.

Escamillo *fights* with José; Escamillo *allows* José the victory but *promises* to *return* for Carmen.

ACT IV

Escamillo *parades* Carmen on his arm before the bullfight (but *does not insist* that she watch him fight.)

Once Escamillo wins Carmen, he does not seem wildly interested in her. Perhaps, as the "Toreador Song" suggests, he is too self-involved, or too needy of adulation, to devote himself to another person, but, whatever the cause, he appears to offer Carmen just what she seeks—passion without possession.

Micaëla's major actions are as follows.

ACT I

Micaëla *delivers* a letter and a kiss from José's mother.
She *leaves,* but only after she *arouses* José's nostalgic feelings for the life he has left behind.

ACT III

Micaëla *searches* for José in the mountains.
She *urges* him to return to his dying mother.

Like Escamillo, Micaëla is not possessive; however, she is as self-deprecating as Escamillo is self-absorbed. For her, love involves obedience and self-sacrifice. She offers José the devoted love he needs, but, tragically for them both, without the passionate challenge he craves.

When you consider the actions of all four main characters, it is clear that "The price of love is death" is not sufficiently inclusive. At the same time, you can see that all the main characters could have found love if Carmen and José had been able to turn to the suitable person at the right time (Carmen to Escamillo at the beginning of act II; José to Micaëla in act I or III.). Therefore, you might fashion as your theme statement "Mismatched needs in love lead to disaster."

Use a Plot Summary Based on the Functions of the Characters

Identify the characters by the functions they serve in the action. In *West Side Story* the roles include the Good Guy, the Girl, the Girl's Brother, the Good Guy's Best Friend, the Authority Figure, and the Trusted Advisor. (Remember, terms like Good Guy, Bad Guy, or Authority Figure are convenient labels for purposes of analysis, not judgments.)

The action uses the love triangle plot. The Good Guy, Tony, is a young Polish-American, the Girl, Maria, is a teenaged recent Puerto Rican emigré, and the Bad Guy is not a person but the force of hatred—personified by the rival American and Puerto Rican–American gangs.

At the Girl's request, the Good Guy tries to stop a fight between the gangs. When the head of the Puerto Rican gang kills the Good Guy's Best Friend, the Good Guy flies out of control and kills the killer—who turns out to be the Girl's Brother.

The Good Guy confesses to the Girl what he has done. She forgives him, but the members of the Puerto Rican gang seek revenge. The Good Guy successfully evades the gang, but when he is told that the Girl is dead—a lie created out of the hatred between the gangs—the Good Guy seeks out death at the hands of his rivals. After he is killed, he is mourned by the members of both gangs.

Two different possible theme statements are suggested by this summary. If you focus on the love between the Good Guy and the Girl, you can interpret the theme as "The triumph of love over hate." If you focus on the Good Guy's death, you can fashion your theme statement as "*West Side Story* mourns the destruction of love by hate."

The music, words, and actions of the final scene are pivotal in helping to clarify which of these two possible themes will bring the piece to life most effectively. The music, although somber, paints a picture of harmony and hope. It is, after all, the music for the song "Somewhere" and, indeed, those optimistic words are sung one final time. The action of the original production, in which the members of both gangs joined hands, reinforced that hope.

You may interpret the actions and their development in *Carmen* or *West Side Story* differently, in which case you would fashion different theme statements. As a result, you would end up with different portrayals of José, Carmen, Tony, and Maria. For instance, if you fashioned "Passion is punished" rather than "Mismatched needs in love lead to disaster" as the theme of *Carmen,* you would likely create a more reckless José, a yet more unpredictable Carmen, a more pathetic Micaëla, and a more narcissistic Escamillo. Since, as already discussed, there is no such thing as a definitive interpretation of a work of art, these differences are to be expected and can offer varied, enriching insights into a piece.

Fashioning a Theme Statement Using Research

So far I have considered ways to fashion a theme statement based on examining information in the score. Doing research into the materials on which the libretto is based, the lives and other works of the composer and librettist, and any relevant history can also yield useful clues. Sometimes the clue is a revelatory fact or statement; sometimes it provides a new perspective that opens up the creators' viewpoint or intentions.

Your research will be most productive if, as you are doing it, you constantly ask yourself how you can apply the information you are uncovering. Keep your mind and your imagination actively engaged.

The Source Material for the Libretto

As you read source material for the libretto, look for similarities and differences between it and the text of your piece; these differences may include the addition or deletion of characters or even whole scenes. Ask yourself how any differences emphasize certain ideas.

Some of the many operas, operettas, and musicals whose sources are plays, stories, novels, or poems are *The Barber of Seville, The Marriage of Figaro, The Magic Flute, Don Giovanni, La Traviata, Rigoletto, Lucia di Lammermoor, Otello, The Merry Wives of Windsor, Macbeth, Faust, Carmen, Romeo and Juliet, La Bohème, Wozzeck, Billy Budd, Lost in the Stars, West Side Story, Peter Pan, The Secret Garden, Les Misérables,* and *The King and I.*

Many operas and musicals are based on myths or historical events that you can usefully research; these include *Orfeo, L'Incoronazione di Poppea, Semele, Les Huguenots,* Wagner's Ring Cycle, *Tristan und Isolde, Hansel and Gretel, The Rape of Lucretia, Elektra, Into the Woods.* Some are based on historical events that were made into plays or novels before becoming the source of a music-theater libretto and so can be explored both from the perspective of history and literature. *Don Carlos* and *Les Misérables* are two such.

If you are trying to fashion a theme statement for a nineteenth- or twentieth-century art song or lied, check whether the text is a poem by an established poet. If so, read the original and study how the composer has emphasized certain words or lines by the way he has set them. Pay particular attention to any words or phrases the composer repeated. Observe how his choices bring forth particular ideas.

Biography

When you research biographical material for clues, see if you can find anything the creators themselves may have said about the piece. For pieces composed after the latter part of the nineteenth century, search for direct quotations in newspapers, magazines, and theater programs. For earlier works you will usually find that letters are the best sources. Look for letters not only by the composer or the librettist but by people who performed the piece, or who witnessed the original performances. You will often find these and other primary source material quoted in biographies.

Other Works by the Same Composer or Librettist

When you research other works by the composer or librettist, begin with any they created together. (Mozart wrote three operas with da Ponte; Verdi wrote several with Boito; most of Richard Strauss's operas were written with Hofmannsthal; Weill wrote several pieces with Brecht; and, of course, there are famous creative teams for operettas and musicals, such as Gilbert and Sullivan and Rodgers and Hart.) But whether you study their joint works or simply other works in their *oeuvre,* look for issues, patterns of relationships, or plot elements that show up repeatedly. Then use these similarities to step back from the specific details of your piece to possible larger themes.

If you are researching the theme of an art song or lied, read other poems by the poet who wrote the original text, and look for issues which he repeatedly addresses.

History

You will always enrich your understanding of a piece by reading relevant history. You never know when you will come across an item in your historical research that will help you fashion your theme statement. I found my key to one possible theme for *The Marriage of Figaro* in a historical section of a biography of Beaumarchais (the author of the play on which *Figaro* is based). There I learned that in eighteenth-century France there were two legal systems: the traditional, feudal system, in which the lord of the manor had jurisdiction, and a new, state legal system, in which a state-appointed judge handed down the decisions.

Suddenly, I understood why when act III opens the Count is waiting on the judge, Don Curzio, to decide the case between Figaro and Marcellina—even though he insisted at the end of the previous act that he would adjudicate it. Clearly, it is an example of the new state legal system taking precedence over the feudal one; the Count's power is being curbed. This led me to observe that other situations in which the Count's power is undercut occur repeatedly throughout the opera. I realized that the erosion of the Count's power was a central thematic idea.

Do research about both the period in which the piece was created and the period in which the piece is supposed to take place. (You can expect to find some history in a good biography.) Sometimes you can find books or articles that bring together relevant historical and biographical information, like "Verdi's Italy" or "Mozart's Vienna."

If in your research you come across someone else's statement of a possible theme, use it to stimulate your own thinking. Ultimately, you may decide to adopt it, but test it first to be sure that it really suits your understanding of the piece.

Troubleshooting

When you attempt to fashion a theme statement, what you are developing is no more than a working hypothesis. Bear in mind that you are not stuck with your choice. You can change it as you fashion your super-objective, objectives, acting beats, and subtext, and as you coach and rehearse the piece.

If you are stumped, unwrap your imagination and try some of the following procedures.

Review your list of conflicts and explore what is at stake in each one. Ask whether the same stakes are at issue more than once. Assume that the conflicts are designed to escalate in intensity and explore what feelings become more intense and what issue(s) generates the feelings. Explore whether there is a pattern to the kinds of choices the major characters make when they are in conflict. For instance, the Count in *The Marriage of Figaro* repeatedly loses his temper. Why?

Write out a plot summary like the one I made for *West Side Story,* labeling the characters with their functions and relationships. Step back and ask what ideas the plot illustrates. If there are several plot lines, look for the issues that the plots have in common. If you can draw a moral from the plot, you have the foundation for a possible theme statement. Mozart's *Cosi fan tutte,* for instance, ends with everyone singing the praises of the man of reason who is able to laugh at life's difficulties. Perhaps the theme of the opera is "Don't take life too seriously" or "If you let yourself follow your feelings you will suffer."

Make a list of the four or five most important characters. Chart how they relate to each other. Examine what connects them. Is it class, family, money, politics, religion, love, hatred? If there are important characters who don't relate to each other, figure out what issue requires them to be in the same piece.

Look at the title page. As discussed in exercise 4 "Questions" (chapter 5), think of the title as an arrow pointing to the center of the work. As an example, consider *West Side Story.* Why is it not called *Tony and Maria* like its model *Romeo and Juliet?* Are we being encouraged to see the piece as exploring a social dilemma rather than the suffering of individuals?

Sometimes, particularly in eighteenth-century operas, you will discover that a work has two titles. Consider both. For example, *Don Giovanni* is subtitled *Il dissoluto punito* ("The Dissolute One Punished"), which certainly suggests a possible theme.

Look for an indication of a genre such as "tragedy" or "comedy." It can help you ask useful questions. *Don Giovanni* is labeled a "dramma giocoso" (light-hearted drama). If you combine this information with its subtitle, you may be prompted to question how seriously you are to take that punishment. Does the piece support a pious theme statement?

Look for the date when the work was premiered. It gives you the historical period within which you can most fruitfully interpret the piece. (Most pieces are published within a few years of their premiere so you can use the publication date as your guide.) The date of the premiere of *The Beggar's Opera* is 1728; that of *Die Dreigroschenoper* is 1928. With this knowledge you have an important key to understanding why, although *Die Dreigroschenoper* is built on *The Beggar's Opera*, their themes are different.

Examine the last scene to see how the conflicts are resolved. Identify the obstacles that the "good guys" have overcome. If, for example, the piece ends in a marriage, identify what previously kept the couple apart—money, class, appearances? Ask what (not who) stood in the way of the resolution.

For instance, I have mentioned that although the toreador, Escamillo, in *Carmen* might seem to be the obstacle to a happy union between Carmen and Don José, it is really their psychological needs that stand in the way. Similarly in *The Barber of Seville*, the obstacle appears to be the Bad Guy (Bartolo, Rosina's guardian), who wants the Girl (Rosina) for himself; however, the obstacle is actually created by the Good Guy (the Count), who insists on wooing the Girl in disguise.

If the Good Guy had started by announcing himself as the aristocrat that he is, the Bad Guy, who is not of the nobility, would probably have felt obliged to bow out. (When the Good Guy secretly reveals his true identity to the Bad Servant (Basilio), the Servant immediately withdraws, which suggests this point.) The Good Guy insists on his disguise as a poor student, because he wants to make sure that the Girl loves him for himself. When he chooses his wife on the basis of their mutual love, he is taking a revolutionary step: he is avoiding the marriage that his noble parents normally would have arranged for political or economic reasons.

By identifying the obstacle, you can see that the theme of *The Barber of Seville* revolves around the Count's rejection of the conventional aristocratic approach to finding a wife. Therefore, you might try "Marriage for love as a revolutionary act" as a theme statement.

Look at the words of the final chorus if there is one. You will often find them to be either summaries of the action or statements of a moral—either of which can be helpful.

Work on fashioning your character's super-objective and objectives as described in the next two chapters. As you understand them, you will get insights into the theme.

Summary

When you fashion your theme statement for a piece it should encapsulate your interpretation of the big idea that holds the music, words, and actions of a piece together. It should also concisely capture the viewpoint embodied in the piece toward this central issue or question. To fashion a theme statement, scour the score for possible clues and explore relevant research material. Then, stand back from the piece and using your imagination and intelligence, look for its overall patterns. Although it can be a challenge, once you have fashioned a viable theme statement, you have a powerful tool with which to organize your entire vocal and dramatic interpretation of a role.

Exercises

EXERCISE 1. (I)   *Create a Scenario Around a Theme*

Objective: to get a sense of what a theme statement may be and how it functions.

Instructions:

Create the scenario for a piece to a theme of your own choice. Start by choosing a theme and your point of view about it. Then create a cast of possible characters and make an outline of the actions of the first three scenes.

For example, the theme might be abortion; the point of view might be pro-life, pro-choice, or a complex mix. (Equally interesting themes might be euthanasia, the difficulties of an illegal immigrant, overpopulation, the dilemma of a young man whether to reveal that he has been molested by his priest, or the impact of rapid change.)

The characters for a piece on abortion might be: a pregnant teenage girl, her boyfriend, a doctor, a clergyman, the girl's mother, and the boy's father.

The first scene might take place in the girl's bedroom; she is just finishing using a home testing kit. She discovers she is pregnant and breaks down crying. She phones her boyfriend and insists that he come over right away.

The second scene might take place in the clergyman's office. The girl's mother has come for advice; she is worried that her daughter is sleeping with her boyfriend. The clergyman gives her counsel. (What counsel he gives will depend on the point of view you want to develop. Does he tell the mother not to worry—the daughter is "a good girl?" Does he suggest that she give her daughter advice about abstinence or about contraception?)

The third scene might take place in the girl's bedroom. The boyfriend has arrived. Depending on the point of view you want to explore, the boyfriend might offer to marry her, urge her to have an abortion, or walk out.

EXERCISE 2. (I) *Analyzing the Familiar*

Objective: to practice creating theme statements by using pieces you know extremely well.

Instructions:

Choose one of your favorite movies.

Analyze what about its content appeals to you. Use that insight together with your knowledge of the plot and characters to fashion a theme statement.

Do the same for your favorite television program or series, or for a favorite song.

EXERCISE 3. (I) *Point of View*

Objective: to distinguish the theme from the plot.
Instructions:

There are several stories that have been adapted by more than one composer. Among the most readily available are Monteverdi's and Gluck's *Orfeo; The Beggar's Opera* by Gay and *Die Dreigroschenoper* by Weill; Verdi's *Falstaff* and Nikolai's *The Merry Wives of Windsor;* Gounod's *Faust* and Boito's *Mefistofele;* and Puccini's and Leoncavallo's *La Bohème.*

Familiarize yourself with one of these pairs. Then create a theme statement for each that captures how their points of view differ.

EXERCISE 4. (I/G). *Applying Your Theme Statement*

Objective: to explore how the theme statement will shape a production.
Instructions:

Here are two theme statements for *The Marriage of Figaro:*

The Marriage of Figaro applauds the erosion of aristocratic privilege.
The Marriage of Figaro explores reconciliation as the maturation of love.

Here are two theme statements for *West Side Story:*

West Side Story celebrates the triumph of love over hate.
West Side Story mourns the destruction of love by hate.

1. Choose a role from one of these pieces that you would like to perform. Pick the theme statement that seems most potent to you or create your own.

Make a list of character choices you would make to help your character illustrate the theme. What personality aspects would you emphasize? How might you alter your physicality?

Pick a particular scene. Explore what choices of dynamics, word emphasis, or vocal colors you might want to use to reinforce your character's contribution to the theme. Pick a specific action your character might do. How might you vary it so it helps reinforce your theme statement?

2. Imagine you are the conductor. How might you shape the musical values of the same scene to clarify the theme? What tempos would you use? What dynamics, which instrumental colors might you emphasize?

3. Imagine you are the stage director. How might you stage the action of the scene you chose to clarify the theme?

4. Imagine you are the scene designer. How might you design the set for your chosen scene to emphasize the theme? What colors would you use? What kinds of spaces would you create?

EXERCISE 5. (I) *Pondering Your Artistic Responsibility*

Objective: to consider the impact of your own values on your role as an interpreter.

Instructions:

Write a brief essay about your mission as an artist. Since as an actor-singer you will usually be cast in the role of an interpretive artist, how will your mission affect your interpretations? Do you feel that your artistic mission involves social responsibility? If so, how do you plan to exercise it?

CHAPTER 8

Your Character's Heart's Desire: Fashioning Super-objectives

Defining a Super-objective

Your character's super-objective is a simple statement of the compelling need that drives her through an entire piece. With it you establish consistant, effective motivations, and a driving energy with which you make her words and actions believable.

You fashion your character's super-objective (also known as a "through-line of action") within the framework provided by your theme statement so that your character's actions help to illuminate the theme. For instance, if (as discussed in the previous chapter) the theme of *The Barber of Seville* is marriage as a revolutionary act, then useful super-objectives for the Count and Rosina might be:

> *I*, the Count, *want* to marry a woman who loves me for myself.
>
> *I*, Rosina, *want* to marry a man I love.

Notice the form in which a super-objective is most usefully phrased: "I (your character's name), *want* (*need, must,* or *must have*), followed by a verb and a short object. This form forces you to be concise, to imagine yourself in your character's situation, and to think in terms of actions; it reminds you that you will be using yourself in service of your character.

The Qualities of the Most Useful Super-objectives

Your super-objective should help you to actively engage with the other characters. If you need their help or cooperation, you will have a clear point of reference from which to respond to everything they do and say. For instance, your super-objective is "I *want* to marry my girlfriend to help create a multigenerational family." To achieve this goal, you need not only your girlfriend's consent but also the cooperation of both her parents and yours. Therefore, you will evaluate and respond to everything that each of them says and does on the basis of whether it promotes or hinders your prospects.

Your super-objective should facilitate the actions of the other characters. If you are playing the Count in *The Barber of Seville,* don't choose "I, the Count, *want* to find a woman I can possess," because Rosina *needs* a man who loves her as an equal, not as an object.

Your super-objective should capture the unique qualities of your character. Avoid "I *need* security" or "I *want* happiness," since they apply to almost everyone. Instead, fashion your super-objective so that it captures the particular way your character's need for security or happiness manifests itself:

I, Tony, and I, Maria, *need* to find a partner who understands me.

I, José, *need* to possess a woman who excites me.

I, Carmen, *need* passion without possession.

Your super-objective should generate things you can do to manifest how your character feels. For instance, clearly delineating Carmen's dual needs for passion and freedom explains what motivates her to sing both the "Habanera" and the "Seguidilla." Avoid "I *want* to love," since, as already discussed in chapter 4, you can't act love. Use instead verbs such as "I *want* to support," "I *want* to possess," "I *want* to marry," or "I *want* to protect."

Your super-objective should emphasize any growth or development that your character undergoes. Usually that will be what is most interesting about him. If you are playing Giorgio Germont in *La Traviata,* and you choose "I *want* my way," you will simply create a frustrated and bitter old man. On the other hand, if you choose "I *want* my children to be happy," you open the door to creating a character who can overcome his own prejudices and grow to become a generous and wise father.

Your super-objective should support everything you must sing and do. This can be difficult if your character does not get what he *wants*—particularly in the many comic operas in which all the characters join together to sing a happy final chorus.

If you are playing a character in this situation, one alternative is to use a super-objective that leaves you angry, frustrated, or hurt at the end—that is, if the music will support it, and if the stage director and conductor agree. In which case you can sing the joyous music of the finale in a fury, sarcastically or through your tears. However, neither the music nor the expectation inherent in most comedies that the world is restored to order will support your character remaining outside the general rejoicing. Therefore, most often you will serve your character and the piece most effectively by fashioning your super-objective so you can happily participate. Here are two examples.

You are going to play Don Pasquale in Donizetti's opera *Don Pasquale*. If you fashion as your super-objective to be "I, Pasquale, *want* Norina for myself," when Norina marries Ernesto at the end, you will be unable to celebrate with the others. If, however, you choose "I, Pasquale, *want* domestic tranquility," then your Pasquale can go through a learning process. You can begin in the belief that you will find what you seek by marrying the young, vivacious Norina. Gradually, you can learn that, to the contrary, your life will be far more tranquil if you remain a bachelor. Therefore, at the end you can be genuinely pleased to marry her off to Ernesto.

You are going to play Anne's father, Mr. Ford, in Verdi's *Falstaff*. If you fashion as your super-objective to be "I, Ford, *want* my way," you will have a hard time joining in the happy finale, since, in fact, things don't go your way. If, however, you use "I, Ford, *want* a happy family," your Ford can learn that trust, not jealousy and coercion, brings happiness. This will allow you to rejoice when Anne marries the man of her choice.

Your super-objective should be stimulating for you to play.

Fashioning a Super-objective

It is helpful to begin with the assumption that your character, just like a real person, does have coherent motivations for what she does. When you make this assumption, you are thinking like a performer—not necessarily like a composer or like your character, who, like any of us, may be unaware of her motivations.

To fashion your character's super-objective, fashion a possible theme statement and then listen to the entire piece from the character's point of view as you follow the score. Consider the music, words, and actions of every phrase she sings or hears as *she* might perceive them. Take note of any interpretations the other characters make about her motivations. Listen to the entire piece again, keeping your theme statement in mind. Repeatedly ask yourself what unifying need or goal lies behind everything your character sings and does. Don't be surprised if you have to repeat this process several times. As any ideas for super-objectives come to mind, write them down.

Once you have a viable candidate that has the useful qualities just discussed, test it. If it doesn't provide a potent motivation for your character's words and actions in every scene, before rejecting it, try shifting the emphasis slightly. There is, for instance, a significant difference between "I *want* power" and "I *want* control." If it still doesn't work, put it aside and try another one. Remember, your character's super-objective is a useful construction that you make for your own purposes, so don't be timid about trying out various possibilities.

If you are able to develop more than one viable super-objective, select the one that supports your theme statement most clearly. Also take your options to the stage director to get her input.

Why a Single Super-objective Is the Most Helpful

Since the purpose of a super-objective is to provide you with a unifying thread through a piece, you obviously will be best served by a single but deeply grounded goal. If you change your super-objective partway through, the transition will create a crisis both for you and for your character. At that moment you will have no motivation for your next word or action, and your character's life will have no direction. It also makes your character less believable.

Real people almost never alter their deepest needs. Even people who undergo religious conversion—a truly profound change—most often are finding new ways to express old needs. For example, one Easter Sunday a singer friend of mine who had always been involved in good causes was attending church. Suddenly, he heard a supernatural voice saying, "T., your calling is to become a priest." Although the experience was certainly miraculous, when T. heeded the voice and changed from musician to priest, he did not change his basic commitment to being socially useful. For the first part of his adult life he served through music. Now he has found a different, more direct, expression for his admirable altruistic desires.

If you were portraying T.'s life, you would capture the truth of his character more profoundly if you used a single super-objective, "I, T., *want* to serve," than if you had two super-objectives—one before the moment of intervention ("I *want* to be a successful musician"), and another one afterward ("I *want* to do God's will").

You can find a single super-objective for a fictional character who undergoes change just as I have done for T.'s life by asking what common motivation drives his actions on both sides of the apparent change. For instance, the main character in *Louise,* torn between her love for her family and her love for her boyfriend, alternates between them. In some scenes she seems to *need* to be an obedient child, in others to *need* to break free. You can motivate all her behavior with a single super-objective such as "I, Louise, *want* to be true to all my feelings," or "I, Louise, *want* to please all who truely love me."

In cases where your character seems to have more than one super-objective, define each one clearly and then ask what need might underlie both. Susanna in *The Marriage of Figaro* appears to have two goals, to marry Figaro and to help the Countess win back the Count. You can unify them with a super-objective like "I, Susanna, *need* to secure my marriage." (Her marriage to Figaro can succeed only if the Count is not pursuing her.)

Troubleshooting

If, after listening to the entire piece several times, you are having trouble fashioning a super-objective, remind yourself that its purpose is to help *you* do your role. Think in the first person as your character: "What do *I*, as my character, *want?*" Try to thrust yourself into his circumstances and imagine saying his words. Remember that even though every character (whether a walk-on, chorus member, or lead) really wants what he *wants*, he may or may not get it. Then try the following techniques.

- Use your theme statement to help you. Ask "What does my character do that develops, illuminates, or reflects the theme?" "What point of view does my character have toward the issue my theme statement encapsulates?" "What does my character *want* that brings the theme into her life?" "What aspect of the theme did the librettist intend my character to illustrate?"
- Focus on the text. Read the words for every scene in which your character is onstage. Scene by scene, make a list both of what he wants from each of the other characters and of what he actually does. Ask yourself why he does each of these things. Look for a single goal that makes both what he wants from each character and what he does necessary.
- Examine your character's three most important scenes. Identify the common need that unifies them.
- Pick one of his important scenes and ask yourself "What analogous situation might drive me to say and do what my character does?" Naturally, your character's motivation may not be the same as yours, but asking this question can help you generate possibilities.

Summary

Your super-objective describes the all-important goal your character pursues throughout a piece. It provides an underlying motivation for everything your character sings and does, and it helps you invent actions to express your character's thoughts and feelings. It also clarifies how your character relates to the theme.

It is a tool you fashion from the information in the score. It is most useful when phrased in the first person using active verbs.

Exercises

Exercises: 1, 2, and 3
   Objective: to practice fashioning a super-objective.
   Instructions:

EXERCISE 1. (I) *Television Heroes***

Pick a character from a television series. Decide what *need* drives him through every program? For instance, if you pick the "good" cop or detective, is his super-objective to prove how strong, how tough, or how smart he is? Is it to confirm that good can triumph over evil or that the law is stronger than criminals? (These last two could also be themes.)

EXERCISE 2. (I) *Ourselves***

We all have super-objectives in our real lives; however, we are usually unaware of them. Sometimes, we can more easily see the unifying *need* that lies behind another person's choices.

1. Choose a public figure: a president, a famous movie star, a sports hero; develop a super-objective for his life. What drove former president Bill Clinton? How does Magic Johnson's decision to reveal his HIV status fit with his life? What drove Marilyn Monroe?

2. Choose a friend or relative. See if you can figure out a super-objective for her life.

3. Analyze your own life for your super-objective. Focus on your big decisions. Why did you choose your career? Why did you choose the place you live? Why did you marry (or not)? Why did you choose your college or professional school? Why did you (do you plan to) have children (or not)? Who are your best friends? Look at these choices, asking "What needs of mine does each choice fill?" Avoid focusing on how outside circumstances may seem to have dictated what happened. If you went to the school your father chose for you, then ask "What need of my own did that fulfill?" Do you see the same need driving several of your big choices?

After you fashion a super-objective for your self, write a five-hundred-word autobiography to support your choice.

EXERCISE 3. (G) *Improvised Characters*

After you finish any group improvisation (see chapter 3), have the group analyze each participant's role for her super-objective.

1. Make an outline of what happened (the plot).
2. Divide the action into "scenes."
3. Look for the consistent thread in the actions of each participant.

EXERCISE 4. (I) *One Super-objective*

Objective: to practice finding the unifying thread.

Instructions:

Choose a character who seems to have more than one super-objective or who seems to change super-objectives. Try to find a single *need* that underlies all of his actions.

Some characters you might want to consider: Figaro in *The Marriage of Figaro*, who gets married in the end of the third act but who is a central player in the fourth; Tom Rakewell in *The Rake's Progress*, who seems to be aimless; Eliza Doolittle in *My Fair Lady* and Tosca in *Tosca*, both of whom seem to change direction in midstream.

CHAPTER 9

Motivating Your Character's Actions:
Fashioning Objectives and Acting Beats

Defining Objectives and Acting Beats

Every character pursues her super-objective with a variety of strategies that generate more immediate goals. Her strategic goal for each scene or stanza is her objective for that section. Each individual strategy she uses to pursue an objective is called an acting beat.

Objectives and acting beats generate specific things for you to do scene by scene and moment-by-moment. They help you to react believably by clarifying your character's feelings about the situation and the other characters.

Phrase your objectives like your super-objective: "I, (your character's name), *want* (*need, must* or *must have*)," followed by a verb—usually in the infinitive—and a short object. "I, Rosina, *want* to prove I'm his equal" or "I, Rosina, *want* to maintain my dignity." Since your objectives should reflect the passion of your character's need, feel free to use colloquial language: "I, Rosina, *gotta* keep my cool!"

Defining the Qualities of the Most Useful Objectives

Your objectives will serve you best if each has the following qualities.

It helps you fulfill your super-objective.
It fits the music and its implications for the scene or stanza.
It supports all your words and actions in the scene or stanza.

It causes you to need something from another character.
It excites you to act it.

Fashioning Objectives for Operas and Musicals

Begin by dividing the piece into scenes. Start a new scene whenever a major character enters or exits. This is the most useful division for acting purposes, since the arrival or departure of a major character inevitably alters the situation onstage and therefore causes the characters to adjust the tactics they use to try to achieve their super-objectives.

You can begin fashioning objectives with any scene you like, whether it is the most crucial one or the one you understand most clearly; however, you will probably find it easiest to work consecutively through the piece. Ultimately, you will want an objective for each scene in which your character appears, whether or not he sings.

If you don't yet have a strong sense of your character's super-objective, you can still fashion immediate objectives. Ask "What is my character trying to accomplish in this scene and what tactics is she using to get to her goal?"

If you have already developed your super-objective, you can fashion your objectives by asking yourself "How does my character pursue his super-objective in this scene?" You will find the concept of strategic *means* to be a good clarifying device. Invoke it by saying to yourself "I, (your character's name), am working toward (fill in your super-objective) *by means of* (fill in a possible objective)." Fashion your answer depending on what you feel the music, text, and the stage directions suggest.

For example, assume that your super-objective as the Countess in *The Marriage of Figaro* is "I, Rosina, *want* to win back my husband." Then, for the scene in act II in which your husband accuses you of being unworthy, you would try "In this scene I am winning back my husband *by means of*. . .? ("How am I trying to win back my husband?") You might answer "by proving I'm his equal" or "by maintaining my dignity."

If using the prompt *by means of* doesn't clarify your objective, listen to the scene several times from your character's perspective. Then answer these questions for her:

How do my actions and reactions relate to the theme?
What do I do, action by action, reaction by reaction, during the scene? (Make a list.)
What do I want from the other characters in the scene?
What do I need in the scene?

What am I trying to accomplish in the scene?

What does the music suggest about my feelings as I sing my text and do my actions?

What single need or goal might motivate all my behavior in this scene?

On the basis of your answers, write down some possible alternatives. Then test them. If a proposed objective doesn't support all your feelings, words, and actions, consider whether a different wording will make it work better. "I *want* to have my way," for instance, although similar, is quite different from "I *want* to manipulate" or "I *want* to dominate."

As a model, let's fashion objectives for the second act scenes between Carmen and José.

José has just been released from jail after serving a one-month sentence for letting Carmen escape at the end of the first act. He seeks her out in the gypsies' disreputable hangout on the outskirts of Seville. They greet passionately, but José quickly becomes jealous when he hears that Carmen has been dancing for some other soldiers. Carmen diverts him by performing. As she is singing and dancing, José hears the army bugle playing "la retraite" in the distance and insists that he must go back to his barracks for evening roll call. Carmen taunts him for being more interested in army regulations than in her, and they quarrel.

In the middle of their argument, José's superior officer, Zuñiga, arrives, sniffing after Carmen. José flies into a jealous rage and draws his sword on the lieutenant. Carmen calls in the other gypsies to break up the fight. Then, in order to protect José from potential court-martial, she persuades him to join her in the mountains.

First, break down their interactions into scenes. (The sound of the bugle is treated as a scene division, because it precipitates a major change in the characters' actions.)

Scene 1: from José's entrance to the sound of the bugle
Scene 2: from the bugle to the arrival of Zuñiga
Scene 3: from the arrival of Zuñiga to his departure
Scene 4: from the departure of Zuñiga to the end

Next look at what the characters do in each of the four scenes, and to help fashion their immediate objectives, either ask yourself how their actions help Carmen and José achieve their super-objectives, or apply *by means of* to those super-objectives. If you use the theme statement and super-objectives developed in the previous two chapters, you will end up with your version of the following analysis.

Theme:	Mismatched needs in love lead to disaster.
Super-objective:	I, José, *want* to possess a woman who challenges me.
Objective (sc. 1):	I, José, *want* to collect my prize.
Objective (sc. 2):	I, José, *want* to stay out of trouble (so I can be with Carmen in the future).
Objective (sc. 3):	I, José, *want* Carmen for myself.
Objective (sc. 4):	I, José, *want* to hold on to Carmen.

Since Carmen has a different super-objective, her objectives for these scenes will be different:

Theme:	Mismatched needs in love leads to disaster.
Super-objective:	I, Carmen, *need* passion without possession.
Objective (sc. 1):	I, Carmen, *want* to seduce José.
Objective (sc. 2):	I, Carmen, *want* to dominate José.
Objective (sc. 3):	I, Carmen, *want* to protect José.
Objective (sc. 4):	I, Carmen, *want* to put José in my debt.

These choices for objectives mirror the music, motivate the characters' actions, help them pursue their super-objectives, and set up needs that only they can fulfill for each other. They create strong conflicts, effectively build toward the climax and resolution, and reinforce the sense that Carmen and José have fundamentally different underlying motivations—which supports the theme.

If you are having difficulties figuring out an objective for a particular scene, try reading the words of a scene aloud to yourself. Stop after each sentence and ask "Why does my character sing that? What does he *want?*" You may have to reread the scene numerous times, but gradually you will think of possible objectives. Another helpful approach is to analyze how the scene and your character function to develop the theme.

To analyze the function of a scene, speculate about:

Why the librettist and composer felt they needed to include this scene
Why this scene has to come at this point in the piece
How this scene illustrates the theme

To analyze the function of your character in the scene, try answering these questions:

Why did the librettist and composer need to have my character in this scene?
What does my character do in this scene that has to be done?

What does my character do in this scene that no other character in the piece can?

The function of the scenes between Carmen and José in the second act might be to show how two people whose needs in love are so opposite can still end up together. Carmen's function in those scenes might be to show how passion can accidentally lead to commitment; José's function might be to show how passion can swamp good intentions.

This analysis might lead you to objectives such as "I, Carmen, *want* to protect José" and "I, José, *must* follow my heart." Once you have opened the door to the flow of possibilities, you can tailor your ideas to the specific implications of the music, words, and actions for each scene.

Fashioning Objectives for Songs, Art Songs, and Lieder

Your character in a song, art song, or lied is the person who is presumed to be singing; she is the "I" of the song. This is true even in those cases where the "I" is narrating someone else's story. To fashion objectives, begin just as you do for operas or musicals. Fashion a theme statement for the piece and a super-objective and Given Circumstances for your character. Often the most fruitful place to begin describing your Given Circumstances in song literature is with the *who* and *want*. As part of the *who,* clarify to whom your character is singing, where that person is, and the nature of your relationship.

Then, treating each stanza or verse as a separate scene, explore how the words and any implied actions further your pursuit of your super-objective. (Using the prompt *by means of* can again be helpful.)

If the piece is not written in stanzas or verses, look for the three or four most important transition points. (They are often indicated by tempo or key changes.) Develop an objective for each major section.

Let's use Schubert's lied "An Silvia" as an example. It has three verses.

1.

(Sixteen beats introduction)
Was ist Silvia, saget an,   What is Silvia, tell me,
dass sie die weite Flur preist?   so that the wide fields praise her?
(Five beats of music)
Schön und zart seh ich sie   Beautiful and gentle I see her approach,
   nahn,
auf Himmels Gunst und Spur   Heaven's favor and mark show,
   weist,

(Five beats of music)	
dass ihr alles untertan,	that to her everything is subject.
dass ihr alles untertan.	

2.

(Fourteen beats introduction)	
Ist sie schön	Is she beautiful,
und gut dazu?	and good as well?
Reiz labt wie milde Kindheit;	Her charm refreshes like gentle child-hood;
(Five beats of music)	
ihrem Aug eilt Amor zu,	to her eye Amor hastens,
dort heilt er seine Blindheit,	there he heals his blindness,
(Five beats of music)	
und verweilt in süsser Ruh,	and lingers there in sweet peace.
und verweilt in süsser Ruh.	

3.

(Fourteen beats introduction)	
Darum Silvia tön, o Sang,	Therefore, Silvia sound, oh, song,
der holden Silvia Ehren;	the lovely Silvia's honor;
(Five beats of music)	
jeden Reiz besiegt sie lang,	long may she surpass every attraction,
den Erde kann gewähren:	that the Earth can offer:
Kranz ihr und Saitenklang,	Crown and serenade her. (*literally:* Garland for her and the sound of strings).
Kranz ihr und Saitenklang.	

(Fourteen beats postlude)

One viable interpretation is that the "I" of the song is a young man who has fallen in love with Silvia from a distance. He is talking about her with a mutual friend. This might yield the following analysis:

Theme:	Silvia's perfection
Super-objective:	I *want* to share my excitement about Silvia, or I *want* my friend to introduce us.
Objective (first verse):	I *need* to know who Silvia is.
Objective (second verse):	I *want* to confirm her virtue.
Objective (third verse):	I *want* the world to endorse my feelings.

If, as part of developing your interpretation, you were to research the source of the text, you would discover that the original words appear in Shakespeare's play *The Two Gentlemen of Verona*. They are delivered as a serenade by a young man as part of his attempt to seduce his best friend's beloved, which he does while pretending to further the suit of someone else. Shakespeare has him sing:

Who is Silvia? what is she,
That all our swains commend her?
Holy, fair and wise is she;
The heaven such grace did lend her,
That she might admired be.

Is she kind as she is fair?
For beauty lives with kindness:
Love doth to her eyes repair.
To help him of his blindness;
And being help'd inhabits there.

Then to Silvia let us sing,
That Silvia is excelling;
She excels each mortal thing
Upon the dull earth dwelling;
To her let us garlands bring.

In contrast to the previous analysis, the Given Circumstances of Shakespeare's character suggest the following super-objective and objectives:

Theme:	Sylvia's perfection
Super-objective:	To win Silvia
Objective (first verse):	To remind her of her several loves (Silvia has other admirers in the play; he is hinting that she is already "playing the field.") Or to praise her (suggesting that many admire her)
Objective (second verse):	To insinuate that beauty imposes obligations
Objective (third verse):	To flatter her

As the interpreter, you will have to decide which version Schubert's music supports, or perhaps you will develop another viable interpretation.

Using Objectives to Strengthen a Role or Scene

As you analyze a piece, it is always helpful to assume that the words, music, actions, and characters in each scene are well written. However, that is not always the case. You can shore up places that are underwritten or in which your character's words or actions are unclear by the way you fashion your objectives. Sometimes the trick lies in creating appropriate objectives for earlier scenes.

For instance, Violetta's decision to leave her lover in the second act of *La Traviata* can easily seem insufficiently motivated. You can make it compelling if, in the first act, you establish how deeply you as Violetta regret the way you have wasted your life. Use objectives like "I, Violetta, *want* to be a virtuous woman," and "I, Violetta, *want* to be forgiven for my evil ways." Then, when your lover's father insinuates that if you leave his son you will be rewarded in heaven, you have set the stage to make your decision believable.

Similarly, Don Ottavio in Mozart's *Don Giovanni* can seem weak, because, although he swears to avenge the murder of his fiancée's father, he procrastinates until the opera is almost over. If, however, as you swear your oath, you use the objective "I *want* to do the right thing," you will create a character with a compelling dilemma: you want to help your fiancée, but not if you must accuse another falsely. Since you cannot believe that a fellow nobleman could do the evil deeds of which Giovanni is accused, you are paralyzed. However, when at last Giovanni's villainy is clear and you jump into action—actively participating in his downfall—you make your Ottavio heroic; you overcome your profound misgivings and do the right thing. (This line of analysis works best in an interpretation of the opera in which Giovanni's punishment is meted out by men, not by heaven.)

You can also use your objectives to strengthen a role that is not well fleshed out. Imagine that you are in the gypsy chorus at the end of act II of *Carmen*. In the score you have no name and are assigned no individual actions. You and your fellow gypsies have gathered at a disreputable inn to prepare to smuggle contraband through the mountains. You witness Carmen convincing an unknown corporal (José) to join your troupe. After you hear her celebrate the virtues of the roving life, you join the other gypsies in singing:

"Come with us across the countryside, come with us into the mountains. When you get used to it you will discover how wonderful the roving life is. The world is your country; your wish is law. Freedom is the best of all!"

If you are a woman, you could decide that you really resent the way Carmen dominates the group. You could turn this attitude into actions with a super-objective like "I *want* to humiliate Carmen" or, perhaps, "I *want* to be the leader of the gypsy women." In which case you might fashion "I *want* to destroy

Carmen's plans" as your objective for this scene. This might inspire you to try to get José for yourself. Obviously, you could accomplish your seduction more easily if he joins you in the mountains. Therefore, you can sing your words with calculating enthusiasm as you focus all your charms on him.

You could approach your role equally effectively with the attitude that you admire Carmen and would like her to teach you all she knows. In which case you might fashion "I *want* to be the center of attention (like Carmen)" as your super-objective, and "I *want* to ingratiate myself with Carmen" as your objective for this scene. These choices would probably inspire you to focus your attention on Carmen and to support her in all she suggests. They would also motivate you to sing your words with vigor and conviction.

If you are a man, you could use either of the previous super-objectives, but with different objectives. You could also try a super-objective like "I *want* to become the leader of the troupe." Then you could use "I *want* to recruit more men" as your objective, which would believably motivate your enthusiastic words.

Since you have only limited evidence in the score to help you choose the most effective alternative, you may want to test your choices with the following questions. "What actions do they suggest?" "Are they appropriate?" "Will they help me sing my words with feelings appropriate to the music?" "What difficulties might they create?" "Will they enrich my role?" "Will they fit the blocking I have been given?" "Will they fit well with what my colleagues have to do?" Naturally, you should always discuss your super-objective and objectives with the stage director, so that you can integrate your choices with his vision of the piece.

As another example, imagine you are a character who has nothing to sing or say at all. You are a nameless servant whose only actions are to take coats and hats from arriving guests in the first scene, and to serve tea in the second. The orchestration during your actions suggests neither the way you do them nor the way the others react to you.

Your analysis of this servant's function suggests that he is there to establish the main characters as respectable and upperclass. Although "establishing respectability and class" is not actable, you can see that you will serve the piece best if you execute your actions in a point-perfect manner. Therefore, you need objectives that will make this possible.

If this is a serious piece, you might fashion "I, Jasper the Servant, *need* to earn a big Christmas bonus" as your super-objective. (Assigning yourself an appropriate name helps make it easier for you to believe yourself.) As your objective for the coat scene, try "I, Jasper the Servant, *want* to make each guest feel personally welcomed"; for the tea scene try "I, Jasper the Servant, *want* to anticipate each guest's every desire." These objectives will motivate you to do every action meticulously; thereby you will establish the sense of a very proper household.

You can increase your involvement with your objectives if you create a compelling *why*. Do you have a secret child who needs a life-saving operation? Do you have creditors who are threatening to expose your large gambling debts to your employers? Either choice will create urgency, but in the first case you will be motivated primarily by feelings of love whereas in the second feelings of fear will predominate, so your choice will subtly affect the way you do your actions.

If you are performing the same servant role in a comedy, assuming the director agrees, you can make your character into a source of fun. To this end you could fashion "I, JuJu the servant, *want* to get fired" as your super-objective, and "I, JuJu the Servant, *want* to insult each individual guest" as your objective for the first scene. In which case you could drop the coats and, perhaps, step on a hat. For the tea scene you could choose "I, JuJu the Servant, *want* to see how much damage I can do with the tea." This might motivate you to put sugar in the tea of a guest who requested it without, and to spill the tea when you pour. Since you still have to fulfill your function of establishing the respectable social standing of the main characters, you would have to carry out these actions in such a way that it is clear that you are choosing to misbehave. If your employers are astounded by what you do, that would, of course, help. Again, you will be well served if you make your objectives urgent by fabricating a compelling *why*.

Fashioning Acting Beats

A character will try anything that is consistent with her moral code and personality to get what she wants. If her objective in a particular scene is "I *want* to keep my beloved from leaving," she might begin with flattery. If that doesn't work, she might try reasoning, cajoling, threatening, seducing, bribing, or even blackmail. We call these various strategies acting beats. Acting beats are mini-objectives that clarify the relationship of your character's individual thoughts and actions to her objectives.

You can fashion your acting beats, whether for operas, musicals, songs, art songs, or lieder, most effectively by once again using the device of *means*. Say to yourself "I want to carry out my objective *by means of*. . ." Or you can ask "What do I do in this scene to achieve my objective?" As you do for objectives, concisely phrase acting beats in the first person using an active verb that helps you generate actions.

As an example, let's fashion Carmen and José's acting beats for their first scene in the second act. First identify the major actions in the scene:

1. José arrives singing a song.
2. José and Carmen discuss his willingness to be imprisoned for her sake.

3. Carmen provokes his jealousy.
4. Carmen begins to dance.

Ask how these actions further each character's objective. Your answers might result in the following analysis for José's first objective:

Theme:	Mismatched needs in love lead to disaster.
Super-objective:	"I, José, *want* to posses a woman who challenges me."
Objective:	"I, José, *want* to collect my prize."
Acting beats:	*By means of* (1) announcing my victorious arrival.
	By means of (2) demonstrating how much I care for you.
	By means of (3) proving how much I want you.
	By means of (4) watching and listening with rapt attention.

Carmen's involvement in each of the actions is as different as her super-objective and objective, so an analysis of her acting beats for this scene might result in the following analysis.

Theme:	Mismatched needs in love lead to disaster.
Super-objective:	"I, Carmen, *need* passion without possession."
Objective:	"I, Carmen, *want* to seduce José."
Acting beats:	*By means of* (1) preparing myself to receive him.
	By means of (2) demonstrating my impatience.
	By means of (3) proving how desirable I am to others.
	By means of (4) exciting him.

Using Acting Beats to Motivate Repeated Text

In their passionate intensity, characters often repeat words or phrases. You can make these repetitions dramatically believable by fashioning a separate acting beat for each one.

Begin with the following three assumptions. First, like a real person, when your character repeats something, he has a reason. Second, like a real person, your character cannot repeat anything without making subtle variations. Third, like a real person, your character, whether he resists or evolves, is always challenged by ever-changing aspects of his circumstances. These assumptions encourage you to see each repetition as an expressive step in an emotional journey and underline the fact that each repetition is unique and necessary.

As already discussed, when a character launches into an aria or song, he begins with strong feelings. As he spins out the notes and words, he develops or explores those feelings. As a result, by the end of the piece he has arrived at a different emotional place. This is true even if he ends with exactly the same words and music, as he will in a *da capo* aria or in a song with a repeated refrain; the very fact of having explored his feelings all but guarantees that those feelings will have changed; he is more stuck, more confused, or more deeply in love.

Let's suppose you are working on a song in which your character sings "I love him" six times in one section. You have fashioned "I *want* to find the man of my dreams" as your super-objective and "I *want* to erase any doubts (that I love him)" as your objective for this part. First, generate a list of possible acting beats that might justify repeating "I love him." Generate several more than you need without worrying about how you will use them. For example:" I *want* to erase any doubts *by means of* . . .

> *telling* myself that it's true"
> *questioning* whether it's true"
> *convincing* others that it's true"
> *trying* out how I feel"
> *denying* that it's true"
> *asking* others whether it's true"
> *proclaiming* that it's true"
> *collecting* evidence that it's true"

Then listen to the music for clues as to the feelings underlying each repetition. Consider not just the details of the harmonies and orchestration but also the melody and its rhythm. Consider your Given Circumstances, the psychology and *needs* both of your own character and of the character(s) to whom you are singing. On the basis of these considerations, you usually will be able to lock in acting beats for at least one or two phrases. Build the rest of the sequence around them, discarding the options that fit least well.

If the contextual clues for the repetitions are ambiguous—for instance, if the music is exactly the same—then you are free to arrange your acting beats in any order that, within your Given Circumstances, creates an effective and believable emotional journey. In the absence of clear musical information, the following sequence would work well for our example. "I *want* to erase any doubts *by means of* . . .

> *trying* out how I feel"
> *questioning* whether it's true"

denying that it's true"
asking others whether it's true"
telling myself that it's true"
telling others that it's true"

You have taken your character on a journey from a state of uncertainty through a series of feelings and actions to arrive at clarity.

Summary

A crucial step in creating believable characters is to give their actions, text, and the music that accompanies them specific and coherent motivations. You can accomplish this effectively by fashioning immediate objectives that define what they *want* in each scene as they pursue their super-objectives, and then further subdividing those objectives into acting beats. Objectives clarify and motivate your characters' thoughts and actions and shape their relationships to the other characters on a scene-by-scene basis; acting beats justify the specific actions they take and each phrase they sing as they strive to fulfill each objective.

To fashion your character's objectives, complete the sentence "In this scene, I (your character's name) am working toward (your super-objective) *by means of* (fill in your objective)." Or ask "What do I say and do in this scene to achieve my character's super-objective?" To fashion your character's acting beats, complete the sentence "With this thought, phrase, or action I (your character's name) am working toward (your objective) *by means of* (fill in your acting beat)." Or ask "How does this thought, phrase, or action clarify my present objective?"

Exercises

EXERCISE 1. (G) *Exploring Objectives*

Objective: to explore the power and utility of objectives.
Instructions:
Here are two different set-ups to improvise. In each there are alternative objectives for the participants. Choose one of the set-ups and improvise it twice. Use a different objective each time.

SET-UP 1

The scene is a line at an airport customs counter in the United States. One of you is an American returning from a trip to a foreign country and trying to smuggle something through customs. Decide what it is and how much of it you have, and invent a compelling reason why you are smuggling it. (Remember, smuggling is a criminal act, but what you are smuggling does not have to be an illegal substance!). For instance, you promised to bring your fiancée a bottle of her favorite perfume back from Paris, the only place where it is available. She is planning to wear it at your wedding in two weeks. Last night, your last in Paris, you went on a shopping spree and spent all your remaining money on presents. You don't have anything left with which to pay the duty on the perfume. (Customs will not accept checks or credit cards.)

You are in line at the customs counter; what you are smuggling is in your pocket or in your personal luggage. Improvise a scene with the objective "I *want* to get through customs without getting caught." Then improvise the same situation with the objective "I *want* to get someone to help me to get through customs so I won't get caught."

If you are participating in this improvisation as one of the other people in line, you might have as your objective the first time, "I *want* to get through customs as quickly as possible." (Your wife, whom you haven't seen for six months, is waiting.) The second time you could try "I *want* to test how thorough the customs inspectors are." (You are spying for a group that smuggles expensive French chocolates.) The improvisations will be more interesting if you don't discuss your *want* or *why* with each other.

If you have participants in your group who are fluent in languages other than English, let them use their skills. Have them play the smuggler(s) or some of the people in line. You can also change the situation so that an English-speaking person is trying to get through customs in a non-English-speaking country—in which case, the customs officer as well as some of the people in line could speak foreign languages.

SET-UP 2

The scene is a job interview. (Choose a job that both participants know something about.) If you are the applicant, you might use "I *must* have this job" as your objective the first time and the second time try "I *need* to get this interviewer to give me the job." If you are the interviewer, you might first try "I *want* to make sure I choose the right person," then try something quite different such as "I *want* to please my boss."

When you repeat the improvisation, keep the *where, when,* and *who* the same but adjust your *want* and your *why.* Do not discuss your objective (*want*) or your *why* with your partner in advance.

After you have improvised either of these set-ups with two different objectives, discuss how changing your objective changed the actions you chose, and the feelings you experienced.

EXERCISE 2. (G) *Developing Objectives*

Objective: to practice extracting objectives from a scene.

Instructions:

After you have improvised a scene—either those in exercise 1 or some other—work together as a group and review the improvisation in terms of each participant's objectives. Fashion a theme statement for the scene and a super-objective for each participant. Then make a list of as many things each participant did as you can collectively remember. When you finish the list, put it into the first person. ("I, the interviewer, walked slowly all around the person seeking the job. I paused when I was standing behind him. I went slowly to my chair. I stood behind the chair with my hands resting on the back and stared at the job-seeker," etc.). Try to fashion objectives for each participant.

EXERCISE 3. (I). *Weak to Strong*

Objective: to clarify how you can improve a "weak" scene using objectives.

It is very hard to give more than a perfunctory performance of a scene or piece of material that strikes you as dramatically unmotivated or unconvincing— material one might call "weak." This exercise is intended to help you clarify why a scene may seem weak to you, to help you describe it in terms that will allow you to see it more sympathetically, and to give you insights as to how you can shore it up by choosing helpful objectives.

Instructions:

Choose a song or scene that you consider weak.

1. Describe what makes it weak. Be specific: is it unclear, does it lack shape, is it inconsistent, are important emotional transitions left out?

2. Create a super-objective for your character (or the "I" of the song). Read through the text and music again. Fashion objectives that mesh with the clues in the score.

3. Change the song or scene in any way you like to make it work better for you. This can include changes in the music, the words, or the way they are set. When you are finished, answer the following questions: Why are your changes an improvement? Do they make the song or scene seem more logical, clearer, deeper, more moving, more entertaining? Have they involved adjusting your super-objective or objective(s)?

4. Again change the song or scene so it works better for you, but this time restrict yourself to changes that are stylistically and thematically consistent with the original and that you believe the librettist and composer might have approved. Again consider whether your changes seem to require adjustments in your super-objective or objective(s).

5. Reconsider the song or scene again. Building on what you have discovered from the previous steps of this exercise but without changing it, invent a super-objective, objectives, and Given Circumstances that make the song or scene work better, that make it more intriguing for you. Sing the song or act the scene using the approach you have just created.

Choose a song that is not necessarily "weak" but that you dislike.

1. Repeat steps 1–5. (Be very specific in describing what you dislike about the song.)

2. Without changing the song, find a way to change your feelings about it.

- Try making a list of at least five things you like in the song. They can be as small as a single syncopated rhythm or a single word choice. Consider the melody, the harmony, the rhythm, the character of the "I" of the song, and the situation.
- Describe why the thoughts, actions, or responses of the "I" of the song to his situation might be appropriate. Why does he need to sing?
- Try to define the fundamental emotional dilemma or source of feeling in the song.
- Recall a time when you have had a similar dilemma in your own life; then examine whether the song captures any of the feelings that dilemma aroused in you. If the song is more of an emotional outpouring ("I love you!!"), explore how the music of the song evokes or supports the feeling.

Capture your understanding in a super-objective and objectives for the song that you would find intriguing to perform.

EXERCISE 4. (I) *Fashioning a Dramatic Analysis of a Song*

Objective: to practice creating objectives and acting beats with material for which the Given Circumstances are not well defined.

Instructions:

Choose a song or lied that you know well but that is not explicit about the *where, when,* or *who.* Using the tools you have developed in chapter 2, construct a complete set of Given Circumstances for the "I" of the song. As discussed earlier, start with the *who* and include a full description not only of your character but (unless she is talking to herself) of the person to whom she is singing. Use your imagination to fill in as necessary. After you have created the Given Circumstances, write out a dramatic analysis of the song: the theme, your super-objective, objectives, and the acting beats.

Practice singing the song, using your analysis to shape your phrasing, dynamics, vocal color, and inflection.

EXERCISE 5. (l).   *Motivating Repeated Text*

Objective: to practice finding motivations for repeated words or phrases in a song or aria.

Instructions:

Choose a song or aria in which a word or, more likely, a brief phrase is repeated a number of times. Create motivations for each repetition by developing acting beats for them. Begin by creating the Given Circumstances of the "I" of the song. Then make a dramatic analysis of the piece as described in exercise 4. When you fashion your acting beats, create a list with several more options than you will need.

Listen closely to the music, paying particular attention to any differences in the melody, harmony, instrumentation, rhythm, or stress in each repetition of the word or phrase. On the basis of your observations, assign as many as possible of the acting beats on your list to particular phrases as you can. Then choosing from the acting beats left on your list, assign actions to the remaining repetitions to create a sequence that will unfold as a compelling emotional journey.

Try singing the piece several times. Make a point of interpreting all repeated words and phrases so that each overtly expresses the acting beat you have chosen. Don't hesitate to adjust the sequence or substitute a different choice of acting beat if you feel either doesn't work well. I recommend that you write the acting beats directly in your music, so that you don't have to try to reconstruct the sequence from memory.

Record yourself singing the song as expressively as you can. Listen to make sure that your interpretation is coming across.

CHAPTER 10

Your Character's Inner Voice:
Fashioning Subtext and an Internal Dialogue

Defining Subtext

As Carmen returns José's ring at the climax of the opera, she sings, "You once gave me this ring—take it!" Her literal meaning is unambiguous: "Take back your ring." But what is Carmen saying emotionally? "I hate you? I feel sorry for you? I adore you? I find you repulsive? I want your body?" Should you sing the line sweetly, lovingly, bemusedly, teasingly, thoughtfully, seductively, provocatively, sarcastically, ferociously, tauntingly, disgustedly, or angrily? How can you know?

Whenever you sing or talk, you are always communicating simultaneously on both a literal and an emotional level. In the theater we call the literal words your "text" and the emotional level your "subtext."

Your character's subtext is the main source of his internal dialogue, the chatter of his inner voice expressing how he feels about what is happening. It is usually subconscious, just out of his awareness, and it complexly feeds into and is fed by his emotional life. When you fashion subtext for each phrase of your text and complete it with internal thoughts for all the places where you don't sing, you make your character into a multi-level communicator like a real person, and you take a giant step toward being believable on stage.

Considering the Score as a Source of Subtext

As you begin to fashion the subtext and internal thoughts for a new character, you are like someone conversing with a stranger who speaks in a monotone and makes no gestures—you hear her words, but you are not quite sure of the subtleties of her meaning. In daily life you figure out these subtleties by combining what she says with clues from her body language, from the music of her inflections, and most of all from the context in which you find yourselves—your Given Circumstances. These involve when and where the conversation is taking place, your relationship to the speaker, what has been said before, and who else is present. When the "stranger" is not a literal person but a role, you will find all those clues (except body language) in the words and music of the score.

The music provides a gold mine of information about your characters' subtext, since, as already discussed, the music is usually composed to express the characters' feelings. This is the function of the key, time signature, tempo, pitches, intervals, rhythms, dynamics, tessitura, and style of your vocal line, of the melody, harmony, rhythm, dynamics, and instrumentation of its accompaniment, and, most often, of any introductions, interludes, or postludes.

The music defines not only the particular nuances of characters' feelings but when they arise and how long they last. For example, in Figaro's famous aria "Largo al factotum" from *The Barber of Seville*, when Figaro starts complaining about how busy he is, and the music is not bitter, angry, or sarcastic but cheerful, you understand that in some fundamental way he enjoys even the demanding aspects of his trade. Rossini fixed the spot where Figaro moves from overt pleasure in his work to complaining; he composed the duration of the complaint and the manner in which Figaro explores it, as well as the exact spot at which the performer must move on to congratulating himself with "Ah bravo Figaro."

Indeed, music provides such an evocative emotional voice that, unless your subtext and ultimately your character's entire internal dialogue reflects the feelings and transitions the music suggests—unless they support the tempo, shape, and any pauses in your melodic line—you create a jolting discordance between your performance and what the ears of the audience lead them to expect. If this discordance is too great, you shatter any chance of seeming believable.

Fashioning Subtext

Naturally, before you can develop your subtext you need to understand the text. If you are approaching a piece in a foreign language in which you are not fluent, you need to make a literal word-for-word translation. There are an increasing number of books and internet sites with literal translations you can check. Translations in CD liner notes can also be useful guides, but be sure to do some checking using a dictionary to test how acurate any of these translations may be. On the other hand, do not rely on the translation printed in your music; it is almost never literal but only a free paraphrase designed to be singable.

When you come across a phrase that when literally translated makes no sense, it may be either an idiom or an archaic usage. For such phrases, try comparing several different translations or, better yet, consult with someone who knows the language.

After you know what each word and idiom means, make a paraphrase that captures the meaning of your literal translation in good, natural English.

Before you fashion your subtext, you also need to be familiar with the way the individual composer uses music to express feelings, both throughout the piece you are learning and for your particular character. To improve your general familiarity, listen to the piece while following the score and ask yourself "When characters have strong feelings, what do their vocal lines sound like? What does the accompaniment sound like?" To explore how the composer portrays your particular character's feelings, look for patterns. Is your character associated with a specific instrument, orchestral color, rhythmic figure, or melodic phrase? If so, explore the feelings that the color, pattern, or phrase evokes. For example, depending on how it is used, syncopation can suggest either light-heartedness or confusion; the bassoon can evoke foolishness, as it does for the exit of the Sacristan in *Tosca*, pompousness and menace, as it does for the entrance of the Grand Inquisitor in Verdi's *Don Carlo,* or great longing, as in Nemorino's aria "Una furtiva lagrima."

After you have a sense of how the composer uses music to evoke feelings and you know exactly what the text means, pick one scene to work on. Listen to the music that your character sings or that accompanies her actions in that scene. Ask yourself "What feelings does the music I sing and its accompaniment suggest?" "What mood(s) or feeling(s) is evoked in any music between the segments I sing?" "What kind of portrait is the composer painting?"

Now focus on the first two phrases you sing in the scene.(For the purposes of this exploration, consider a phrase to be the same as a breath.) Read the words aloud several times. Think about them in light of everything you know about your role. Ask "What do I as my character *want* in each of these two phrases?" "What thought(s) do I as my character really want to express?" "What feeling(s) do I as my character wish to express?" Then invent a couple of possible alternative subtexts and jot them down.

As you develop possibilities, remember that subtext usually proceeds by phrases rather than individual words. For example, you can logically sing the line "You once gave me this ring—take it!" with one subtextual expression such as "I hate you!" You can also do it with two: "You romantic slob—you disgust me!" However, if you divide it up further, you risk making it illogical and confusing.

Don't waste time composing your subtexts in good English or complete phrases. They can be as simple as sounds that evoke feelings, like "Grrrrr!" "Aaachh," or "Aaiyeee." They can be reactions like "Fantastic!" or "Disgusting";

They can be short phrases like "I can't stand you!" or "You make me sick!"; you can use colloquialisms like "Bug off!" or "Cool it!" or "Come here, baby" (or stronger and more colorful terms that I can't print here). Do not try to fashion subtext out of stage-direction adverbs like "sarcastically" or "sweetly." They come from outside rather than inside the part of your mind where subtext is generated. "Oh yeah!?" or "You're soooo wonderful!" take you into the right space.

Once you have a couple of alternative options for the first two phrases, listen repeatedly to the music that accompanies them. Notice where there is tension and where it relaxes. Consider each word in relationship to the shape of the whole musical phrase. Which words are emphasized by being set high or low, by being held for a long time, by being spread over several notes or by including unexpected skips or dynamics? Which words are emphasized by unusual rhythms, dynamics, or instrumentation in the accompaniment? What emotions are evoked? Which of your possible subtexts is best supported by the accompaniment?

Sing the two first phrases using each of your alternative subtexts. Which one makes the words seem to express the music better? Which makes the words sound more convincing? Which makes your character seem more believable? Which best fits your objective?

If the two phrases are not preceded by an introduction or interrupted by orchestral or piano interludes, write your best choice in the score and proceed to the next two phrases. If there is an introduction or interlude, you need to take its subtextual implications into account before finalizing your choices.

Fashioning Internal Thoughts for Music Without Words

Assume that every musical passage before, between, and after each of your sung phrases is intended to illuminate your character's feelings. Listen repeatedly to any music that directly precedes your first sung phrase. Then improvise a spoken dialogue to that music as if you are your character talking to himself. Refine this improvised text so that it:

- is exactly the right length for the music;
- leads logically into the words you sing;
- causes you to inhale with the appropriate feeling for the words that follow;
- reflects the phrasing and character of the music and clarifies it as an expression of your character's internal life.

After you have refined a dialogue, using a recording or working with an accompanist, test it by speaking it aloud over the music, making a direct segue into singing your character's words. Repeat this several-step process for each place in the first two sung phrases where you have more than a short rest. Remember that your internal thoughts for each musical interlude have to create a bridge from what your character was feeling to the feeling he is about to express next. Even if music that precedes or interrupts your sung phrase does not seem to be about your character's feelings, you still need to develop internal thoughts for it; otherwise during that music your character will die, and you will just be you standing there waiting to sing.

The introduction to the duet in *Lakmé* between the Princess Lakmé and her servant, Mallika, is an example of music that does not seem to be about the characters' feelings; it appears to simply evoke the gentle lapping of water. If, however, you can hear it as capturing Lakmé's struggle to appear calm in the face of her anxiety about her father and Mallika's need to try to help her find that calm, you have the basis for effective internal thoughts.

After you have developed internal thoughts for any introductions or interludes, combine them with your most promising subtexts for the words of the first two phrases to create a continuous internal dialogue. Finalize your choice on the basis of what feels dramatically and musically right to you and what suits your voice.

Write your best candidate in the score. Use pencil, so that you can modify it as your ideas develop and in response to any input from the conductor and stage director. Work your way through each scene in which you appear using the same approach.

Integrating an Internal Dialogue into Your Dramatic Analysis of Operas and Musicals

To complete your understanding of a role, it is enormously useful to assemble all the elements of your dramatic analysis—including your character's internal dialogue for every scene in which he participates. Write down the most promising candidates for your theme statement and your character's super-objective. Then begin to work scene by scene. Write out your objective for a scene and write out the text of that scene, leaving space for additions below each line and blank spaces where you have musical introductions, interludes, or postludes. Divide the text into acting beats, indicating each division with a slash. To the right of each slash write a phrase that encapsulates the beat. Then fill in your internal thoughts for places where you have music without text and below each line of text write your subtext. If you are working in a foreign language, first write in your literal translation, below that your paraphrase, and then below that your subtext.

Let's reconsider the subtext for Carmen's line "You once gave me this ring—take it!" There is no orchestral accompaniment under the line to help narrow your subtextual choices. However, there is a helpful stage direction in the original score; it states that Carmen pulls the ring from her finger and throws it at José *à la volée*—with reckless abandon. This suggests that singing the line, sweetly, lovingly, bemusedly, teasingly, or thoughtfully is inappropriate; however, it could support a seductive, provocative, sarcastic, ferocious, taunting, disgusted, or angry interpretation.

(If you can, check the source of stage directions before using them to shape your choices; often what is printed in your music is only some director's interpretation. For operas, usually the best source is a reprint of the first edition of the orchestral score.)

To choose between the remaining contenders, examine the shape of the vocal line. Each word is set on one of two low notes, except "take it." At that moment, the vocal line jumps up an octave and is marked fortissimo. This suggests that Carmen sings it with passionate anger, disgust, or ferocity rather than seductively, sarcastically, or provocatively.

To narrow your choices further, reexamine which of your proposed subtexts best clarifies the theme, your super-objective, your objective, and the acting beat. Here is a hypothetical dramatic analysis for Carmen's line:

Theme:	Mismatched needs in love leads to disaster.
Super-objective:	"I, Carmen, *need* passion without possession."
Objective:	"I, Carmen, *must* get free."
Acting beat:	"I, Carmen, *must* get free *by means of* breaking every bond."
Text:	"Cette bague, autrefois, tu me l'avais donnée, Tiens!"
Literally:	"This ring, another time, you gave me, there!"
Paraphrase:	"You once gave me this ring—take it back!"
Subtext:	"I hate you!"
Or:	"You romantic slob, you disgust me!"
Or:	"Stay away from me! I despise you!"
Or:	"Let me go!!!!"
Or:	?

Integrating an Internal Dialogue into Your Dramatic Analysis of Art Songs, Lieder, and Songs

You create internal dialogues for art songs, lieder, and songs the same way you do for dramatic roles. As an example, let's return to Schubert's "An Silvia" and create subtexts for the opening words and internal thoughts for any musical interludes for each of the interpretations explored in the previous chapter.

1. A young man who has fallen in love with Silvia sings to a mutual friend.

Theme: Silvia's perfection
Super-objective: I *want* to share my excitement about Silvia.
Objective (first stanza):   I *need* to know all about her.

Let's begin with the introduction. It is four measures long; you can hear that it has a curious tension on the ninth beat, that its high point is on the twelfth beat, and that there is a slight sense of relaxation from the twelfth beat to the first word.

With your first objective in mind, knowing that you want your internal thoughts to parallel the music, that you want them to express your character's internal life, and assuming that you need to inhale on the fifteenth beat, you might try:

FIRST STANZA

Literal Text	*Subtext/Internal Thoughts*
(Sixteen beats introduction)	"I know she's wonderful (beats 1–4), I know she's fabulous (beats 5–8), but (beat 9) actually I know nothing (beats 10–12), so you must tell me (beats 13–15)."
What is Silvia, tell me,	"Oh please, talk to me."
So that the wide fields praise her?	"Her beauty's making me crazy."
(Five beats of music)	"Oh, how do I find out more?!"
Beautiful and gentle I see her approach,	"She's looking this way!"
Heaven's favor and mark show	"I'm dazzled!"
(Five beats of music)	"Tell me all about her."
that to her everything is subject,	"I am her slave."
that to her everything is subject.	"Help!"

SECOND STANZA

Objective:	I *want* to confirm her virtue.
(Fourteen beats introduction)	"Tell me everything, every detail (beats 1–8)! No (beat 9), say nothing (beats

10–12), her beauty says it all (beats
13–15)."

Is she beautiful,
and good as well?
Etc.

"Ayyyy!"
"Is anyone more perfect?"
Etc.

2. A young man wants to seduce Silvia.

Theme: Sylvia's perfection
Super-objective: I *want* to seduce Silvia.
Objective (first stanza):   I *want* to remind her of her several loves. (Sil-
                              via has other admirers in the play; he is
                              hinting that she is already "playing the
                              field.")

FIRST STANZA

(Sixteen beats introduction)   "How will I get her? What will I say
                                  (beats 1–8)? Available (beat 9) she
                                  certainly is (beats 10–12), but how to
                                  snag her (beats 13–15)?"
Was ist Silvia, saget an,   "What sort of woman are you really,
    dass sie die weite Flur   hiding behind your beauty?"
    preist?
(Five beats of music)   "I can have you."
Schön und zart seh ich sie   "I undress you as you approach me."
    nahn,
auf Himmels Gunst und Spur   "You are perfect."
    weist,
(Five beats of music)   "I must have you."
dass ihr alles untertan,   "Others have had you,
dass ihr alles untertan.   I will have you!"

SECOND STANZA

Objective: I *want* to insinuate that beauty imposes
                                      obligations.
(Fourteen beats introduction)   "Will you resist me? Turn me down
                                      (beats 1–8)? No (beat 9), never (10–
                                      12). You're too beautiful to be pure
                                      (beats 13–15)."
Ist sie schön und gut dazu? etc. "Can't fool me," etc.

Troubleshooting

If you are having difficulty hearing your character's music as subtext or internal thoughts, try any of these three approaches:

- Listen to other music by your composer or by his contemporaries with an ear to how they portrayed feelings in music.
- Do exercises 3 and 4 at the end of this chapter.
- Apply exercise 4, "Questions," from chapter 4 to a page of your piece.

Summary

Your subtext and internal thoughts are the flow of feelings embodied in your character's music, text, actions, and accompaniment turned into words to create an internal dialogue. Your subtext enables you to simultaneously deliver your character's words on a literal and an emotional level just as people do in real life. In combination with your character's internal thoughts it puts you inside your character—converting him from a stranger to an intimate friend. It motivates everything you do, so your character is believable.

If you could fashion a "perfect" subtext and "perfect" internal thoughts, they would be so completely developed into a continuous internal dialogue expressing your character's feelings, and so absolutely appropriate to the implications of the music and the words, that you would make each note, rest, transition, word, and action into the perfect expression of your character and her situation. You would make it seem that, rather than re-creating an existing score, your character is inventing the music and words in the moment, and that the sounds of the accompaniment are coming from inside her!

Exercises: Decoding the Subtext

Objectives: to help you to hear the composer's musical choices as subtext or internal thoughts, to learn to fashion possible subtexts, and to become proficient in delivering subtext.

EXERCISE 1. (I/G) *Words Without song***

Instructions:

1. Choose a song, aria, or lied on which you are working in English. Fashion a theme statement and objectives. Then go through the text to make sure

you know both the literal meaning of each word and the meaning of each phrase. Since songs usually have poetic texts, to make sure that you have a good grasp of the words, make a paraphrase of each phrase. For instance, here is the text of the first lines of Henry Purcell's "Music for Awhile." I have put the literal meaning of the unusual words directly below them in brackets and a possible paraphrase in italics

Music, music for awhile
A little music
shall all your cares beguile,
                    [amuse, charm]
will temporarily relieve you of your worries
shall all, all, all, shall all, shall all your cares beguile:
will relieve you of every single one of your worries.

Read the original words aloud as if they are a dramatic text that has never been set to music. At first you may find it difficult to keep the composer's music out of your head. If, however, you focus on expressing the meaning of the words, after several repetitions you will be able to free yourself from the conditioning the music has created.

Go through the text of the piece breath-phrase by breath-phrase. Decide how each one relates to the theme and to your objectives. Mark the most important words in each phrase. (Underlining the most important word twice and the second most important once is a good system.)

Read the piece aloud, clearly emphasizing the words you have marked while maintaining an expressive flow. You can create emphasis by changes in volume, pitch, and rhythm, as well as with strategic pauses.

Using a clear subtext, read the words aloud to someone who doesn't know the piece. When you are finished, ask the listener what she thinks the song is about. If your subtext didn't get across, don't explain yourself. Read the piece again, making your subtext clearer. You may have to repeat this process several times.

You will probably be surprised both at how much subtlety you can convey and, simultaneously, at how clear and specific you have to be to get your subtext across.

2. Choose an aria, song, or lied that you are working on in a foreign language. Begin by making a literal, word-for-word translation. Write the literal translation either in your score under the printed words or on a separate piece of paper on which you have written out the text. Below your literal translation write your paraphrase and your subtext. Then repeat the previous exercise.

When you read the words aloud as a dramatic text, first read the original language with feeling, and then do the same with your English paraphrase. Practice reading the original aloud until you can put as much feeling into it as you can into your paraphrase.

EXERCISE 2. (G). *Song Without Words*

Instructions:

Choose a song you don't know. Have someone play two or three phrases of the melody and its accompaniment. Ask yourself what feelings are evoked by the music and analyze how the composer evoked them. Then have the person play the melody again while singing the words. Examine in what ways the music seems appropriate (or not) to the feelings and meaning suggested by the text.

EXERCISE 3. (I) *Words Are Music*

Objective: to tune your ears to hearing music as subtext.
Instructions:

1. Make up a short phrase of text ("Shut the door"; "Don't you look nice"). Fashion a subtext for it. Say the phrase aloud, expressing the subtext very clearly. Repeat it several times. Record yourself.

2. Listen to the rise and fall of your voice, listen to which words and syllables are emphasized; listen to which are quicker and to which are slower. Keeping the same inflection, repeat the phrase, substituting the syllable "la" for the words.

3. Roughly notate the "melody" and "rhythm."

4. Sing your notation.

5. Repeat the exercise, using the same phrase with a different subtext. For example, for the phrase "Shut the door" first do the exercise with the subtext "I don't care what you do." Then repeat it using "Do what I say!" Try the phrase "Don't you look nice" first using the subtext "Undress me, baby!" and then using "Did you find that dress in the garbage?" Do steps 2, 3, and 4 with the alternative subtexts. Compare the results.

6. Imagine yourself in the following scene. You are standing in the doorway of your house or apartment saying goodbye to your boyfriend or secret lover. Your text is "I love you." Try saying the text aloud with each of the following intentions: "to get rid of him," "to get him to stay," "to determine if he loves me," "to get him to marry me." (Fashion a clear subtext to express each intention before you speak.) Record yourself.

Listen to your melodic and rhythmic inflection and then abstract it into music. Try singing each version.

EXERCISE 4. (I) *Hearing Music as Feeling*

Objective: to hear different styles of music as subtext.

The following exercises are particularly useful if you are working on a piece for which you are having difficulty decoding the composer's emotional vocabulary. They are just as applicable to an operetta by Gilbert and Sullivan in which all the music may sound glibly superficial to you as to one of Handel's operas in which all the music may sound distressingly similar.

Instructions:

Choose a vocal piece for which you have difficulty hearing the music as subtext. Get a score and a recording.

1. Read through the text. On the basis of the story, choose three highly emotional moments that have strongly contrasting feelings. Basing your interpretation exclusively on the words, write down what you see as the dominant feelings in each of the three moments. Then, as you follow the score, listen repeatedly to the music for the three moments you have selected. Listen for similarities and differences. Use your understanding of the text to help you hear the emotional "storytelling" elements in the music.

2. Pick two characters of the same sex from the piece who have very different roles: the king and the young male lover, the young female lover and her female servant. Repeatedly listen to the music for each member of the pair and notice similarities and differences. Ask "How are the characters portrayed in the music?" "Are any elements of the melody, harmony, rhythm, or instrumentation repeated each time one of the characters appears?" Pay close attention to how the character's words are set.

PART III

PREPARING FOR PERFORMANCES

This last part focuses on how you can optimize the way you audition, rehearse, and perform. It presents techniques to help you to prepare before you enter the stage, to heighten your feelings and energize your voice and body for large spaces, and to handle a variety of performing problems—all so you can be believable as your character each time you perform.

CHAPTER 11

Being Believable in Any Role on Any Stage: Heightening

Defining Heightening

How can you create a believable character when you are singing in a cavernous theater over a noisy orchestra while executing the gestures of people who are exploring the extremes of human feelings and who moreover may be from distant epochs and an unfamiliar social class?

Just as the solution to being heard is not singing loudly but rather correctly placing and supporting your voice, so the solution to these acting challenges is not making your feelings and gestures big but rather motivating, focusing, and energizing them. I call this process "heightening." You can use it to fill any auditorium with nuanced gestures, as well as to make the stylized movements of period pieces and the magnified emotions in melodramas and farces believable.

Heightening Your Feelings and Gestures by Energizing Your Body and Breath

Energizing Your Body

The simplest thing you can do to heighten your presence is to place your weight slightly forward over your toes as you perform. When you sing with your weight back over your heels you seem to the audience to be pulling away, whereas if you are slightly forward you engage them. Probably more effective but slightly more complex is to initiate each phrase you sing and action you do with a strong impulse of intense, motivated feeling. You can evoke that impulse by engaging in a vivid internal dialogue, making your character's Given Circumstances compelling or charging your imagination with the Magical *if.*

Once you have activated an impulse, pay attention to where in your body you experience the intensified feeling. Then intentionally send the feeling flowing out from that spot. Be aware of it as it leaves the spot and as it energizes your muscles and the pathways of your nervous system on its way through your body to initiate a sound or a gesture. Let it continue as feeling-energy to stream out through your voice and gestures toward your partners and the audience.

For example, you are playing Susanna in the first scene of *The Marriage of Figaro.* It is the morning of your wedding day. You have just put the finishing touches on your bridal bonnet, and you *want* Figaro, your fiancé, to admire it. As you sing "Look a moment at my little hat," you have a spontaneous urge to glance over your right shoulder toward Figaro; at the same time, you find yourself lifting your left hand in a coquettish gesture toward your hat.

To heighten your gestures, begin by intensifying the urge that stimulates them: "Figaro, you *must* notice my hat; I *need* your attention/approval/admiration." Notice where in your body you experience Susanna's need. Let's assume it creates a deep ache in your gut. Let the *need* flow from your gut, up your spine, and through both your neck and your left shoulder. Let the feeling-energy that flows up through your neck cause you to glance to the right, and let it shoot out of your eyes toward Figaro and beyond. Let the feeling-energy that flows through your shoulder continue down your arm, through your wrist and hand, and out of your fingertips, suffusing your entire head with a halo of appeal. Let it continue to flow outward toward Figaro and the audience. Let it also be manifested in an energized delivery of your text.

In this example and others that follow, the process of heightening may seem mechanical, and, indeed, initially you may have to execute it as a mechanical procedure. However, with practice it can become a natural, integral outgrowth of your desire to express yourself. You may also discover that, although most of us in Western societies experience our strong feelings in our stomachs, guts, or chests, there are some feelings you may experience in your throat, very high in your chest, or in your shoulders. Since that is less than optimal for good singing, you will want to move them lower. Fortunately, you can usually do that as an act of conscious will.

Energizing Your Text

As mentioned earlier, the words that you sing are usually not the language of daily life, but rather some form of poetry. For instance, in "Tonight" Tony begins by singing

Tonight, tonight won't be just any night.
Tonight there will be no morning star.
Tonight, tonight I'll see my love tonight.
And for us stars will stop where they are!

Not only does this teenager from the streets of New York employ imaginative imagery, but formal rhyme!

By the time you perform Tony you will have long since made the words he sings simply part of who he is. However, to heighten your performance it is useful to re-examine the poetry of the words you sing. Since poetry is itself a form of heightening, a larger-than-life form of expression, bringing some of your awareness to it can serve as a foundation on which you can stand as you expand your performance. Notice the scansion, rhyme, and images in your text. Feel the power they lend to your character's expressiveness. As you sing let that power fuel the motivations you have already developed, and be sure to take advantage of it as you employ the techniques of heightening your breath and gestures described in the sections that follow.

Energizing Your Breath

You can use your breath to help heighten your gestures by building on the intimate connection between the initiation of a gesture and the impulse to inhale discussed in chapter 1. For any phrase on which you intend to gesture, let the emotional impulse that causes you to inhale to sing also activate your body. As you begin to exhale, also begin the gesture. You can increase the effectiveness of the heightening process if you not only coordinate the beginning of each gesture with your in-breath but also execute it with a focused awareness of the phrase you are singing—including its poetic elements. After you initiate the gesture simultaneously with your breath, let the gesture unfold—experiencing it as your character expressing himself though the music and poetry. Let your gesture come to a brief rest as the phrase ends. In this way your gesture becomes a physical illustration of the phrase, and the music itself makes your gesture more visible.

The next step of using your breath to heighten your gestures is to energize the breath itself with feeling. Begin by intensifying the specific feeling or thought you want to communicate until it is ready to explode inside you. (Your internal dialogue and your Given Circumstances, particularly *what* has just happened, will help.) Then inhale, filling your in-breath with the thought or feeling. Now as you exhale to sing, initiate a gesture and imagine that you are sending your breath through the gesture as you let it unfold.

You can notch up the heightening process still one more step by energizing your body and breath together. As before, evoke a strong impulse of motivated feeling and locate just where in your body you experience the feeling. Then inhale—imagining your breath flowing into that exact place. Now exhale with the sense that you are generating your gesture, your breath, and your sound from that spot. Let the energized gesture unfold, animated by the musical phrase and filled with your feeling-breath. When you breathe the feeling in this way, you energize not only your gestures but also your text and your sound.

Heightening Your Gestures for Period Pieces

As you prepare to apply heightening to gestures in period pieces, remember that characters—no matter in what epoch they live—most often give their gestures no conscious thought. Like yourself, as they grew up they absorbed certain expectations of their period and class, including assumptions about how and when it is appropriate to make different kinds of gestures.

There are three important exceptions to this generalization. Two are obvious: when your character is learning new behavior (like Cherubino in *Figaro*) or when she is trying to impersonate someone else (like Adele in *Fledermaus*). The third exception is presented by characters in Baroque operas.

During the Baroque era, members of the upper class (as well as actors, dancers, and singers performing for upper-class audiences) made a fetish of paying exquisite attention to their gestures as a kind of conscious, stylized, non-naturalistic body language. Therefore, when you perform a Baroque piece in period style, you should consciously execute all your movements in the manner of the time. Bear in mind that their actions (including taking snuff, using a fan, and bowing) arose out of clear motivations and were seen as not just decorative but intensely expressive.

For example, if you want to perform the leading role in Monteverdi's *Orfeo* (Mantua, 1607) in period style, your every gesture should be elegant and balanced and should reflect the period conventions. At the same time, Orfeo's feelings must penetrate his every move. You would want to appear fearful but undaunted in the face of Charon and devastated by the loss of your beloved Eurydice. Monteverdi and his audiences expected no less.

In the final analysis, music-theater pieces of every period and genre are about the characters' conflicts and feelings, not about the style in which they express themselves. Ultimately, therefore, your task remains to make the style of your singing and acting serve your character's feelings and to move the audience. However, if you want to understand your role in depth and want to bring the music and text to its highest realization, you will be well served by grounding your performance in a thorough understanding of the original context and performance style.

Often this will require both research and special coaching. The style of a piece is dictated by its era, the nationality of the composer (or the affiliation of his compositional style), and the form: an English melodrama from 1920, a French farce from 1870, an Austrian comedy from 1780, an Italian tragedy from 1640. (For information about how to research period practices in music and movement, including suggestions of possible sources, see appendix 4.)

Combining Your Research, Analysis, and Heightening to Make Your Performances of Period Roles Believable

Here are three examples that suggest how to integrate your research and analysis with heightening techniques as you develop a period role. They include hypothetical input from the director or conductor or both.

La Calisto (Cavalli; Venice, 1652)

You are playing the role of Destiny. You appear in the prologue, in which the supernatural forces Destiny, Nature, and Eternity lay out a metaphorical framework for the piece.

The conductor is committed to Baroque musical practice and expects lots of ornamentation, which she wants you to improvise in each rehearsal and performance. The stage director, building on a convention of the Baroque period, has decided that you are to hold statue-like poses. He asks you to develop several evocative possibilities.

You have researched seventeenth-century Italian musical conventions and practiced them with an expert, so you are ready to improvise your ornaments; you have studied Baroque sculpture and painting, so you have a clear image of how the Greek gods were portrayed; and you have done some research into how destiny was perceived. On the basis of your dramatic analysis you have fashioned "I *want* to control all that happens" as your super-objective, and you have fashioned an objective and subtext for each segment of the prologue.

Combining the elements of your research and analysis, you are ready to fulfill your assignment. You create several poses that are appropriate for Destiny and for the objectives you have chosen. You continuously enliven those poses with heightened energy springing from your sense of *who* you are, what you *want*, and *why*. (You can apply the Magical *if*. For instance: "I am going to behave *as if* I am so potent that I dominate the argument with my impressive presence.") As you inhale for each phrase, you breathe from the place in your body where you experience your *want* and bring that energy to your text, so your singing and all your vocal ornaments become passionate expressions of your character's needs.

Cenerentola (Rossini; Rome, 1817)

You are Tisbe, one of the stepsisters, in this version of the Cinderella story. For the second act sextet in which the characters sing their words broken down into syllables, you learn that except for any coloratura runs, the conductor expects you to treat the words as pure sounds, which you are to deliver as sharply separated staccato notes: "Ques / t'è un/ no / do / a / vvili / lup / pa / to . . ." In your research you have already discovered that in his comic ensembles Rossini not infrequently uses words more for their musical effect than for their literal sense, so you are prepared for the conductor's choice.

The stage director, reinforcing the confused astonishment of the characters' reactions and the words about tied-up knots and tangled cat's-cradles, asks that after you start to sing you should make a different gesture once every two measures, which you are then to hold for eight counts. The gestures should suggest that you are so befuddled that you are tying yourself into knots.

On the basis of your analysis you have fashioned as your super-objective, "I, Tisbe, *want* to marry nobility" and as your objective for this sextet, "I, Tisbe, *want* to eliminate Cenerentola" (who is the cause of the confusion and an obstacle to getting the Prince). You develop an internal dialogue that involves getting rid of Cinderella *by means of* beating, stabbing, poisoning, garroting, pounding, drowning, and stoning. You use this internal dialogue to motivate your staccato syllables and to heighten and energize your gestures so they are compelling.

Das Rheingold (Wagner; Munich, 1869)

You are Fasolt, one of the two giants who have built the gods' new home, Valhalla. The stage director wants you to do your movements in slow motion to suggest that Fasolt symbolizes "brawn."

You know from your research that Wagner intended his characters to function on both a realistic and a metaphoric level. You have explored how the words he wrote for Fasolt and the way he supported them with music (including leitmotifs) facilitate combining personality and abstract ideas. Therefore, you are prepared to work in the direction the director requests.

You also know that you cannot act "brawn" any more than you can act "love"; however, you can believably create your slow motion movements either by treating them as a physical reality of your character like Rigoletto's hump, or by using the Magical *if:* "I will behave *as if* my limbs are dragged down with weights."

On the basis of your analysis, you fashion "I *want* what I deserve" as your super-objective and "I *want* to get my way without the use of force" as your objective for this scene. Thereby you justify and energize your words and actions.

(You also create a psychological motivation for your slow movements: they are the result of restraint.) If, in addition, you imagine yourself with giant-sized passions seething in your guts, you have created the energy with which you can heighten your gestures.

Heightening Your Gestures for Melodramas and Farces

The world of melodramas and farces is one of extremes. In melodramas the actions tend to be more sensational and extravagantly emotional than in tragedies; those in farces more broadly humorous than in comedies. The main characters usually do not introspect or question but instead maintain a tenacious, single-minded focus on getting what they want. Any event that takes them even the slightest bit closer to their goals is cause for elation, while any little thing that moves them farther away causes desperation. These characters impose acting-singing demands not unlike those in the period pieces I have been discussing— the need to motivate extreme behavior believably.

The first step is to accept that even characters in farcical and melodramatic pieces are convinced that they are real, and that therefore they believe in their situations and their responses. However, since characters in melodramas and farces often are pretty minimally developed, as you do your dramatic analysis you may have to search deeper, expand small hints in the text further, and engage your imagination more than you do for the more developed characters in comedies and tragedies. You may find it helpful to substitute a very urgent *want* for their underdeveloped *why*. Researching the background, the period, and period practices in movement, gestures, and performance is just as helpful in creating and heightening believable characters in melodramas and farces as it is for other works.

Combining Your Research, Analysis, and Heightening to Create a Believable Character in a Melodrama

Verdi's *Il Trovatore* (Rome, 1853) is a good example of an operatic melodrama; the characters are not introspective, and they suffer a lot as they attempt to resolve conflicts that are chosen not for their probability but to arouse a continuous flow of intense feelings.

For instance, if you are Azucena, the gypsy servant, the first major action you take (which actually precedes the opera) is to murder your infant son. If you are Leonora, a young noblewoman, your last major action is to swallow a slow-working poison.

Let's first assume you are preparing Azucena. From your research you learn that in the Middle Ages, when *Il Trovatore* takes place, a nobleman like your master, Count di Luna, had complete authority over his subjects; you also learn that burning women who, like your mother, were accused of witchcraft was common.

To create the kernel of intense feeling that might believably motivate you to kill a child, take these bits of factual knowledge and intensify them with your imagination. What *if* you, as Azucena, were forced to watch as your mother was burned at the stake for a crime she didn't commit? Really imagine it.

You are seventeen years old. You are being held by two huge soldiers who practically thrust you into the fire to make you watch. You can feel the heat of the flames scorching your face. You close your eyes, but you can't keep out the stench of your mother's burning body. You hear the sizzling sounds of her cooking flesh, mingling with her screams of agony. After long minutes of this hideous suffering, your mother cries out to you "Avenge me," and dies.

You decide to exact revenge by killing the Count's son, whose nursemaid you are. Imagine that late that night you sneak out of the castle with your two small charges, the Count's child and your own infant son, who happen to be about the same age, and return to the site of your mother's suffering. The great logs are still smoldering; suddenly the sights, sounds, and smells from earlier in the day come rushing back to you. Might you not be sufficiently distraught to make a mistake in the dark and hurl the wrong bundled-up child into the fire?

Imagine how you would feel when you discovered your error! Could those feelings be the foundation for a life of rage and hatred? Wouldn't a useful super-objective be "I, Azucena, *want* revenge?"

Now imagine your plight as Leonora. You love Manrico, the troubadour, with such passion that you cannot imagine marrying anyone else. With equal intensity you despise Count di Luna, Manrico's rival and a powerful nobleman who effectively rules Aragon, where you live. From your research you know that in the Middle Ages virginity was so prized that an upper-class woman deflowered before her marriage was considered ruined. You also know that even as a noblewoman you are at the mercy of a nobleman whose rank is superior to yours, so when di Luna offers to spare Manrico's life if you will satisfy his sexual desires, you do not see any alternative. And yet your deepest desire (your super-objective) is "I, Leonora, *must* be true to Manrico."

Caught in this insoluable dilemma, you determine to take poison. To create a kernel of intense feeling that might believably motivate you to take this terrible step, would it help to imagine that Manrico is your first love—that love that combines infatuation and admiration with total surrender? Would it help you to imagine that you find the beauty of Manrico's voice totally seductive? Have you known the despised di Luna all your life? When you were children, did he and his friends strip you naked and make you dance for them? When you were twelve, did he try to force his body on you? Use the Magical *if* to thrust yourself into Leonora's situation or to magnify feelings that you have really had. Try recalling a relevant situation from your life that you can embellish with imaginary details to mine as a source for appropriate actions. (Bear in mind that your preparation work is private; so as long as your choices are compatible with the facts of the piece and facilitate everything you and your colleagues have to sing or do, you are free to make up and use whatever works for you.)

Combining Your Research, Analysis, and Heightening to Create a Believable Character in a Farce

Let's assume that you are preparing the role of Mustafà in Rossini's *Italian Girl in Algiers* (Venice, 1813). This opera is a typical early nineteenth-century Italian comedy with some farcical scenes and one farcical character, Mustafà, a potentate in Algeria. It revolves around Mustafà's repeated attempts to make Isabella, a beautiful young Italian woman who has been shipwrecked near his palace, the crown jewel of his harem.

Rossini's comedies have been staples in the repertoire since their premieres, so you can easily find material on the singing style, the period, and its stage conventions. If you dig a bit, you can find some information about harems and about North Africa in the early nineteenth century. From this material you are likely to discover that minor Moslem dignitaries rarely had the opportunity to interact with foreign women. Therefore, Mustafà might indeed find an Italian woman totally extraordinary.

In the opera's climactic farcical scene, Isabella prepares to escape by bamboozling Mustafà. She promises him honorary membership in an order dubbed "Pappataci." She stipulates, however, that first he must pass an initiation by eating a huge plate of spaghetti and drinking a great deal of wine without looking to the left or right. Mustafà agrees, hoping that his cooperation will win her.

You can believably motivate Mustafà's behavior out of your *need* to win Isabella. You are smitten by this foreign beauty, who, unlike the docile women of your harem, is immune to your well-tried seduction techniques. The more she rejects you, the more infatuated you become. Finally, in desperation, you go along with the strange initiation she proposes.

To bring your actions to farcical size, heighten your *need*, so that it becomes even hotter than that which you might use for a less exaggerated comic character. Behave *as if* you are totally consumed by your passion for Isabella. You can think about nothing else day and night. You cannot sleep. You are obsessed; you will do anything to win her.

Resist the temptation to choose stupidity as the foundation of Mustafà's behavior. First of all, you cannot act "stupidity," because like love, it is not an action. (Probably the most effective way to appear stupid is to try extremely hard to understand.) Second, if you make Mustafà stupid, you will almost inevitably filter out much of what is happening around you—drastically restricting your range of reactions. Finally, as Mustafà you need to present a formidable obstacle to Isabella; if you seem stupid, she will not seem clever. Like the other genre, farce proceeds by conflict; if you take the guts out of the conflict, the piece will not be funny!

Using Heightening to Support Hyper-melodramatic and Hyper-farcical Roles

Hyper-melodramatic Roles

There are numerous opera roles such as Salome, Elektra, and Brünnhilde in which the characters engage in serious actions that seem at first glance to be beyond normal behavior. I would point out, however, that every day the news is filled with reports of people topping these characters in both the fierceness of their emotional commitment and the extremity of their actions: people indulging in totally bizarre sexual behavior, people committing terrifyingly brutal murders, ordinary people immolating themselves in support of political causes. Therefore, the issue in acting hyper-melodramatic roles is not *whether* the behavior can be believable but *how* to make it so.

The first step is to put aside judgments belonging to the world outside the role. Accept your character's actions as human and embrace her as doing what she must. The next step is a clear analysis. For hyper-melodramatic roles you may want to add some analytic tools beyond those I have discussed. It can be useful, for instance, to understand how such characters relate to basic human archetypes, and then to search for the "hero," "caregiver," or other archetype in yourself.

It can be helpful to read accounts of how ordinary people find the strength to do superhuman acts. However, most often when such people are interviewed, they say "You would have done the same thing if you were in my place." In other words, just as for a character, you need to understand their Given Circumstances as *they* perceived them.

Another very useful approach is to figure out what "flaws" or propensities contribute to your character's choices. After all, not every daughter participates in matricide because her mother betrays her father, but Elektra does.

If you reexamine the analysis of Salome in chapter 2, it is certainly possible that the need to defy your stepfather and win personal freedom described there would not be enough to motivate you to the extremity of Salome's actions. You may need to add to the equation further analysis of the peculiarities of her personality. Is it a mix of a Hamlet-like anger and jealousy, combined with an incredible need to be loved, inflamed by a particularly profound sense of powerlessness, embodied in an oversexed teenager that leads Salome where she goes?

If this is an accurate analysis, then your task is to use your acting tools to heighten your anger, jealousy, need for love, sense of powerlessness, and frustrated sexuality. (Remember that if it works better for you, you have the option of using the Magical *if* to intensify your behavior without necessarily engaging your personal feelings.) Do not expect to achieve performance-level intensity instantly. Creating a character is a developmental process; you build gradually, step by step, to the point at which, within the framework of the piece, you can believably behave as your character does.

Hyper-farcical Roles

Instead of an empathetic bond based on feelings, hyper-farcical roles substitute a bond between characters and audience that is grounded in irony or intellectual understanding. This understanding is most often founded in social, political, or sexual satire. Some hyper-farcical characters exist with an awareness of themselves as entertainers; some interact with the audience. Occasionally, they exist both inside and outside their roles and create both empathetic and intellectual bonds. Naturally, such roles present acting challenges that are different from more naturalistic ones.

The operettas of Gilbert and Sullivan offer many examples of hyper-farcical roles. In *Pirates of Penzance*, the Modern Major General's behavior is motivated by the protective and loving feelings of a widower for his daughters, but this supposed rationale is exaggerated to the edge of absurdity. Similarly, the Sergeant, who sings "A Policeman's Lot is Not a Happy One," is thrust into a sketchily developed emotional dilemma in which he must enforce a law with which he doesn't agree. It serves as enough of an impulse to make him break into song, but the piece clearly exists primarily to make a satirical social comment.

Once you are freed from the boundaries of believability you are faced with difficult decisions as to how outlandish you should be. You no longer have the useful yardstick that the audience will only believe that which is believable to you. However, even the behavior of a hyper-farcical character consists of responses to his needs and the conflicts he experiences. (As I indicated, both the Modern Major General and the Sergeant are given at least the outlines of an emotional dilemma on which you can build.) Therefore, it is useful to define his Given Circumstances; analyze what he *wants*, what the obstacles are, and who embodies those obstacles. Then support his actions and text, however absurd or outsized, with heightening.

Troubleshooting

If you have difficulty applying heightening to a character in any kind of music-theater piece, realistic or otherwise, consider the following suggestions.

Give yourself permission to be expansive. Literally say to yourself before you work: "I give myself permission to feel and to express my character's feelings fully—whatever they may be."

Build step by step. Begin by activating feelings (or behaviors) in which you can believe and then gradually expand them. To achieve the heat of passion that José feels for Carmen in their final scene, you might start with attraction, then build through desire, lust, and obsession until you can experience (or believably portray) desperation. Be patient. After all, José didn't reach his peak of desperate, jealous passion without weeks of emotional "preparation."

Refine your internal dialogue so it is potent and continuous.

Increase your bodily awareness and control. An effective way to do this is to take classes in dance (particularly "modern"), body movement, yoga, tai chi, or the Alexander technique.

Work on your vocal technique so you can sing with a variety of vocal colors that subtly reflect your feelings and without inappropriate tension in your face and body.

Summary

You can use heightening techniques to increase the carrying power of your feelings and gestures so they are precisely appropriate for the piece, its period, your character, and the size of your performing space and still be believable in your role. They can help you be believable even in roles that are stylized, oversized, farcical, or melodramatic.

The steps to heighten a gesture or feeling are:

- Ground yourself in knowledge. Use research to develop a clear understanding of the musical and theatrical expectations of the period. Thoroughly explore your text and music to create a detailed analysis of your role.
- Go through your role phrase by phrase. Develop a kernel of intense feeling in which you can believe for each phrase.
- Connect each kernel of feeling with the spot in your body where you can experience it and imagine breathing through that spot.
- Imbue your breath, the words you will sing, and any gesture you wish to make with feeling-energy, starting from the spot where each feeling springs. Send it in a continuous energy flow to and through the parts of your body

with which you wish to express yourself and out toward the other per-formers and to the farthest reaches of the auditorium beyond.

Exercises**

EXERCISE 1. (I) *Breathing and Emotions*

Objective: to integrate your breath, gestures, feelings, and sounds in your body.

The region across your midriff, between your lower abdomen and lower back, is what you might call an "acting-singing" center. This is where you experience your diaphragmatic breathing and gut feelings, and, because many gestures radiate from the base of your spine, from it you initiate many of your gestures. This confluence makes heightening your feelings and gestures much easier.

Instructions:

1. Choose a feeling that you can experience in your gut. (Fear or anger are likely candidates.) Heat up the feeling until you actually physically experience it and have an urgent need to express it in sound. Inhale with a deep diaphragmatic breath, letting your breath connect with your gut feeling. As you exhale, sing a word or expressive sound; it can be a howl, a growl, a scream, or whatever feels right to you. Simultaneously, initiate a large arm gesture from your lower back. Let loose and allow the chosen feeling to flow out freely through your voice and gesture, until the space in which you are standing is completely filled with your sound and the feeling-energy behind it. Let the gesture unfold for the entire duration of the breath.

2. Repeat this exercise a number of times, using different feelings, different sounds, and different gestures.

3. Repeat "Inhaling the Idea" (chapter 1, exercise 3) with the following modifications: Choose two phrases from a piece each of which expresses feelings that you experience in your gut. Concentrate on intensifying the first feeling until it is ready to flow out. Then, when you do step 4, heighten your sound and gesture. As you exhale with an expressive sound, make a large gesture using one or both arms. Repeat these same steps for the second phrase.

In this same way, add gestures as you exhale in steps 5, 6, 7, and 8. You may change your gesture as you add words and music. When you link the two phrases in step 6, create the impulse for a new gesture as you inhale for your second breath.

In each step of this exercise strive to:

• Fill each in-breath with feeling
• Initiate each gesture from the same impulse that makes you inhale
• Begin the gesture as you exhale

- Feel the gesture starting from the base of your spine
- Sustain and energize the gesture for the entirety of your out-breath
- Experience the feeling breathing out through your gesture

* * *

Exercises 2–6

Objectives: to energize your body, to free the pathways of your muscular and nervous systems, and to let your feelings fill your performing space.

As you do these exercises it is helpful to remember three points from chapter 1:

- Every movement you make is a response to input from your senses
- Every movement you make begins as an impulse from your brain
- Every movement you make radiates outward from your spine

EXERCISE 2. (I) *Pathways***

Instructions:

Place the palm of your left hand on your lower back slightly to the right of the base of your spine. As you do each of the following movements, feel the muscles moving under your left hand. The amount of detectable movement becomes increasingly subtle with each step of this exercise. This exercise will help you experience the reality of the song that claims that the ankle bone is connected to the head bone.

1. Shift your weight onto your left foot. Take one large, slow step with your right leg. (If you don't feel movement at the base of your spine, move your hand until you find the place on your lower back where you do.)
2. Standing with your feet about twelve inches apart, keep your weight on your left leg. Lift your right leg with your knee bent so your knee is approximately hip height.
3. Swing your raised leg from the knee.
4. Keeping your right leg raised, flex your right ankle.

With your left hand in the same position, do the following upper-body gestures. As before, be aware of the muscles moving under your left hand and expect the amount of movement to become increasingly subtle with each step of this exercise.

1. Slowly swing your entire right arm in a large arc. (If you don't feel movement under your hand at the base of your spine, move your hand slightly until you find the place where you do.)

2. Raise and lower your right shoulder.
3. Hold your right arm partially extended to the side at shoulder height, and move your forearm in and out.
4. Hold your arm fully extended to the side at shoulder height with the palm of your hand down; then point your index finger in a gesture that includes a slight rotation of your wrist, so your palm turns toward the ceiling.

EXERCISE 3. (I) *Expanding*

Instructions:
Stand with your feet the width of your shoulders apart in the middle of a large room. Close your eyes; extend your arms out to the side at shoulder height. Imagine yourself slowly getting taller and taller until you can feel the top of your head touching the ceiling. Then, retaining the feeling of height, imagine your arms slowly getting longer and longer until you can feel your hands touch the walls. Imagine yourself expanding to fill the entire space of the room; encompass everything in it with positive, vibrant energy.

Retaining this expansive feeling, slowly lower your arms, open your eyes a crack, and walk slowly around the room. You should feel as if you dominate the space with positive feeling.

EXERCISE 4. (I) *Bigger Circles*

You used the image of an expanding circle of light to improve your concentration when you did "The Circle of Concentration" (chapter 4, exercise 4). You can employ the same image to fill your performing space with your (character's) feelings.

Instructions:
Stand in the middle of the stage or a large room. Choose an intense feeling or *need* appropriate to a character you are studying. Arouse that feeling or *need* in yourself by focusing on a few details of your character's Given Circumstances and applying the Magical *if*. Now imagine that you are standing in a small but very bright circle of light—like that of a follow spot. Experience the chosen feeling or *need* as an energy that fills to bursting the small, intense circle.

Slowly expand the circle. As it grows, keep it filled with the radiating energy of the specific feeling or *need*. Continue to increase the size of your circle until it reaches the walls of the room or the theater so that the particular feeling you have evoked is bathing everything within the circle's outer reaches—including any objects or other people.

You can further heighten your ability to fill a big space with particular feelings by converting the circle of light into a sphere. Summon up the chosen feeling as before, then imagine yourself at the center of a ball of light with rays of that particular feeling-energy shooting out in all directions from your gut or heart. Let the rays radiate down your legs, up through your head, and out through your front, sides, and back until you feel them hit the floor, ceiling, and walls of the room all around you.

EXERCISE 5. (I/G) *Sending Energy*

Instructions:

1. Invent a situation in which you *need* to drive another person out of the room but don't want to touch him. Your *need* is so intense that it renders you speechless, so you must get him out solely by the force of your gesture. Develop Given Circumstances. For instance, you are having a terrible fight with your husband/boyfriend. You have just screamed "I'm not saying another word. Now get out!" You don't dare allow yourself to touch him for fear you will do violence.

Locate the physical origin of the feeling. (Most people experience rage as a gut feeling.) Be aware of the connection between the physical locus of the feeling and the muscular impulse at your spine.

Let the feeling rise up your back and out through your shoulder like a searing, red-hot flame. Keeping your elbow bent and your hand near your chest, let the intensity of your *need* lift your arm to shoulder height. Let it deliberately unfold your arm and energize your elbow, forearm, and wrist. As it passes through your wrist, let it extend your index finger. Be aware of an uninterrupted connection between the physical origin of the feeling and the end of your finger. Then shoot the energy of your *need* out of your finger—driving the person away.

If you are doing this exercise by yourself, use the energy flaming up your spine and out of your finger to burn a hole in the wall opposite you.

If you are working with a partner, have him stand seven or eight feet away. Without moving your feet, see if you can drive him backward with the feeling-energy of your gesture. Try to let the energy shoot out of your eyes as well.

2. Repeat the exercise, adding sounds or words that express the feeling you are sending.

EXERCISE 6. (G) *Tuning In*

Instructions:

Repeat "Private Scripts" (chapter 2, exercise 3). As before, you and a partner each privately choose an intense emotional experience you are willing to share, and write it out. Then sit facing your partner close enough that your knees almost touch. Take turns reading your own essays silently to yourselves and "listening" to the other person read. When you are reading, focus on fervently reliving the experience, but do not mime or act it out in any way. When you are listening, pay attention to everything you experience. Do not bother trying to guess what your partner is reading; rather, listen with empathetic intensity, using all your senses.

After each of you has read his essay once silently, without discussing the experience, move apart to a distance of five feet and repeat the exercise. When you are reading, intensify the sense of your feelings, but do not *do* more. When you are listening, expand your "circle of concentration" and extend your empathetic antennae.

Repeat the exercise a third time at a distance of fifteen feet, with each participant expanding his "circle of concentration" to include his partner. Don't rush your readings. Take the time to make the experience of the feelings in your essay even fuller. Listen more acutely.

After the third silent reading, discuss your experiences. Explore how they were different at the different distances. Discuss what you received as the "listener" at each.

EXERCISE 7. (I) *Preparing an Aria from a Period Piece, Melodrama, or Farce*

Objective: to develop a vocal piece that requires heightened gestures.

Aside from improving the expressiveness of your voice, face, and body, increasing your facility with the Magical *if,* and developing your emotional range with improvisations and other acting exercises, the only way to work on the problems presented by period pieces, melodramas, or farces is to tackle one.

Instructions:

Choose an aria or song from a piece written before 1850, or from a melodramatic or farcical one that you and your voice teacher feel is suitable. Prepare it for performance in the appropriate period and style.

Be aware of this project as a *process* that you will be repeating throughout your career as you master more repertoire. Pay attention to exploring *how* you do it, as well as to the details of what you are learning. Begin with research. You might want to start at the library. Familiarize yourself with the kind of information you can find in the basic references books such as *Grove's Dictionary of Opera, The New Kobbe's Opera Book,* or the *Encyclopedia Britannica;* find out what a reference librarian can do for you and how to borrow materials using interlibrary loan. Or you can start on the internet to see what information may be available there. Check out your community to find out what institutional resources it may offer (including museums and colleges) as well as what kind of individual experts may live in your area. The latter may include specialized scholarly or private collectors, experienced performers, directors, choreographers, historians, or people with knowledge about the country or period of the piece.

Experiment to find out whether using written notes, audiotape, or videotape is the best way for you to document the information you are collecting, so you can review it, absorb it, and make it part of your integrated approach to the piece.

As you would for any piece, develop a theme statement and your character's Given Circumstances, super-objective, objectives, acting beats, and subtext to supply motivations for your words, music, and actions, so you can execute them with complete understanding and commitment. Practice singing and moving as your character in the style and period of the piece. To do this, it helps to find an appropriate costume (or approximate one as best you can). Suitable shoes are especially important in creating a foundation for your movements.

Try to find a knowledgeable choreographer or director who can coach you and let you know whether you are believable.

CHAPTER 12

Getting the Part: Auditioning

Introduction

Your auditioners want you to succeed; they are searching for the performers who meet their needs. Assure them that you do, and you'll get the job. In the following pages you will learn how to manage your audition so that you will present yourself at your best.

Like you, the auditioners are under stress. In a few brief minutes they have to make choices that will inalterably determine whether their venture will be a success. Your job is to present affirmative answers to the many unspoken questions they have to decide: Is your voice suitable for the role(s) they are casting? Do you have a good vocal technique? Are you musical and able to learn music accurately? Can you act and move well? Will your voice, physical characteristics, and personality enhance the role(s) and fit with the other members of the cast? Will you be a responsible and cooperative team member?

A good way to make sure your audition will be effective is to examine your choices from the auditioners' point of view: "If I were auditioning someone for the role of 'X,' or for a production of 'Y,' what would I like to hear? To see? To know about the person?"

Preparing to Audition

Your Resumé

Your resumé should help the auditioners evaluate how you can be useful to their project on the basis of what you have done, and the skills you have mastered. It should reflect where you are in your career. It is perfectly all right to be an emerging artist; however, you want to be sure that your resumé presents your experience and abilities in the best possible light. Lead with your strengths: your most recent work, your most significant roles, or the most prestigious companies with which you have worked. Make it clear, well organized, and brief—one page is standard; two is maximum. Use one side of the page only. Print your resumé with a high quality printer.

Your contact information is the most important; put it at the top. Include your name, voice category (coloratura soprano, lyric tenor), address, telephone numbers(s), and e-mail address. Many people also list their age or the age range in which they are believable, and any union affiliations.

Divide your experience into categories: opera, musicals, oratorios, plays, films, television, commercials. Prepare different versions of your resumé to use when you audition for different kinds of work. For opera auditions, you should have a version that lists your opera experience first; for musical comedy auditions, you should lead with your experience in musicals.

Each entry should include the role you played, the piece it is from, the company it was for, and when you did it. If there was something special about the production such as having a famous conductor or an extended tour, you may certainly include that to your advantage.

If you have won any significant musical contests or prizes, include that information in its own category.

In the early years of your career you may want to list your educational experience, internships, teachers, coaches, and any important conductors you have worked with. Under a heading such as "roles prepared," you may list roles that you know but have not yet performed. Be sure to include only roles that you know in their entirety and that are close to performance ready.

Have a category of "special skills." Include your dance experience, instruments you play, languages you know fluently, and unusual skills that might be useful in a production such as dialects, fencing, acrobatics, pantomime, or gymnastics.

Tell the truth. The musical world is small; if you lie, there is a fair chance you will be caught. If you are caught, you will not be cast. More important, since art is about exploring ultimate truths, how can you be an artist and lie about yourself?!

Your Photograph

Your photograph presents your public image and reminds the auditioners who, of the many people they heard, you were.

Choose a photo that is a good likeness; otherwise, you serve neither the auditioners nor yourself. Choose one in which you are alert, focused, relaxed, well dressed, well groomed and in which you like the way you look.

Use an 8″ x 10″ glossy "head shot" (head and neck); it is the trade standard. Have it done professionally—your competition will. (You may deduct the cost of having the photo taken and duplicated from your income tax as a professional expense.) If you specialize in "character" or comprimario roles, consider a composite photo with a standard head shot and a couple of small inserts with images of you in contrasting roles.

Update your photo periodically as you mature.

Label the back of the photo clearly with your name, address, and telephone number(s) and staple it to your resumé.

Your Clothes

Your auditioning outfit (one is all you need) should be flattering in cut and color, allow you to move easily, and make you feel good about yourself.

Since you are selling your voice and performing abilities, not your clothes or body, avoid tight clothes and loud colors. Don't wear jewelry that makes noise or calls attention to itself. When in doubt, make the conservative choice. If you are a woman, wear an outfit with a modest neckline, and with a hem that comes at least down to your knees. If you are a man, wear a coat and a tie. (For opera auditions, a suit is usually preferable to a sports coat and slacks.)

Dress your feet. If you are a man, wear polished, leather dress shoes; if you are a woman, wear a dressy shoe with a low heel. Choose shoes in which you can walk and stand well and in which you have practiced singing.

If you are going to an audition call for a pants role or a specific character— particularly in a musical—you may want to ignore usual dressing guidelines and instead wear clothes specifically appropriate for that part.

Your Repertoire

Choose pieces that are suitable for your voice, for which you might conceivably be cast, and with which you can show the range, timbre, size, and flexibility of your voice, the clarity of your diction, the accuracy of your pitch, your musicality, and your interpretive sensitivity. They should also be pieces that you know well and feel secure enough performing to demonstrate your most beautiful and expressive singing. (It helps if you have already done them in public.)

Solicit suggestions for suitable repertoire from professionals who know your voice, such as your voice teacher or your vocal coach. But since you will sing your best when you perform material you love, you should make the final choices.

Tailor your repertoire and style of presentation for each audition. If, for example, you are going to a general audition for an opera company, be sure you know whether that company performs pieces in their original languages or English, so you'll know which to feature. Find out whether the company emphasizes singing or acting-singing and adjust the number of gestures you make appropriately. (See the section "How Much to Move" later in this chapter.) Choose pieces that are related to the repertoire in the company's upcoming season(s), but unless they specifically ask for it, avoid pieces from the repertoire itself as their preconcieved notions may keep them from hearing your potential. If they're doing *Don Pasquale*, sing an aria from another Donizetti comedy or perhaps one by Rossini; however, it's a good idea to have an aria from *Pasquale* ready should they ask for it. Similarly, if they are planning *Oklahoma*, sing a song from another Rodgers and Hammerstein hit but have your song from *Oklahoma* polished up.

If you want to perform in musicals, you should have two spoken monologues—one serious and one funny—that you can perform on demand. They should be less than two minutes long. You should have them memorized and worked out in full physical and dramatic detail, using the techniques of analysis and character development outlined in chapters 6–10. If you need suggestions for material, bookstores and libraries have books of monologues preselected by genre, sex, and period.

Your Music

Make it easy for the pianist to give you the excellent support he wants to provide. If your music is photocopied, put it in a three-ring binder with two-sided copies or with the pages mounted back to back to create the minimum number of page turns. Better yet, if it is not too cumbersome, tape the photocopied pages together so they can be laid out flat on the music stand, eliminating all page turns. (Do not give the pianist loose pages; if they fall off the music rack, you'll be in trouble.) If your music is bound, break the spine of the book so it will stay open easily.

Make sure that any cuts or repeats are clearly marked. Imagine how you would like the music to be prepared if you had to sight-read it in public.

The Day Before

Develop a routine that prepares you to do your best at the audition. It is helpful to:

- Check that you have updated copies of your resumé and photo.
- Check that your music is ready; that you have all the pieces you plan to sing and that they are properly marked.

- Lay out your audition outfit; make sure all the elements are ready to wear.
- Sing (or mark) through each number you plan to perform; think about dynamics and interpretation; review your objectives and subtext so they are fresh in your mind.
- Eat well.
- Get a full night's sleep.

On the Day

- Do a thorough warmup before you go to the audition space. You can't be sure what facilities, if any, will be available to you there.
- Arrive early.
- Use your waiting time constructively. Review your music, text, and dramatic intentions. Do quiet relaxation and concentration exercises. (There are some at the end of chapter 14.)

Doing Auditions

Creating a Public Persona

Whenever you have to appear on stage without the cover of a role, as when you enter to sing an audition, it is useful to have a Public Persona. Your Public Persona is the person whom you want to present to the public. It is not you being fake or insincere; it is a preselected you that emphasizes positive aspects of your personality. Clothed in your Persona, you can be available, natural, and true to yourself without feeling naked. (No plastic smiles, please!)

To create your Public Persona, develop a list of four or five qualities that you want to project. For auditioning, you might choose: expressive, electric, confident, and sincere. Develop them using the Magical *if* and improvisation, or use exercise 1 at the end of this chapter.

At the moment when you want to summon up your Persona, for instance, just before you enter the audition space, activate it with the Magical *if*. "I am going to behave *as if* I am expressive, electric, confident, and sincere."

You can fruitfully combine your Persona with a set of Given Circumstances. For auditioning, use the actual *where* and *when* of the audition, but for your *who*, imagine yourself to be a successful performer with a flourishing career, or a singer who is both sensitive and fearless. For your *want*, you could try "I *want* to prepare myself and the auditioners for an emotional music-theater experience." For your *why*, consider "More than anything else, I love to share myself and my feelings through singing." You can add other imaginary details like "I've secretly been told that I am the preferred candidate for several roles."

Entering the Audition Space

Most often you will not be familiar with the setup in the auditioning space; you won't know how long a walk you will have to the piano, how many auditioners will be in the room, whether they will be close or far away, whether they will be paying attention, or who the pianist is going to be. Your Public Persona will help you gracefully handle whatever you encounter.

Since you may have very little time between the time your name is called and the time you enter, you may want to assume your Public Persona while you are still waiting.

Immediately before you actually walk into the auditioning space, repeat your auditioning super-objective. I recommend "I *want* to do my best possible work."

When you are about one-third of the way to the piano, pause briefly to make contact with the auditioners. Look out with a natural smile that says "I'm glad to be here, and am looking forward to singing for you"; then proceed.

You and the Pianist

If you have your own pianist, she should carry the music, enter immediately after you, and walk directly to the piano, passing behind you as you pause to make contact with the auditioners.

If the pianist is someone whom you don't know, give her the respect owed to a competent professional. Quickly introduce yourself and explain anything that is absolutely critical for her to know—although if you have prepared your music well, you should not have to say much. Do give a clear indication of your tempo. (You are much more likely to catch the tempo accurately if you softly sing the first phrase than if you beat it out.) Do tell the pianist how you will indicate when you are ready to begin.

Announcing Your Selection

After your brief interchange with the pianist, move to the crook of the piano. Continuing to maintain your Public Persona, stand with your weight on both feet, alert and breathing from your diaphragm, until at least one of the auditioners looks up, acknowledging that you should begin. Say your name loudly, slowly, clearly, and confidently. You want the auditioners to know who you are, and to feel assured that you are taking charge of your presentation. Try using the subtext "I like my name, and I am looking forward to singing for you."

Clearly announce the name and composer of the song or aria. (Be sure that you have practiced saying them aloud, and that your pronunciation is correct.) A good subtext is "I really like this piece and know it well." Since the auditioners may hear only one selection, start with the one that is the most relevant, that you think shows off your voice to best advantage, and that you like to sing the most.

There are no absolute rules about introducing a piece, except that you always want to give the name of the piece and the composer. (The name of most opera arias is the first sentence in the original language.) However, "I will sing" or "I'm going to sing," is stronger than "I want to sing" or "I would like to sing." "I will begin with" is not a great opening, because it presumes on the auditioners' prerogative to choose whether you will sing more than one selection.

A good clear introduction for an aria would be: "I will sing Figaro's aria 'Aprite un po' quegl' occhi,' from the fourth act of Mozart's *Le nozze di Figaro*."

If the piece is originally in a foreign language, but you are singing it in English, you may want to give the opera's name in English. For example, "I will sing Figaro's fourth-act aria from Mozart's *The Marriage of Figaro*" or "I will sing Figaro's aria 'Aprite un po' quegl' occhi' from the fourth act of Mozart's *The Marriage of Figaro*." Do not say, "I will sing Figaro's aria, 'O Fellow Man, Be Smarter' from the fourth act of Mozart's *The Marriage of Figaro*"; it gives the impression that you don't know the name by which the aria is normally known and therefore makes you seem unprofessional.

Getting into Character

After you have announced yourself and your selection, take a brief moment to make the transition from your Public Persona to the "I" of your song or aria. For a serious selection, you can create a private space for this preparation by looking down toward the floor; for a comic piece, you should keep your preparation as public as possible. In no case should you take longer than fifteen seconds to prepare, or you will lose the auditioners' attention; however, if you have practiced, fifteen seconds are plenty.

Begin by grounding your breathing with a couple of good diaphragmatic breaths. (Use whatever terms your teacher uses with you.) Remind yourself of the super-objective and the first objective of the "I" of the song or aria. Then apply the Magical *if* to *what* has just happened. Use it to plunge yourself into your character's Given Circumstances, and to arouse an urgent need to express your character's feelings.

For example, you are going to sing Figaro's "Aprite un po' quegl' occhi," in which he is suffering because he thinks his bride, Susanna, has betrayed him. You have fashioned "I, Figaro, *want* to restore my equilibrium" as your super-objective for the piece. Your first objective is "I, Figaro, *want* the understanding of other suffering men." For your *what*, you have created the following fantasy, in which you have personalized Figaro's situation. "What *if* my girlfriend of several years walks up to me, and says, out of the blue, 'I'm not going to the movies with you tonight, I have a date with X; we've been having an affair for three weeks,' turns on her heel, and walks away?" Maybe all you need is the image of yourself standing alone as she disappears in the distance.

Beginning to Sing

As soon as your preparatory thoughts or image arouse the necessity to give voice to your (character's) feelings, you are ready to begin. Take a distinct in-breath and look up in character. This signals your pianist to begin, and does not require you to disrupt your concentration by having to look or gesture to her.

With the same in-breath, keeping your weight on both feet, subtly shift your weight forward so you feel as if it is over your big toes. This increases your presence and engages the audience. At the same time, begin your character's internal dialogue to motivate any introduction and lead you to the feelings of your first words. Think your internal dialogue actively, and *allow* your feelings to show on your face. When it's time, inhale with the feeling of your first words and sing.

Performing Your Piece(s)

Your goal as an actor-singer should be to use your voice, face, and body (as appropriate) beautifully and believably to portray the emotional implications of the music and words. You want to bring the "I" of the piece to life.

Between Pieces

At the end of each piece, remain in character until after the last note has sounded. When it has died away, do not bow, but return to your Public Persona. Usually the auditioners will tell you what they would like you to do next. If you feel that they are waiting for you, either announce your next selection or offer several alternatives and ask which they would like to hear.

If you have the opportunity to sing a second or third piece, remember to take a private moment to prepare each time.

If the auditioners stop you while you are singing, immediately assume your Public Persona and wait for them to tell you what they want you to do. Bear in mind that if they stop you it does not mean they don't like your work; they simply have heard what they needed to hear.

Exiting

When the auditioners indicate that they have heard enough, thank them and, still wearing your Public Persona, exit.

Solving Auditioning Problems

How Much to Move?

Adjust the amount of movement you make depending on the kind of opening for which you are auditioning. If it is an oratorio, a church job, or a lieder recital, use movement sparingly or not at all; rely on your voice to convey expression. If you are auditioning for an opera, operetta, or musical, use well-chosen gestures. You want to let the auditioners know that you can use your body expressively and extend your interpretation into gestures that have a natural relationship to the meaning of the text.

Use upper-body gestures while keeping your feet still. Be sure that every gesture you make has passion and conviction and, as discussed in chapter 11, that all gestures are connected to your breath. Ideally, you will vary your gestures for each selection to specifically reflect the personality of the "I" of that song or aria. If it is a comic piece, you will probably want to gesture more freely and frequently than if it is a serious one. When you are not gesturing, it is important that your body remain still, and in any case, you should be extremely restrained about moving away from the piano. You do not want to lose contact with your pianist.

Where to Focus

When you speak, look directly at your auditioners. However, if you look straight at them while singing you may make them uneasy; therefore, it is safest to send your voice, gestures, gaze, and energy just over their heads. If they are in a darkened space so you can't see them, embrace the entire space with your presence and focus toward the back. The exercise "Bigger Circles" (chapter 11, exercise 4) can help you.

Fixing Wrong Tempos

If the pianist takes a tempo that is only slightly too fast or too slow, you can easily change it: slow your in-breaths to pull the tempo back or anticipate them slightly to push it ahead. If the tempo is seriously wrong, stop immediately. Since everyone at your audition wants you to do your best, there is no point in continuing if you will have to constantly fight the tempo. Apologetically tell the auditioners that the tempo is wrong, and ask if you may start over again. Establish the correct tempo with the pianist. (Take the time to make yourself clear, because you definitely should not start over a third time.) Be sure to re-enter your character's reality before you begin again.

Memory Lapses

Should you have a momentary blank, try to keep going. If you demonstrate composure as you get back on track, you will not be penalized. If you have a serious memory failure, you may have to stop. Don't make excuses; ask politely if you may go back a phrase or two. Be clear and specific with your pianist about where to start. Then be sure to take a brief moment to pick up the thread of your character's inner life.

How you will be judged for forgetting depends on how well you handle it and whether you appear to have just had a momentary blank or to be unprepared. In any case, you can't undo what is done, but you can impress your judges with the quality of your composure and with the excellent, highly concentrated performing you do thereafter.

Dealing with Rude Auditioners

If your auditioners seem rude, *do not take it personally.* If they are talking to each other, just tell yourself they're figuring out how much to offer you, and you won't mind so much. If they are eating, it is probably because they have been auditioning for many hours and don't have time for a break. If they suddenly laugh, it may be that one of them just had four pens fail in three minutes. You can't know.

Your most effective response is to enter more deeply into the feelings and meaning of your material and to commit even more fully to sharing your internal dialogue through your expressive singing. If anything will command your auditioners' attention, that will.

Handling Disasters

If some unexpected mishap occurs, such as the inseam of your pants tearing or the pianist knocking the music off the stand, calmly do what needs to be done. Do not spend even a split second on regret or blame, but if you do have to stop, always take a moment to get back into your material before you resume singing.

Dealing with Rejection

When you aren't chosen, remember that you don't know on what basis the decision was made, and that your singing and acting were only two of the many factors that the auditioners considered. You don't know what commitments they already had, what particular slant they planned, or even who your competition was. You may have been perfect in every way, but have been up against a singer who had previously sung with that company, or who had already had great success performing the role for which you were being considered. You can be sure, however, that when you are not chosen, it is not because you are a bad person.

You should also ask yourself whether the auditioners might not have been right. You should want to be cast appropriately for your vocal development, voice color and size, acting skills, experience, and maturity. If you are miscast, you will be at least as miserable as the audience and your employers.

Try to use the fact that you were not chosen as an impetus to cooly examine what you could have done better. Consider all the elements of your audition, not just your actual singing and performing.

If you did your best in an audition, you should feel good; you can't do better than that!

How to Improve

Auditioning is a skill, so you can improve by practicing. Wearing your auditioning outfit, go through all the steps with your voice teacher or vocal coach. Start auditioning for small companies—not with the anticipation that you will be cast, but rather to gain skill and confidence. Take advantage of the opportunity to observe how other people dress and, if you can, to see how other people present themselves in their photographs and resumés.

A Final Note

Ironically, in spite of the fact that the auditioners are eagerly seeking the perfect person for each role, you usually have their undivided attention for only about a minute. Therefore you want your announcement to be polished and your preparation to be short and effective. You want to give your all to each piece, starting from your first in-breath. Most important, you want to sing every note with beauty, passion, and expression.

Summary

An audition is a specialized form of performance in which how you sing, act, and present yourself are evaluated as an example of your potential. Not only are your voice and technique judged but also your musicality, your interpretive abilities, your performing skills, and your qualities as a possible team member.

Polish every aspect of your presentation to put forward your best professional self in each: your resumé, your photo, your auditioning outfit, your entrance, your announcement, your choice of repertoire, and, of absolutely the
greatest importance, your singing, your performing, and your dramatic and
musical interpretation.

Afterward, evaluate your audition not on whether you got cast, which is
based on innumerable factors that are out of your control, but on whether you
did your best.

Exercises

EXERCISE 1. (I) *Perfecting Your Public Persona*

Objective: to develop a useful "public self."

As you work on your Public Persona, your goal is to select positive aspects
of yourself and express them in a way that is flexible, natural, and honest. Your
auditioners, judges, and audiences want to meet you, and they want to be assured that you have the potential to deliver the goods; using your Public Persona can help you fill those expectations.

Instructions:

1. Choose two qualities that you would like to project as part of your Public
Persona. You might try "calm" and "professional" or "positive" and "prepared."

2. Make a list of physical and mental attributes that you feel typify each.
Use the Magical *if* to project yourself into each quality, one after another. To
clarify for yourself what traits of movement and speech convey the quality you
are exploring, try creating an opposite quality. For "calm" your might try
"chaotic"; for "professional" try "amateurish."

3. Try walking so that your walk manifests each quality. Be aware of how
you hold your head, neck, and back. Be aware of the length of your stride and
of how your feet touch the ground.

4. Try slowly sitting, eating, or dressing yourself while manifesting each
quality. Be aware of your body. In what ways are you adjusting your normal
movements?

5. Try talking to yourself aloud in a way that manifests each quality. Say
your name and the titles of some of the pieces you sing.

6. After you have gotten the feel of each quality individually, try the two
together.

7. After you have worked on the two qualities, practice in front of some
friends who will be your audience. Try making an entrance and introducing
yourself and your selection while wearing your Public Persona. Don't tell your
audience what qualities you are going for. Let them tell you what they get.

8. Take your Public Persona to a lesson or coaching to get feedback from a professional.

EXERCISE 2. (I/G) *Practicing Parts*

Objective: to improve the way you present yourself on stage.

Every successful performance is the sum of numerous parts. You are already practicing many of them when you work on your singing and musicianship. This exercise gives you a chance to work on some others: your entrance, your announcement, and your exit.

This exercise is done most effectively with a group of colleagues and in a large room, but you may also do it by yourself. The first part requires a recording device. The second requires a video camera.

Instructions:

1. Set up a recording device across the room and practice your announcement. Start with your name. Say loudly: "Hello. My name is . . . " (It is equally appropriate to say "Good morning," "Good afternoon," or "Good evening." However, it is best not to use "Hi"; it is overly casual and may lead your auditioners to think you don't respect the importance of the process.)

Listen to your several recorded "takes." Do you sound positive and confident? Check that you don't inflect your phrases upward at the ends, which suggests doubt and hesitation. If you are working with colleagues, let them tell you what they hear.

Add the name of your piece after your name, and record yourself. Check that you are easy to understand. Is your projection good, your diction clear, and your tempo moderate? Again, listen to whether you sound positive and confident. Practice with the recording device until you feel that all the spoken elements of announcing yourself are under control.

2. Set up a room as it might be arranged for an audition, with a grand piano in the middle of one end and chairs for auditioners partway back. If that is not possible, simulate the situation as best you can. Place a video camera with a good view that includes the entrance and the space around the piano.

Record yourself in both a full body shot and a closeup focusing on your face as you walk to the piano, stop at the crook, and announce your name. Study the tape to see what kind of statement each part of your presentation makes. Is your walk jerky or insecure? Is it nervous? Is it pompous? When you stop at the piano, do you stand with your weight on both feet and your body erect? Notice whether you make any nervous motions. Look at your facial expressions. Do you come across as master of your material? Do you seem natural?

Practice finishing your performance and leaving the space. Speak the last phrase of your song, then say "Thank you" as you might in an audition, and leave. Look at the video. Does your exit make a positive statement, or does it send a less desirable message, like "Whew! I'm glad that's over!"? It is ideal to practice in front of some colleagues, both so that someone can run the camera and so that you can get their feedback.

EXERCISE 3. (I) *The First Breath*

Objective: to begin each selection in your audition with a vivid emotional impulse.

Instructions:

Revisit "Inhaling the Idea" (chapter 1, exercise 3), using one of your audition pieces as your material.

Fashion a complete set of Given Circumstances for the piece. Be particularly detailed with your *who* and *what;* include to whom you are singing, where that person is physically located, and a detailed description of your relationship. Boil down your *what* to one or two sentences that embody your character's dilemma and that set your emotional juices going. For instance, if you are going to sing Carmen's "Seguidilla," you might try: "He's tied my hands; he's going to lock me up! But he's a man; I bet I can manipulate him." Use the Magical *if* to develop your Given Circumstances into kernels of intense feeling. Then use your heightening techniques to expand them until they are appropriately scaled.

Now, as if you were about to begin to sing, practice taking the following three steps. (1) Remind yourself to breathe from your diaphragm. (Use whatever terms your teacher uses with you.) (2) Say to yourself your character's super-objective and her first objective. (3) Revisit with conviction *what* just happened. Next, practice adding a diaphragmatic in-breath that is imbued with the feeling with which you want to fill the first phrase of music—sung or not.

Put the whole package together. Get the pitch for your first note. (Since you are only going to sing the first phrase, you don't need a pianist.) Stand with your weight on both feet, your eyes cast downward, and do all three preparatory steps. Then, as you inhale to start the music, fill that in-breath with *what* just happened, shift your weight slightly forward, and look up. Speak aloud your internal dialogue for any introduction and then inhale to sing the opening phrase. If there is no introduction, sing on the in-breath with which you look up.

EXERCISE 4. (I/G) *Gestures*

Objective: to control your gestures selectively.

Instructions:

1. Select a piece that would be appropriate to use for an oratorio or lieder audition in which you will only want to make a few gestures. Take the idea to

the extreme, and choose one word near the climax of the piece on which to make a single gesture. Practice saying the phrase in which the word lies and making an effective gesture.

Videotape yourself singing the entire piece and making the one gesture you have chosen. Is the gesture convincing? Natural? Effective? Is it distracting? Does it seem like the right word on which to make your only gesture? Does it seem to be the right gesture for that word? If not, try a different word or gesture.

Equally important, during the rest of the piece, are you standing still, with your weight slightly forward—free of nervous twitches or half-started movements? Practice singing the song, using the video as your teacher, until you are able to perform it standing still, being fully expressive with your face and voice and effective and engaged when you gesture.

2. Select a piece that you might use to audition for an opera or musical with which you want to show the auditioners your ability to be dramatically effective with your body. First sing through your piece, gesturing wherever it feels right. Do not worry about which gestures you make. Then read through the text and mark the most important word in each phrase. Sing the piece again, gesturing only on the words you have chosen.

Sing through the piece a third time, selectively gesturing only where it feels important. Be sure to make several gestures, but don't worry about what they are. Videotape yourself. Review the tape and critically evaluate how many gestures you make, when you make them, and whether they are effective. The object is ultimately to include only gestures that are engaged, convincing, and evocative of the feelings you want to express.

Repeat the process of alternately singing through the piece with gestures and then watching the video until you can consistently make well-chosen gestures just when they seem most urgent. You may either memorize your choices or recreate them spontaneously, whichever works best for you. Between gestures, your body should be energized but still.

CHAPTER 13

Getting Good: Rehearsing

Introduction

Rehearsals are the laboratories in which you work out how you will interpret and perform a piece. Together with the other performers, the music director, stage director, choreographer, and designers, you search for the choices that will illuminate the work in an appropriate and aesthetically pleasing manner and will make your character believable.

Once you establish your choices, you rehearse them again and again. Paradoxically, the reason for repeating them so often is to make all your character's thoughts, feelings, and actions seem spontaneous. If you repeat your choices often enough, they can become second nature, and then you are freed to subtly vary each choice in response to the tiniest nuances of your colleagues' behavior. Then each time you perform, working within your well-rehearsed boundaries, you can spontaneously reinvent the piece with your partners! (See the next chapter for an example of how this can work.)

Spontaneity, more than any other quality, will make your character believable.

Preparing to Rehearse

Preparing for Musical Rehearsals

You are expected to be note perfect and to have your music fully memorized when you arrive at the first musical rehearsal for any professional engagement.

(If you are one of the many performers for whom memorization is difficult, there are a variety of effective techniques that can help. Exercise 2 at the end of this chapter outlines one.)

You should also be familiar with the entire piece and your character's place in it. You should have begun your background research on the period and style. If you are working in a foreign language, you should have learned the meaning of not only every word you sing but every word that is sung while your character is on stage. If you arrive prepared in this way, you will be ready to participate in the real purpose of musical rehearsals, which is interpretation and ensemble work.

Bring your score and a pencil, so that you can mark in indications of tempi, breaths, dynamics, and phrasing.

Preparing Recitatives

In most operas written before 1820, particularly those written in the French and Italian styles, much of the action and dialogue is carried forward in "recitatives." Recitatives are text set to music that attempts to capture the rhythm and feeling of natural speech without developed melody. French-style recitatives are to be delivered as notated, both pitches and rhythms. Italian-style recitatives can vary. When they have orchestral accompaniment (*recitativo accompagnato*), they are to be performed just as notated. On the other hand, when they are accompanied only by a few instruments—harpsichord or piano and maybe a single cello or bass—it is another matter. These *recitativo secco* (literally, "dry recitative") are meant to imitate the pacing of spoken dialogue. So, although (with the exception of appoggiaturas) the pitches are to be followed strictly, the notated rhythms are to be used only as a general guide and are to be flexibly altered, according to the meaning of the words and the characters' intentions. It is usual to sing *secco* recitatives with less vibrato and to release the final note of each phrase quickly to give more of a sense of speaking.

When preparing *secco* recitative, beginning from a literal word-for-word translation is clearly essential. Next, learn the pitches and rhythms exactly. (Do learn the rhythms as the composer wrote them, both because often he has embedded in the rhythms clues to the characters' intentions and feelings and because there is a wide variation in how much freedom your conductor may want you to take.) Now, combining everything you know about your character, his objectives, his subtext, and the action of the scene, begin to experiment with various ways of delivering the recitative: sing the text strictly as written, speak the text of the recitative as your character, sing the pitches exactly while subtly adjusting the rhythms to convey your character's thoughts and reactions. Slightly shorten the notes for words you want to de-emphasize and lengthen those for words you want to stress. Try adding brief hesitations at points where your character has a change of idea, or when he needs a moment to think. The end result should be that the flow of the text reflects your character's mind at work.

You can expect that the choices you make during your preparation period will undergo considerable refinement as you work with the musical and stage directors, as you develop your staging and as you complete your internal dialogue.

Preparing for Staging Rehearsals

You may be able to begin musical rehearsals before you have learned the literal meaning of every word or having your part fully memorized, but you definitely cannot go in to staging rehearsals without this work behind you. You should also have developed some preliminary ideas about the theme of the piece and about your character's super-objective and objectives. Only then will you be prepared to learn your staging, develop your role, and participate in shaping the scenes in which you appear.

Because it takes a long time to get a character's physical characteristics ingrained, it is useful to begin working on them in advance. You will want your character to have an appropriate walk, posture, and repertoire of gestures and facial expressions. Study the text for information about the character's age, size, shape, class, education, nationality, occupation, physical condition, psychological nature, and the era in which he lives, all of which will influence his movements. Consider, also, how his life experiences might have shaped his body and face.

Listen to the music as a subtext that suggests not only what you do but how you do it. Are there any evocative rhythms? Do they suggest fluid or jerky movements? You will certainly hear suggestions about your character's temperament. Is she basically suspicious, puzzled, joyful, accepting, or angry? Explore how her attitudes might affect your physical appearance. Is your brow furrowed? Do you scowl a lot? Is your face creased from smiling?

Observe people of the appropriate nationality. How much do they gesticulate? Observe people who are the appropriate age, or who have a psychological or physical likeness to your character. How do they move their hands? How do they walk? How do they hold their bodies? Do some research. Look at paintings, photos, and sculptures of people from the period and class of your character. Search out appropriate videos and films.

As you begin to have a sense of the character's physical characteristics, explore how they are manifested in all aspects of his movement: his gait, the rotation of his head, the way his arms swing, and so on. Spend time working specifically on each of those things. Practice doing the dishes, brushing your teeth, or eating with his physicality. The process is the same whether or not the character is similar to you, or if he has a deformity like the hunchbacked Rigoletto.

The Rehearsal Process

Preparing for Rehearsals

You are expected to arrive ready to work. You should be vocally and physically warmed up, and, as much as possible with your "real-world" worries parked outside.

Arrive early so you have time to relax and focus. (See exercise 1 at the end of this chapter.) Review the sections you will be rehearsing and clarify your goals for the rehearsal. If for reasons out of your control you can arrive only at the last minute, get your thoughts focused on the work of the rehearsal even while you're on your way.

Dress appropriately. Often in early staging rehearsals it is useful to wear clothing that you don't mind getting dirty and in which you can move freely. But as rehearsals proceed and you delve more deeply into your character, choose clothes from your personal wardrobe that reflect your character's attire. At the very least, if your character wears dresses or skirts, so should you; if your character is going to be wearing a suit or a frock coat, wear a sportcoat or suit jacket. Pay particular attention to your footwear. It's hard to get a feel for Don José if you're in sandals!

The best way to approach each rehearsal is as an artistic adventure in which you are curious and eager to explore and develop the piece and your character.

Staging rehearsals have four major goals:

- To develop bonds of trust with your colleagues: the other singers, instrumentalists, technicians, conductor, and director.
- To explore how deeply engaged you can get in your character's feelings without adversely affecting your singing.
- To forge a complete vocal, physical, and psychological interpretation of your role, of which the linchpin is a continuous internal dialogue for every moment you are on stage.
- To develop your staging and integrate it with your expressive singing.

Developing Trust

You earn trust by giving trust (chapter 4). Practice sympathetic listening. When your partners are singing or saying their lines, tune in to the nuances of their delivery. Listen to the emotional subtext as much as to the words themselves. Subtly respond as your character to what you hear. Don't be negatively critical of your colleagues while you are in the process of working together. Remember that like yourself, they will improve during the rehearsal period.

Play theater games and improvise together. Improvising is particularly useful for developing trust because it requires all the participants to journey together into the emotionally unknown.

Develop your own role thoroughly and allow yourself to manifest your character's feelings. Your example will encourage your colleagues to trust you in your work together and inspire them to trust themselves.

Exploring How Far Is "Too Far"

If you are like many singers, you are hesitant to get too deeply engaged in your characters' feelings out of fear that you will get so emotionally involved that you can't sing beautifully, that you will go "too far." In fact, the question of how far is "too far" is a complex one.

When Rodolfo sings "Mimi!" as he collapses over his girlfriend's dead body at the end of *La Bohème,* should he make a gorgeous, perfectly placed, vibrant, pearly sound? Or should he use his vocal expertise to fill his voice with grief and even, perhaps, to let it be distorted by tears? Could the more truly "beautiful" sound for this devastating moment be the more interpretively appropriate one?

Let's say that you are rehearsing Rodolfo, and when Mimi dies, you actually do cry. You are wonderfully believable, but you get so much phlegm in your throat that you are unable to make *any* sound. Since one of the basic rules of music-theater is that you have to sing all of your notes, you have in fact gone "too far."

First give yourself credit for summoning up feelings adequate to the emotional climax of your role. Then figure out what you thought about and what you did to get to that state. Immediately before you rehearse the scene again, instruct yourself not to go quite so far: "I want to get deeply engaged in Rodolfo's grief at Mimi's death, but I only want to tear up and not actually cry." Then reactivate the crucial elements that allowed you to cry, but do not focus on the possible results. Most likely you will achieve exactly the degree of grief that you want. If not, since it is only a rehearsal, nothing is lost. You can revise your instructions to yourself and at the next rehearsal, try again.

Most often, however, the dilemma is not how to pull back because you have gone "too far" but how to find your way to going far enough. Generally, "too far" is *much* farther away than you think; the only way to discover where the boundary lies is to explore the possibilities. Consider constructing improvisations or probing relevant experiences from your own life. Try freeing yourself to respond by choosing a very potent *want* and *why* and giving yourself permission. For a scene like that from *La Bohème,* try telling yourself " I, (your name), give myself permission to break down in tears when I see that Mimi is dead."

Even if your preferred mode of acting is to reproduce the exact appearance of believable behavior from the outside rather than involving yourself emotionally, it is still worthwhile to experiment with arousing your own feelings in rehearsals. By reaching toward "too far" you will almost surely discover unexpected but evocative actions that you can intentionally use to make your character more believable.

Whatever your decision about what feels "too far," use your rehearsal time to learn how to create a sense of total commitment to the demands of the piece and how to work just inside of that extreme at moments of highest drama. Remember that rehearsals are not performances, they are places to experiment. You can learn as much from your "failures" as from your "successes."

Forging an Interpretation and a Continuous Internal Dialogue

As already discussed, you begin to forge your interpretation by creatively building on your research and on material in the score. Here are two principles to keep in mind as you work toward the right balance between your research, your analysis, and the way you develop your role:

• Since your primary task is to use your voice, face, and body to make the thoughts and feelings of your character clear and believable, the goal of your research and analysis is to help you understand the piece, not to set yourself up to demonstrate your expertise.

When you arrange flowers as Cio-Cio-San in *Madama Butterfly*, use the action to express your excitement at Pinkerton's return, not to show off how cleverly you have learned the principles of Japanese flower arranging. Similarly, if you are singing Cleopatra in *Julius Caesar*, ornament an aria like "Piangeró la sorte mia" to express her grief more vividly, not to show how well you know Baroque musical practices.

• The *truth* of each action springs from its feeling-impulse and touches something universal. But the *way* each action is executed is shaped by your character's culture, class, education, personality, the period in which she lives, when and where the piece was composed, and, of course, by who you are and the interpretation you are pursuing.

Cio-Cio-San chooses death from her sense of shame, betrayal, and abandonment—truths that transcend the literal details of her situation. But the way in which she carries out her choice—the honorable ritual of stabbing herself in the gut—is appropriate for her character and reflects Puccini's fascination with local color.

Although in previous chapters you have garnered the information you need to construct a dramatic analysis of a character on your own, in practice you will finalize your interpretation as a member of a team. For auditions and juries, you are the captain of a team that includes your voice teacher, vocal coach, drama coach, and pianist. For recital work, sometimes you are captain and sometimes it's more of a shared command with your pianist. But for operas and musicals, the conductor and stage director are the captains; they have the ultimate responsibility for all the artistic choices in a production. You may be expected simply to be their pawn, or you may be encouraged to participate as an active player. In either case, you will usually find that the captains' game plan actually strengthens the constructs you made yourself or is so useful that you can happily adopt it. And in either case, as soon as it is prudent you should seek out an opportunity to share your thoughts about your character.

No matter how the team is constituted or what the rules of play turn out to be, when you rehearse you will be working out and refining your character's motivations and internal dialogue. Even if your character's motivations are dictated to you by the stage director, it is still crucial to develop your character's internal dialogue on your own. After all, the internal dialogue is the way *you* think as your character.

Your internal dialogue is complete when it is continuous from your first entrance to your final exit, when it seamlessly connects your subtext and your internal thoughts, and when everything you sing, say, hear, or do on stage feels directly connected through it to achieving your character's objectives. It is just as important to have this sort of fully developed internal dialogue for pieces you perform standing by the piano or in front of an orchestra as it is for dramatic roles. Even though in the first two cases you will not be in costume or moving around, you still want to deliver a clear and believable characterization.

Once your internal dialogue is continuous and you are comfortable enough with all the details of the performance to subtly adjust it to the slightly changing nuances that you continuously receive from your colleagues both on stage and in the pit, you are almost surely ready for performance. (In the next chapter there is a detailed example of possible internal dialogues for Carmen, the chorus, and José in their first scene, illustrating this interaction.)

Developing Staging and Integrating It with Your Expressive Singing

Note: If there are terms in this section with which you are not familiar, check the glossary in appendix 3.

* * *

It is helpful in your early discussions with the director if you talk not only about your character's super-objective but also about your character's physical characteristics and find out what your costume will be like. Then as you develop your blocking and business, you can consciously practice doing your actions with your character's physicality, confident that your choices fit with the director's concept. With repetition, you will be able to associate the way you do your actions with the gestures themselves, and gradually the character's physicality will become an automatic part of your every move.

Rehearsals to develop blocking, business, and your character's physical characteristics can be done in a variety of ways, reflecting how the stage director sees his role as a captain. At one end of the spectrum are rehearsals in which the director tells you exactly what you are to do; at the other end are rehearsals in which you have the major inventive initiative or in which the production is developed collectively. Most rehearsals fall somewhere between the two extremes.

If the stage director expects you and your colleagues to develop blocking or business on your own, it is helpful to begin by discussing each of your characters' Given Circumstances and how the particular scene and the characters in it function to develop the theme. Then you can invent actions appropriate for your characters that illustrate your insights. If for some reason you are unable to discuss these questions with your colleagues, answer them for yourself.

Integrating Your Feet: "Sharing," "Cheating," and "Commanding"

As you develop your blocking and your character's walk and stance, you want to get used to optimally positioning your feet. You want to arrange them so you can see the conductor as necessary, be easily heard, and, most important, have a believable connection with the people to whom you are singing and listening. To achieve all these goals simultaneously, you will want to "share" or "command" the stage and "cheat" as is appropriate.

When you are having a conversation on stage with a partner that moves relatively quickly and equally between you, the two of you should stand facing each other with your feet slightly apart. The toes of your upstage feet (the ones farther from the audience) should be in the same plane and exactly opposite each other, while the toes of your downstage feet should face toward the audience. With your feet in this open stance, a sort of spread "fourth position," you will find that your bodies are at a forty-five-degree slant to each other. You are thus literally "sharing" the stage, positioned to receive equal attention. "Sharing" allows each of you to look directly into the other's eyes when that is most effective, or to subtly swivel away to send your voice past the end of the other's nose, "cheating" it out toward the audience without losing contact with each other. In this position you can also easily catch a cue from the conductor.

When you are having a conversation in which one person sings for a long time before the other responds, the two of you should stand so that the listener is not on the same plane with the singer but slightly downstage of him. When it is the listener's time to respond, shift. If his response is extensive, the singer should move slightly above the listener, because from an upstage position you can sing to your partner(s) and at the same time have your body optimally positioned in relation to the audience. You are the most "commanding" when you stand above the people you are addressing. When you stand downstage of (below) the people you are addressing, you may feel more important because you are closer to the audience but actually you appear less so; from below you put yourself in the weak position of either having to turn your back to the audience to see the people to whom you are singing or of singing outward to the air, which is seldom very believable.

Although you make the adjustments of sharing, cheating, and commanding for technical reasons, it is crucial in order to sustain the believability of your character to motivate them from his needs.

Integrating Your Hands and Gestures

Like most performers, you probably have good natural instincts about when to gesture, particularly as you begin to get into a role. (This will be increasingly true as you work on the exercises in chapter 11.) Therefore, when you feel the slightest impulse to gesture in a rehearsal, unless the director is dictating your every move, act on it. Any gesture will do to begin with. As you continue to rehearse, bearing in mind that audiences read every gesture as a significant piece in the puzzle they are assembling, you can refine them and decide how long to sustain them or how subtly to shape them; you may also decide to eliminate some as superfluous or repetitive. Ultimately you want to be sure that each one is evocative.

You can give clear gestural expression to extremely complex feelings or states of mind if you do your gestures as a sequence. First execute a gesture that clearly evokes a particular thought or feeling, then do one evocative of a different thought or feeling and so on. Even if your character's feelings are contradictory, you can evoke them clearly and believably if you give them expression one at a time.

In her final moments with José, Carmen is fearful, defiant, and resigned. Clearly, no single gesture can express these three contrasting feelings. However, you can express all of them by doing three separate gestures in sequence—perhaps a glance to the ground, followed by squaring your shoulders as you look up, and then slowly letting your shoulders drop. Naturally, your gestures can flow one into another, or you can interrupt one gesture with another or alternate between them. If your choices spring from your sensitively developed internal dialogue, they will automatically reflect the music and the way it moves.

If a thought or feeling is important, you can reinforce it through several different actions. For instance, José's obsession with Carmen is crucial to his character. Therefore, you will serve your José well if, in addition to the opportunities suggested in the score, you find other moments to reinforce his mania. For instance, in the scene that follows your first meeting, you might take out the flower Carmen threw at you and smell it from time to time. After you have clearly established that you keep it hidden in your inside breast pocket, you could occasionally just touch that spot and smile.

Once you have discovered and developed gestures that are expressive of your character and his feelings, you are free to slightly modify them to reflect the subtle changes in your internal dialogue stimulated by your colleagues. This is equally true whether you allow your gestures to spring naturally from your character's circumstances or whether you consciously select and repeat them until they are automatic.

As you know, for vocal competitions, recitals, and oratorios you are basically expected to stand still. This places enormous emphasis on manifesting a believable internal life through your voice and face using only sparing, carefully chosen gestures. Therefore, it is even more crucial than in staged operatic performances to make these gestures seem like natural and necessary expressions of your character's thoughts or feelings.

You can still develop them by behaving *as if* you are in your character's situation, and applying a much more stringent filter to decide how much to move. Or you may want to work more consciously, choosing the few ideas that you want to emphasize, selecting gestures using your hands and arms to underline them, and then repeating them until they look and feel natural. In either case, develop a repertoire of gestures, some using both hands, some the right or the left. Be sure to make different gestures for different emotional situations, and to establish a natural connection to your breathing.

If an arm or hand gesture is worth doing, it generally should be done with your hands above the waist. Gestures made below the waist tend to be read as nervousness, particularly when you are standing at the piano.

Handling Your Props

Props (short for stage properties) are any objects that your character handles—a letter, a cane, a gun, a fan, a purse, or a telephone.

Often part of the rehearsal process involves deciding on the perfect prop to help define your character. You will, for instance, create a slightly different color as Micaëla if you arrive with the note from José's mother wrapped in a bandanna than if you have it in a hand basket with other goodies. It is perfectly appropriate to make suggestions for props that you think would help clarify your character and your actions.

Sometimes your prop may be the real thing; more often it will only be a theatrical representation of the object. In either case, props seem exactly as real as you make them. If you handle a wooden gun as if it is deadly, it can be more fearsome than if you hold a real .44 Magnum without conveying an awareness of its destructive potential.

Your character may have a strong point of view about a particular prop—a telephone can be terrifying, a bottle of poison her path to salvation. If you are Rigoletto, a cane may be your friend or a curse, a strength or a weakness, depending on how you use it. This reality, too, is yours to create.

Often characters have personal props that are part of their daily life—a policeman's night stick, a woman's purse. If you are playing an eighteenth-century character you might have a fan or a sword. It is essential to learn and master any etiquette associated with such props, so that you can use them to express your internal dialogue as is appropriate.

Notating Your Blocking and Business

In staging rehearsals you almost always work without the score, so that your hands are free to develop your gestures and business. However, you are expected to write down what you have worked out after you have finished a scene or when you have a break.

When you make your notes, record both what you are to do, including any business with props, and when you are to do it. You can put your instructions directly above or below the staff or line of text—perhaps circling the note or word on which you begin the action. Or you can put a number at the precise spot in the music or text where you begin an action and write your notes next to a corresponding number in the margin or on a facing page. Quick diagrams to show where you stand and which way you are facing in relationship to the furniture or other people are very useful. They can be extremely simple: people can be represented with xs or circles, and the direction they are facing with a small arrow. Always use a pencil; directors are allowed to change their minds, and often do so.

You may use any notation that makes sense to you; however, your notes should be sufficiently clear that you can use them to practice on your own, and so you can reproduce your blocking and business precisely even if several weeks have elapsed between rehearsals.

Creating an Integrated Performance Focus

Since, as already discussed, the audience reads your conscious thoughts as your character's, so your character's internal dialogue provides the perfect core around which you can integrate everything you want to do as your character. It is continuous and is the character's mind at work. In chapter 1 we saw how you can use it to integrate your vocal technique with your acting, and in this chapter how it can serve as the central thread with which you can integrate your blocking, your character's physical characteristics, and your dramatic interpretation. You can also use it to integrate those moments when you need to look toward the conductor for cues.

You achieve this integration using the same technique with which you integrate your vocal demands: repetition and association. If, for instance, you need to get a cue from the conductor, but you are blocked so you actually have to turn your head to see her hand, first establish exactly when you need to look and what sort of information you are looking for—a tempo, an entrance, dynamics. Then use your internal dialogue to generate a motivation for looking in the conductor's direction. Practice alternately looking for the information and allowing yourself to glance in the conductor's direction as part of your character's life. After sufficient repetition, your glance will become your character's action, and you will also get your cue.

Integrating All the Elements—The Final Rehearsals

In the final stages of preparing a musical or opera you need to integrate your staging and musical work with the orchestra and with all the other production elements including your costumes, wigs, and makeup, and the scenery, lighting, furniture, and props. You need a chance to work out your part in relation to the entire production, starting at the beginning and making your way through to the end. To achieve this integration, it is usual to have a series of rehearsals with different emphases, beginning with a technical rehearsal.

A technical rehearsal (abbreviation: "tech" rehearsal) is one in which the details of the physical production are worked out. It gives the technicians the opportunity to rehearse with you, so that you will have light when and where you need it, your props and furniture will be in the right place, and the curtain will open and close at the right moment and at the right speed. At a technical rehearsal you may go "cue to cue." This means that you will rehearse only those moments where there is a technical cue like a light change.

Around the time of the technical rehearsal, you will usually also have rehearsals with the orchestra in which you do little or no movement, followed by a piano dress rehearsal and one or more orchestra dress rehearsals. In preparing an opera, it is standard practice to use the German names for the several kinds of musical rehearsals preceding the dress rehearsals.

A *Sitzprobe* (zitz´-pro-bah), literally, a "sitting rehearsal," is a rehearsal with orchestra at which you are seated, so you can focus on the musical aspects of the show. Often it is the first time that you will rehearse with the orchestra. You can expect that the conductor will give instructions as to how she will beat particular measures, or how she will indicate your entrances. You are expected to bring your music and a pencil to the *Sitzprobe,* so you can take notes.

A *Stellprobe* (shtel´-pro-bah), literally, an "in-place rehearsal," is a rehearsal with orchestra in which you only do your major moves, so you are standing in position to sing each line but you are not expected to act.

A *Wandelprobe* (vahndl´-pro-bah), literally a "moving-around rehearsal," is a rehearsal with orchestra in which you do all your blocking as you sing but are still not expected to act.

The *Sitzprobe,* when used, comes first, but sometimes it is omitted and you proceed directly to either a *Stellprobe* or *Wandelprobe.* Either of these last two gives you a chance to learn which instruments you will hear from the various places on the stage where you sing, and gives the conductor a chance to learn where you will be when he needs to cue you.

After the orchestral rehearsal(s), you will have a piano dress rehearsal which is a full work-through of the piece with all the elements of the production—scenery, props, lighting, costumes, makeup, hair—in place as for a performance, except that it is accompanied by a piano rather than by the orchestra.

The final rehearsal is an orchestra dress rehearsal that is like a performance. Sometimes there is even an audience.

Troubleshooting

Handling a "Weak" Partner

Most often you will find a partner "weak" either because he consistently makes musical mistakes or because he fails to deliver his part with appropriate and believable feelings. Sometimes you can address such problems directly by suggesting that you work together outside of rehearsals. You may also diplomatically ask the music or stage director to help.

If neither of those approaches bears fruit, then you need to find a way to neutralize your partner's "unsatisfactory" behavior. If the problem is musical, you can learn to get your cues from the accompaniment and learn his part sufficiently well that his mistakes can't throw you.

If your partner fails to imbue his part with enough feeling to give you something to react to, search for some tiny detail on which you can build what you need. For example, to stimulate feelings of affection, you can use anything about the person that you find attractive, no matter how small: the shape of his earlobe or pinkie finger, the inflection of a single word, the way he sings a particular note. You can substitute this limited attraction for a stronger feeling—

for instance, singing, "I love you, John," while saying in your head, "I love the flare of your nostrils, John." You may also find a personality trait that you can use: maybe he is very vulnerable, or honest or dynamic. Once you identify one attractive trait or behavior, it often opens the door to others.

You can use the Magical *if:* "I am going to behave *as if . . .* I have always loved people who speak very slowly" or "who show very little feeling," or whatever the stumbling block(s) may be. Sometimes to get past your own feelings of disappointment or frustration you may find it useful to add another layer between you and your "weak" partner: "Regardless of how I personally feel, I, (your character's name), will behave *as if* I find my partner's character's behavior charming, provoking (etc.)." You are still reacting to what you are really getting, but you are using it transmuted. You are seeing the world through your character's senses while making whatever your partner does work for you.

A third approach is to redefine the area of difficulty with a positive gloss. Of your partner's slow speech, say to yourself "I admire a person who speaks with deliberate wisdom"; of her wooden behavior, "I prefer people who show great emotional consideration." Then behave *as if* this is true. Similarly, if you are receiving nothing in a situation where your partner's character is supposed to display strong anger or, perhaps, to charm your character with her wit, come up with an interpretation that turns it around. The "nothing" you are receiving is in reality a depth of rage so extreme that your partner's character must totally repress it, or a sense of humor so sly that she shows nothing. You, however, have the sensitivity and intelligence to appreciate her self-mastery or subtlety.

Turn what you get into what you need, so that you don't empower someone else to destroy your good work.

Handling Problems with the Conductor or Director

Occasionally you may find yourself in the unhappy situation of disagreeing with the ideas of the conductor or stage director. Although they have the final call, you are usually allowed to argue your case. You will be most successful if you talk about your disagreements privately and in a non-confrontational manner. It helps to set out the problem in terms of your character's motivation: "I am having a hard time motivating singing 'I love you' with hatred. Can you help me?"

If the director or conductor is adamant about what she wants, don't waste any time resisting. Accept her choices as givens in your character's circumstances and figure out how to make them work. You are responsible for making everything you do on stage seem motivated and believable—regardless of who makes the choices. Fortunately, there are a dozen different ways to motivate any behavior.

Sometimes you will find yourself in the equally unhappy position of not receiving enough guidance from the conductor or stage director. Don't hesitate to ask questions. If you still don't receive what you need, use the tools you have learned in this book to make your own interpretive choices.

Summary

Rehearsal is the final stage of the process whereby you develop a complete vocal, musical, physical, and psychological portrait of your character, so you can be believable in your role. Part of this process is to develop trust in yourself as your character and trust in your colleagues as committed participants in the emotional world of the piece; another part is to explore how deeply engaged you can get in the character's feelings without adversely affecting your singing. A third part is fashioning a continuous internal dialogue for every moment you are on stage, so your conscious mind is always thinking your character's thoughts. The last part is integrating all the elements of your performance around the central thread provided by your internal dialogue.

You rehearse your part, repeating it again and again, until you have mastered all the technical details of your singing and acting, including your blocking, how to stand so you can be heard, believably support your colleagues and get your cues, and how to use your props, so you can put all these details on semi-automatic. Then you are free to respond spontaneously to the details of your partners' behaviors.

A Rehearsal Checklist

This is a guide to help you shape your work for rehearsals.

Pre-rehearsal Preparation

- Do you know the piece thoroughly?
    - Have you read the entire libretto to identify the big ideas?
    - Have you read the entire libretto from your character's point of view?
    - Have you listened to the entire piece? In how many different recordings?
    - Have you become sufficiently familiar with the entire work to hear the music as an expression of the characters' feelings?
    - Have you become sufficiently familiar with the entire work to hear how your character is musically portrayed?

- Have you done background research? Some possibilities:
  - Read the original material on which the libretto is based. Look at pictures and sculptures from the period and country relevant to the piece.
  - Look at pictures of how people of your character's social class, period, and country dressed.
  - Study how people of your character's class, age, and country moved and gestured.
  - Read about social customs of people in your character's period, class, and country.
  - Read history about the relevant period.
  - Research the major concerns of the composer, librettist, relevant period, country, and your character's class.
  - Listen to other music by the composer.
  - Read literature of the relevant period and country.
- Have you tried to imagine how the piece was understood in its time?
  - Have you researched how it was received?
  - Have you read letters of people who saw it, who participated in it?
  - Have you read reviews from the time?
- Have you fashioned an interpretation?
  - Did you do a word-by-word translation, being sure to check out any idioms?
  - Did you make a paraphrase of your translation in usable English?
  - Have you fashioned a possible theme statement?
  - Have you fashioned a super-objective for your character?
  - Did you make a careful analysis of why each scene in which your character appears must be there (its function), and how each scene contributes to your character's development?
- Have you defined your character's Given Circumstances in each scene?

Rehearsals

- Do you arrive at each rehearsal at least five minutes early?
- Do you arrive rested and eager to explore the work further?
- Do you arrive physically and vocally warmed up?
- Have you learned the required material thoroughly?
- Have you reviewed your written and mental notes from the preceding rehearsal(s)?
- Do you wear clothes that help you to be your character, particularly appropriate shoes?
- Do you bring in rehearsal props to help make the scene work for you (if appropriate)?

- Do you bring a list of questions that you have developed since the last rehearsal?

Between Rehearsals

- Do you practice any places where you have had musical, vocal, or textual difficulty?
- Do you mentally review your blocking or, better yet, walk through it?
- Do you continue to develop your interpretation?
  - Honing your objectives?
  - Breaking down each scene into units of action?
  - Fashioning a subtext for every phrase your character sings?
  - Writing out your character's internal thoughts for any rests, pauses, introductions, postludes, and all moments when you are on stage listening?
- Do you practice speaking your text, experimenting how you might make your subtext clearer?
- Do you practice incorporating your character's physical characteristics into her walk and gestures?
- Do you try observing people who might be of the appropriate nationality, age, class, or psychological type?
- Do you work on finding an emotional impulse for each new unit of action?
- Do you try exercises such as imagining your character in other contexts? For instance, do you try going to a restaurant, the library, a class, or even to work with your character's world outlook?
- Do you get together with your partners outside of rehearsals?
  - To talk the piece through?
  - To practice your scenes?
  - To improvise?
- Do you periodically go back and listen to the whole piece?

Exercises

EXERCISE 1. (I) *Breathing for Relaxation*

Objective: to relax and focus your mind.

One of the most successful ways to relax and focus your mind is to control your breathing. It works quickly, can be done anywhere, and takes no special equipment.

Before you begin, make yourself comfortable. Loosen any tight clothing around your neck or waist. If you can, take off your shoes and lie down on your back. If you are sitting, be sure your back is straight.

Instructions:

Close your eyes. Inhale slowly; feel as if you are filling yourself up with air starting from the bottom of your abdomen. Take in as much breath as you can. Keep your shoulders relaxed. Exhale slowly; expel all your air. Focus on feeling the air as it goes in and out. If your mind wanders, just call it back. Take ten deep breaths—gradually lengthening them.

After ten slow breaths, take three breaths in which you sigh a long, gentle sigh on the out-breath. (If you are in a public place, you can sigh silently.) As you sigh, let go of extra tension in your body. Release any tightness in your forehead, your jaw, around your eyes, and in your shoulders.

After the three gentle sighs, imagine yourself floating on a puffy white cloud totally surrounded by a warm, delicious, relaxing sea of blue. Take five breaths in which you inhale and exhale the blueness. Pause briefly both when you are full of air at the top of the in-breath, and when you are empty at the end of the out-breath. As you pause, float out into the blueness.

At the end of this series you will feel significantly calmer. You may then want to energize yourself.

Gradually change your vision of floating in a sea of heavenly blue to being surrounded by vibrant yellow or red. Imagine inhaling the energized color. Take ten breaths, feeling the vibrant color going in and going out. Gradually shorten the breaths. (If you begin by taking ten counts on each in-breath and each out-breath, gradually shorten the count down to five.) At the same time, repeat a positive message to yourself. Try: "I feel full of positive energy," "I am enthusiastic about my work (rehearsal, performance)," "I am ready to do my very best."

Feel free to vary the basic pattern of this exercise as you find works best for you.

EXERCISE 2. (I) *Memorization*

Objective: to memorize accurately and efficiently.

Instructions:

Whether you are a facile memorizer or a slow one, you will find that you can benefit from learning the rhythms, words, and pitches of your pieces separately. Begin by reading and singing through the piece a number of times, so you know its shape and content. If the words are in a language you don't know, directly under the original text write out a literal word-by-word translation (except for any idioms that you should translate for their sense).

Working from the score, start by memorizing the first phrase. Learn the rhythm first (without words or pitches). Tap or clap it out so you experience it physically. After you can tap out the first phrase absolutely accurately, speak the text in the rhythms as written. Repeat the text of the first phrase in rhythm several times. As you do so, focus on the literal meaning of each word (except, of course, for any idioms that you need to think of as a unit).

After you can speak the words in rhythm, learn the melody. First just master the pitches; don't worry about the rhythm or words. After you have learned the intervals, add the rhythm. Tap out the rhythm or the beat as you sing the melody using solfège syllables, numbers, or just "la-la-la." When you can do this accurately, add the words to the rhythm and pitches.

After you have gone through these steps, you will probably be able to do the first phrase from memory. If not, go back through the steps and memorize each one before you proceed to the next. Repeat this procedure—first learning the rhythm, then the words, and then the melody—for each successive phrase. After you master a new phrase, attach it to the phrases you have already memorized and sing the entire sequence. If you work your way through the piece in this manner, you will learn it accurately and have memorized it efficiently.

No matter how well you have learned it, the first time you "go public" with memorized material, you are likely to stumble a bit. Therefore it's a good idea to practice freshly memorized material for friends before taking it into a rehearsal.

EXERCISE 3. (G) *Cheating*

Objective: to learn how to share focus on the stage and simultaneously to get your voice out to the audience.

In this exercise you practice playing a scene that involves exchanging lines back and forth with a partner, using the techniques of "sharing" the scene and "cheating" your voice out to the audience.

Instructions:

1. Pair up with a partner. Choose a topic about which to improvise an unaccompanied but sung conversation. Decide who will start. Stand as if the two of you are at center stage. Define where the audience is. Face each other so that the toes of your upstage feet are in the same plane and are directly opposite each other. Your downstage feet should be a comfortable distance apart from each other, with your toes angled toward the audience.

Practice gently swiveling your upper body to the right and the left, so that you alternately make direct contact with your partner and open out to the audience.

Keeping your feet in this basic position, make eye contact with your partner and begin a singing conversation. The person who is singing should not be either sending his voice into his partner's face or directly out at the audience. He should send his air past the end of his partner's nose so that he is "cheating" his voice downstage at an angle toward the audience.

2. Switch places and practice the same exercise.

3. Practice crossing from a distance and coming to a stop facing each other with your feet in the proper position for "sharing" and "cheating." Do this repeatedly. You want stopping with your feet in the proper position to become second nature.

4. Repeat step 3, but walk and stop with the physical characteristics of a character you are working on or would like to play. After you stop, share singing lines with each other.

EXERCISE 4. (G) *Peripheral Vision*

Objective: to widen your field of vision.

As you doubtless discovered in exercise 3, when you share a scene, you end up looking somewhat out of the corner of your eye to see your partner. When you see out of the corner of your eye, you are using your peripheral vision.

You can combine the shared foot position and peripheral vision not only to interact with your partner but also to achieve good contact with the conductor while still remaining involved in the scene. With a little practice, you can widen the field of your peripheral vision, so as to get all the information you need from the conductor without appearing to look at him, even if you are not facing directly toward him. (Sometimes you may have to convince the conductor of this.)

Instructions:

1. Look straight ahead. At the same time see how far to the side you can see out of the corner of your eye. Concentrate on widening your field of vision.

2. Work with a partner. One person is the "singer"; the other is the "conductor." Stand about ten feet apart. The "singer" stands at right angles to the "conductor" and focuses straight ahead. The "conductor" starts from a position in which the "singer" can easily see her moving her arms. Then gradually the "conductor" inches out of the "singer's" view, as the "singer" practices keeping the "conductor's" motions in his peripheral vision. Alternate roles.

3. Work with two other people. Two of them are "singers"; one is the "conductor." The two "singers" face each other with their feet in the sharing position. The "conductor" positions himself about ten feet away, making the apex of a long isosceles triangle. The "singers" have an urgent conversation or work on a scene, "cheating" their voices out; at the same time, the "conductor" conducts, cuing who should speak when. Using their peripheral vision, the "singers" practice catching the "conductor's" cues.

This can also be done as a dramatic improvisation. Assume the "conductor" has information critical to the topic the "singers" are discussing; however, he cannot let himself be seen by any outsider. For instance "boss" (singer) is interrogating "employee" (singer) about an office theft of which he's suspected.

"Conductor" was an accomplice of the "employee" but has been forced to turn informer. "Conductor" tries to help both sides; the singers must take his cues.

EXERCISE 5. (I/G) *Creating Gestures*

Objective: to make natural gestures.

If in spite of committed work on connecting your body to your feelings and your gestures to your breath, your work on a character is not resulting in spontaneous impulses to gesture, try the following exercises.

Instructions:

CHARACTER QUIZ

Answer the two following questions.

> If your character were a real person, do you think he would make a lot of gestures or some, few, or none? As you decide, keep your character's nationality and personality in mind.
> In your daily life, do you make a lot of gestures or some, few, or none?

If you described yourself as making no gestures, I recommend that you ask a really close friend to watch you for part of a day as you interact with people and have her point out every gesture you make. There will be some—I promise. You will be a more effective performer if you can acknowledge your friend's observations and become aware of this facet of your behavior.

If you think your character makes no gestures, apply the same lesson. Even extremely restrained people do employ some gestures, whether they're aware of it or not, and even extremely self-contained characters are almost always made more effective in the theater by an occasional well-chosen gesture.

If you answered "none" or "few" to either question, you may find it useful to create a gesture "bank" on which you can draw. Invent a small repertoire of gestures that you think might be appropriate for your character without regard to when or where you will use them. Over the course of several days practice making the gestures often enough that they begin to feel natural. Then pick out one or two of your character's most intense, passionate, or revealing moments. Try using one or more of your "banked" gestures while speaking your text.

You may also find it useful to give yourself permission or even to dare yourself to make gestures as your character. Say to yourself, both before you go to sleep at night and directly before your rehearsals, "I give myself permission as (your character's name) to gesture." If you don't succeed, don't punish yourself. Remember that if it were easy for you, you'd be doing it! Rather, be glad for any successes you have and make a new commitment for the next rehearsal.

FREEING

Choose a song or aria that you know from memory. Speak the text while making a gesture on every word—including every "and," "the," and "but." You can make any gestures you like; it is not important that they make sense. You may go as slowly as you like. Think of it as "extreme charades" or as a kind of dance using your arms and upper torso.

This exercise works best with a partner. One person speaks a text trying to make a gesture on every word; the other interrupts every time the speaker says a word without making a gesture. To be most helpful, the person who is watching should be insistent.

Repeat the exercise while singing (slowly).

EMPHASIS

Choose a song or aria that you know well. Write out the text. Underline the most important word in each sentence twice, and the second most important word once. (You may have to try speaking some of the sentences several ways in order to decide which words are the most important. It will be easier if you fashion objectives first.)

Speak through the text, doing a gesture on the most important word in each sentence. It doesn't matter just what gestures you choose.

Sing though the piece, doing a gesture on the most important word in each sentence. Do it slowly first, then up to tempo.

Speak through the text, doing a gesture for each word you have underlined.

Sing through the text, doing a gesture for each word you have underlined. Do it slowly first, then up to tempo.

It is equally fruitful to do this exercise using a spoken dialogue or recitative.

CHAPTER 14

Delivering a Believable Character: Performing

Preparing to Perform

Since it is not easy to prepare yourself vocally and physically to meet the demands of performing, it is worthwhile giving your preparation process special attention and developing procedures that work for you. (You may want to adopt some of the suggestions about preparing for auditions in chapter 11 and look at the relaxation exercises and physical and character warmups in chapter 12.) Unless you know that there is a suitable space at the theater, plan to do most of your warm up at home.

The most useful preparations allow you to leave your "real-world" concerns behind and set you up to concentrate on being in the moment as you perform. They include getting to the theater so you can check that your props are in place and functioning properly at least thirty minutes before the show is supposed to begin, and make up, dress, and be fully ready well before your first entrance. (If you are doing a recital, your props might include a pitcher of water and a glass off stage.) Your preparations should allow you to prime yourself to meet all the demands of the performance in a way that also respects the needs of all your performing and technical colleagues.

Preparing to Enter

You will probably be nervous before your first entrance—most performers are. Welcome the feeling! It means you are getting extra adrenaline that increases your energy, sharpens your senses, and speeds your reactions. If, however, your nervousness interferes with your concentration or tends to make you feel sick, you can probably reduce it by taking the following steps.

Well in Advance of a Performance

• Get your material and presentation down cold. There is nothing that soothes performance anxiety better than the feeling that you really know what you are going to do.

• Try to uncover the fears or fantasies that generate your nervous feelings. Casting a realistic light on them often reduces them to a manageable size.

Let's say that one source of nervousness is the fear that you will crack on your high notes. Ask yourself, "What is the worst thing that can possibly happen if I crack?" Let your imagination run wild: "My teacher will drop me as a student," "No one will ever hire me to sing again," "My parents will disown me." Then compare such worst-case scenarios to the likely and far-from-irreparable reality: "My teacher, my employer, my parents, and I will be disappointed."

Immediately Before a Performance

• Remind yourself that you know your material better than the audience does. Most often the audience won't notice that you made a mistake unless you call attention to it.
• Promise yourself that before your next performance you will work to improve anything that does not go as well as you would like.
• Assure yourself that you will deal with whatever happens, when it does.
• Use controlled breathing (chapter 13, exercise 1).
• Focus on your character's objectives.

Entering

Your performance begins offstage.

Operas and Musicals

Each time you come onstage, you want to enter as your character. Prepare by assuming your character's physicality as you are waiting in the wings. Also review your character's super-objective and think about your relationships to the other characters from your character's point of view. Immediately before you enter, ground your breath, focus on your first objective, and imagine *what* has just happened so that you will be propelled on stage with your character's internal dialogue running.

Oratorios, Contests, and Recitals

The audience doesn't want to see "nervous you." They want to meet you as a self-assured, well-prepared actor-singer who is looking forward to entertaining them with a superb and moving performance. Therefore, even when you aren't playing a role, you want to transform your presence before you enter. Using the Given Circumstances and super-objective of the "I" of the first piece you will sing is an option, but won't help you make a positive first impression if the piece isn't upbeat. Most of the time you will do better to walk on stage and take your place wearing your Public Persona, as developed in chapter 12.

Art Songs, Lieder and Songs

Assume your Public Persona before you enter and cross directly to the piano. Unlike in an audition, there may be applause. If there is, standing with your weight on both feet, alert and at ease, wait until it dies down. Try using the subtext "I love being here and look forward to singing for you." If the applause is sustained, acknowledge it with a modest bow or curtsey. Try a subtext like "Thank you."

Performing Operas and Musicals

Playing Moment-to-Moment

As I began to explore in chapters 4, and 13, the single most convincing quality of a believable character is that he is spontaneously engaged in a first-time reality. To create this quality, you respond within the boundaries established in rehearsal by reacting moment-to-moment to what is actually happening between you and the other performers as your characters. When appropriately done, the resulting adjustments are so small and subtle that the stage director and conductor should feel that the interpretation of the piece and its characters as worked out in rehearsal is being beautifully and appropriately developed, and an audience member watching the show on successive nights would not be able to tell what is different, but only that each time it is somehow fresh and spontaneous.

As examples, let's first examine a very brief moment between José and Escamillo in act III and then we'll make a longer and more elaborate exploration of Carmen's first entrance and opening scene.

Escamillo appears as José is guarding the periphery of the gypsy encampment. Escamillo has heard that Carmen was in love with a soldier who deserted for her sake, but he is sure that the affair is now over, since, as he sings rather matter-of-factly, "Carmen's loves never last more than six months," to which José replies softly, "You love her anyway!" Escamillo responds on a high D-flat, "I love her!" stressing the word "love" by holding it for a half note. José repeats "You love her anyway!" but this time beginning and ending a third higher than before and both starting louder and making a crescendo through the line. Escamillo confirms his love, singing, "I love her, yes, my friend, I love her to madness." In the second repetition the word "love" is set on a high E-flat, while the phrase "to madness" drops in pitch and ends *piano*.

In rehearsal the singers, stage director, and conductor have agreed that José is so dumbfounded that a man could be interested in Carmen without needing to possess her forever that he turns away when he sings "You love her anyway!" the first time and sings the words very softly, as a gasp of astonishment. Escamillo, focusing on his own passion and lust, responds with pleasure, "I love her!" as a public declaration, without looking at José; José, still caught in his own thoughts, gives Escamillo's response only partial attention. However, just before he repeats "You love her anyway!" with greater intensity and an exaggerated crescendo that captures his movement from disbelief to jealousy, he turns and grabs Escamillo roughly by the shoulders. Although taken by surprise, the toreador harbors no animosity towards José, and gives him a pat on the shoulder as he sings, "Yes, my friend." Then he becomes self-involved as he sings "I love her" a second time and is himself slightly surprised by the intensity of his feelings, which accounts for the diminuendo on "to madness."

Let's assume that in today's performance José's attention is caught by the energy Escamillo gives to the word "love" the first time he sings it. This causes José to feel both his disbelief and his jealousy a little more strongly than in the previous performance, so when he grabs Escamillo's shoulders, the motion and the quality of his vocal expression are slightly rougher. Escamillo is not just surprised but experiences a slight sense of aggression; however, as a man very certain of his own physical prowess, he responds with only the slightest increased tone of condescension as he frees himself, and he gives José a couple of small friendly pats rather than his usual single one. None of these adjustments change the plan of the scene, and, if anything, they only deepen the agreed-on qualities of the characters; yet they make the scene seem spontaneous and believable because the performers are playing moment-to-moment.

Now let us examine Carmen's initial scene, in which she interacts with the chorus men and sees Don José for the first time, and observe how moment-to-moment interactions flow back and forth even between the major roles and minor ones.

You are Carmen. Your objective in this scene is "to take control of the situation." This is a step toward fulfilling your super-objective, "to live fully and free."

From the libretto you know that:

- The scene begins after the midday meal.
- You and the other women who work at the tobacco factory are called back by a bell.
- You are the last to enter.
- As always, there are young men hanging around the square in front of the factory waiting to ogle and, perhaps, to pick up women.

To manifest your objective and to reflect the somber fate motif so prominent in your entrance music, you and the stage director have agreed that you enter slowly, preoccupied and angry—smoking a cigarette. At first, you barely notice the men, and when their "There she is" gets your attention, you turn away until they sing the phrase again when you put out your cigarette. After "Tell us on which day you will love us" you begin to look them over. When you see José sitting at a distance, you stop cold. You exchange a brief but electric look with him, and then launch into the "Habanera."

During rehearsals, in consultation with the director, you developed the following story of *what* just happened before you enter: You (Carmen) spent your midday break with your boyfriend. You had a terrible fight over his need to keep you subservient, and broke up with harsh words and bad feelings. When the bell rings, you consider skipping work, but you have been warned that if you are late one more time you will be fired.

Now let's imagine the details of a particular performance with all the excitement of playing moment-to-moment. While still offstage, you as Carmen begin your internal dialogue with the aftermath of this supposed fight, casting your thoughts in the most pungent language that feels like you as Carmen and shaping them to reflect the music, so you can bring the music to life as Carmen's thoughts and feelings.

Right before you enter, you imagine watching the retreating figure of your now ex-boyfriend. You are full of anger and bitterness from the fight—a setback in your need to live fully and free. You are smoking a cigarette to calm yourself and to reestablish your sense of control. In your head you shout after him, "You s.o.b.! Don't you dare to tell me how to live my life!" (You enter.) "That louse!" (Stop; slowly look back in fury.) "Stay out of my life. If you come near me again . . . !"

As you stand there smoking your cigarette, absorbed in your thoughts about breaking up, the men's questions are a minor aggravation like the buzzing of flies—part of your reality but brushed away almost unconsciously. However, "There she is" catches your attention, and you look at the men with annoyance; your subtext: "Men!"

As worked out in rehearsal, one of the chorus men suggestively touches his crotch when he sings the line. At the last performance, even in your annoyance, your Carmen saw his gesture as stupid, which lent a touch of irony to your thought: "Men!" But suppose that today he does the gesture in a way which your Carmen experiences not just as stupid but insulting, so your subtextual "Men!" has an angrier, more dismissive color, and the glance you throw him before your usual turn away is slightly more piercing.

The chorus man, his character ashamed by your glance, looks down. One of his fellow choristers sees the downward look and (rather than giving the smile indicating "man-to-man" approval that the crotch gesture provoked the previous time), this time smiles so as to suggest, "Whew! She's hot today."

The other men nearby, all of whom are also playing moment-to-moment, react to these slightly different gestures, causing a cascade of minute adjustments. Some sing their next "There she is" a bit more tinged with awe than with the somewhat indulgent understanding that was provoked the previous time. This in turn affects the way all the rest of the crowd sees and experiences the moment—causing literally everyone on stage to do whatever they do *slightly* differently. The differences are sufficient to make the scene feel totally spontaneous, but, as I said before, too small to change the characterizations and blocking choices made in rehearsal.

Meanwhile, having snubbed the men, you continue your internal dialogue: "They're all the same. Think they can tell me what to do! Try to push me around." Then you hear the men singing "There she is" for the second time. Previously, you have used some form of the internal thoughts "Yeah! Look, but don't you try to touch!" (done with an angry toss of your head), thrown down the butt of your cigarette, and put it out with your foot as you thought, "Don't mess!" However, this time when you hear the awe provoked by your previous angry glance, their line sounds a bit more like a dare. So you adjust your internal thoughts: "Yeah! Look, but you can't have me!" You toss your head and throw down the cigarette butt, but this time you grind it into the ground more deliberately as if it were one of the men, while you think, "Men are such jerks!"

As they sing their next words, "There she is! There is Carmencita!" the men are supposed to move closer to you. However, in response to your more aggressive manner of snuffing out your cigarette, some of them move slightly more timidly than they did before; others, feeling their characters turned on by the implied violence, cross in with more energy. You respond to the timid ones with disdain, thinking, "Wimps!" and to the bold ones thinking, "Sure, thrust yourselves forward, but you can't have me, because I'm the one who does the choosing. That's right, me!" (With this thought you reinforce your objective of taking control.)

Now, as planned in rehearsal, a new thought begins to crystallize. You can take control by revenging yourself on some man for the anger, rejection, and insult you have just experienced with your boyfriend. This idea grows as the men sing: "Carmen! We are following every move you make. Carmen! Be kind and at least answer us. Please tell what day you will love us. Carmen, please tell us what day you will love us."

"Yes, I *am* going to choose one of you," you think, as the men sing, "At least answer us." Then, as they continue with "Please tell us what day you will love us," you begin to look them over just as originally planned, but in response to all the tiny changes that have occurred, this time you look at the men with a harder edge, perhaps a bit more sadistically.

As you check them out, you say to yourself, "Yes, you mighty men, I'll pick one of you to love like you've never been loved before. I'll destroy you with my love."

In previous performances the chorus men have justified repeating "Tell us what day you will love us" by their *need* to break through your preoccupation. But today the manipulative anger they feel in your look causes some to feel less confident, so they sing this line with a slightly fearful vocal color, whereas others feel even more eager to be chosen and reflect their feeling with a more assertive sound.

You reject one after another as unsuitable for your revenge. Many of them you know; you may have even slept with them. You finish your survey just at the end of the men's plea, then you notice a soldier sitting at a distance whom you've never seen before. You look at him, "Who is that?!" You see him look up; "I like him!" You briefly lock eyes with him; then you see him look down. Intuitively, you know he is perfect as your next conquest; "He's the one!"

You begin a new unit of action: "I want to take control by making this man fall in love with me." As you sing the first words of the recitative leading into the "Habanera," "When will I love you?—I don't know," you are calculating just how to snare José.

If you are playing Don José, since you have nothing to sing in this scene, you will need an especially well-developed internal dialogue to support your moment-to-moment work. Your internal dialogue should form an unbroken commentary from your final line in the previous scene, "I"m going to work on a chain to attach my priming pin to my rifle," until you sing again. It should allow you to be at least somewhat conscious of the activity around you as you work; it should motivate you to glance up at the very moment Carmen looks at you, and then, when she catches your eye, impel you to look down.

If you have fashioned "I, José, *want* to possess a woman of my choice" for your super-objective, then you could use "I, José, *want* to clarify my feelings about Micaëla" for your objective while you work on the chain. Since you have just been told that Micaëla has come to town looking for you, her arrival would naturally stir up memories. You could recall the deadly fight over cards that made it necessary for you to join the army—leaving behind your village, your mother, and Micaëla herself. These thoughts might reinforce how important it is for you to "make good." You could manifest this need by focusing very intently on your tasks as a soldier: alternating diligent work on your chain with frequent piercing checks of the crowd. You could also logically recall your mother's hopes for you and Micaëla, which would cause you to be unsettled by Carmen's burning glance.

Of course, to be effective, you need to actually think the words of your internal dialogue aloud inside your head and allow it to be shaped by the way you experience everything around you. In this instance your internal dialogue does not have to reflect the music, since the music, except at the moment of the glance, is not about you.

* * *

This illustration of playing moment-to-moment should clarify how your performance can be both minutely rehearsed and at the same time be an improvisation born at the intersection where "what you want" meets "what you get." It also illustrates several ideas previously discussed:

- What is real on stage are the other performers, and the way they do what they do.
- Every role (no matter what size) is clarified by vivid objectives and a detailed internal dialogue.
- You can help make your character believable if you behave *as if* you are perceiving the world through the lens of his objectives and Given Circumstances.
- You can help make your character believable by incorporating the six basic human behaviors elaborated in chapter 1.

Performing Art Songs, Lieder, and Songs

Getting into Character

After any initial bow or curtsey at the piano, make the transition from your Public Persona to the "I" of your song or lied. As in an audition, you should not take longer than fifteen seconds. Create a private space for your preparation, ground your breath, review your super-objective and first objective and fully immerse yourself in *what* has just happened. As you inhale and look up to begin the song and your internal dialogue, remember to shift your weight subtly forward so it feels centered over your toes to heighten your presence.

Let's re-examine Schubert's lied "An Silvia" to see how you might prepare yourself for each of the alternative analyses made in chapter 10.

A Young Man Who Has Fallen in Love with Silvia from a Distance Sings to a Mutual Friend

Let's lay out some possible Given Circumstances to help develop an effective *what*:

When: a mid-June evening in the present

Where: a large, elegant party at which Silvia, a lawyer friend of mine, and I are all guests

Who: I am a young lawyer eager to find the right woman. This is the second time I have seen Silvia, who is a fashion model of exquisite beauty. My friend, who was my buddy all through law school, knows Sylvia well.

Want: "I *must* find out more about Silvia."

Why: "I am so infatuated with her, I must talk about her"; or "I need my friend to introduce us."

For these Circumstances, an effective *what* might be: I've been watching my friend talk to Silvia for fifteen minutes. Now he's finally finished, and I corner him. Just before you look up to sing, you say to yourself "You must tell me all about Silvia!"

A Young Man Wants to Seduce Silvia

For this situation, your Given Circumstances might be slightly different:

When: a mid-June evening in the present

Where: a large, elegant party at which Silvia and I are guests

Who: the same as before (except in this interpretation you are singing directly to Silvia, so you don't need to invent a friend)

Want: "I *want* to seduce Silvia."

Why: "I am totally turned on."

An effective *what* might be: I have been watching Silvia in her provocative dress chat flirtatiously with various men all evening. She has just agreed to go out on the terrace with me. Right before you look up to begin, you say to yourself "I must have her."

Beginning to Sing

As in an audition, when your *what* or preparatory image arouses the need to give voice to your (character's) feelings, take a distinct in-breath, and look up in character. (This lets your pianist know that you are ready to begin, as well as serving to start the flow of your internal dialogue.) If the introduction is short, you can sing on the same breath with which you initiate the music. Otherwise, actively think your internal thoughts, which you have practiced to be just the right length to fill the music, until it is time to inhale to sing.

Performing Moment-to-Moment in Solo Pieces

Just as you do when you perform a role in an opera or musical, you can take advantage of playing moment-to-moment to make your solo performances spontaneous and believable. Since your accompanist will not play any phrase exactly the same way twice, and since you will never feel exactly the same way about what you hear, you—listening with the ears of the "I" of the song—are free to let the music affect your interpretation.

Between Pieces

At the end of each piece, remain in character until *after* the last note has sounded. When it has died away, return to your Public Persona and either take a private moment to prepare for your next number or, if it is appropriate, receive the audience's applause with a modest bow or curtsey. As you might for an opening bow, you could think a silent "Thank you."

In recitals of classical music, it has been customary for the audience to applaud only at the end of a set of songs from the same piece. However, sometimes there is confusion; be prepared and don't let unexpected applause fluster you.

Acknowledging Final Applause and Exiting

When you are finished and the audience applauds, enjoy their thanks and acknowledge them with bows or curtseys given with generous warmth and professional calm. Maintain your Public Persona, focusing on an appropriate subtext. Consider "Thank you, I'm really glad you enjoyed it" or "Thank you, I love singing for you." You should have a plan about how you will include your accompanist. It is a very good idea to rehearse your bows together.

Your exit is part of your performance. When you leave the stage, wear your Public Persona—positive, gracious, relaxed.

Troubleshooting

Repeating a Success

One of the most dangerous enemies of a good performance is trying to reproduce a previous success. Concentrating on the past prevents you from tuning into the moment-by-moment nuances of the present and all but guarantees that you will be less successful than before. Indeed, when you focus on any end result, you will almost inevitably fail to activate the preparatory factors that made that moment work. The key to succeeding again (and again) is to accept that although you can never exactly duplicate the past, you can do equally well—or perhaps even better—if you reactivate the process that made a previous success possible.

To re-create a successful vocal performance, don't think about the good sound you made. Instead, review what you did technically and which images and subtext you used that helped that sound emerge. To re-create a successful emotional performance, do not try to reproduce the emotions. Go back to your objectives and use the Magical *if* to revivify your Given Circumstances; trust your thorough preparation and play moment-to-moment.

Handling Disasters

In any live performance you can expect that something will go wrong; you just can never know what. If the problem turns out to be something you can handle, behave as if the stage is your home and deal with it as your character. If a vase falls to the floor, pick up the pieces, dismiss it with a laugh, call the maid, or, as a last resort, call a stagehand. After you have dealt with the problem, go on as if nothing had gone wrong, and you enable the audience and your colleagues to do the same. On the other hand, if what goes wrong is something that cannot be fixed, commit yourself to putting it behind you and keep going. For instance, if your voice cracks, pursue your objectives with renewed vigor and behave as if it hadn't happened.

Summary

Performances are the joyous culminations of an enormous amount of hard work both alone and with your colleagues, on yourself, your voice, your craft, and your piece(s). When you perform, you exercise skills of analysis, control, trust, concentration, and imagination. You believably behave *as if* you are in your character's situation. With this transformation, you set free a flow of empathy between the audience and your character through which you can lift your audiences out of the mundane world into the more clearly delineated and more intense realm of art. On this flow you can communicate truths about the human condition, order, and beauty.

Exercises

EXERCISE 1. (I/G)   *Physical Warmups*

Objective: to warm up and relax your body so you are ready to assume your character's physical characteristics.

Instructions:

Hanging over. Stand with your feet approximately the width of your shoulders apart and with your knees very slightly bent. Hold the fingers of one hand lightly in the other, and raise your arms above your head. (See fig. 1.) Tilt your head up and look at your hands. Continuing to hold your hands lightly together, stretch your arms as high as you can. Feel as if you are lifting your upper body out of your lower back.

Gradually lower your hands passing them close to your forehead, nose and chin, and follow them with your eyes. As you move your hands down in front of your chest, let your chin drop toward your chest; then, continuing to lower your hands, *slowly* bend over until you are hanging over from the waist. (Be sure your knees are still slightly bent.) When you are hanging over as far as you can, fold your arms at the elbows (cross your arms in front of you), so your hands don't touch the floor. (See fig. 2.) Hang over for a minute, or as long as you are comfortable. (Do not bounce; you can pull a muscle.)

When you are ready to stand up, unfold your arms, letting them hang. Gradually straighten up with the feeling of stacking your vertebrae one on top of the other—starting from the base of your spine. (Check that your knees are still slightly bent.) When you have straightened up all but your neck and head, complete the stretch by tucking your chin backward as you raise your head.

Slowly repeat the exercise a couple of times.

Shoulder stretch and side bend. Begin as in the preceding exercise. Remember, as you stretch your arms as high as you can over your head, to keep your knees slightly bent and to lift out of your lower back. Then, looking straight ahead, reach right with your arms (hands lightly clasped), and slowly bend to the right—lifting out of your left shoulder and the left side of your back. (See fig. 3.) Go as far to the right as you comfortably can. As you return slowly to vertical, be aware of lifting out of your right shoulder and right side. Bring your hands down in front of you.

Figure 1

Figure 3

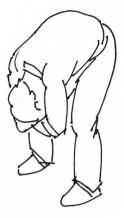

Figure 2

Figure 4

Begin again as before, but this time stretch to your left side—feel the stretch in your right shoulder and right side as you go left, and in your left shoulder and left side as you straighten up.

Slowly repeat this exercise a couple of times.

Leg stretch. Sit on the floor with your right leg stretched in front of you and your left leg resting on the floor, bent at the knee, so that the sole of your left foot gently touches your right calf. Holding the fingers of one hand lightly in the other, reach out both arms toward the toes of your right foot. (See fig. 4.) As you reach for your toes, be aware of stretching your lower back. Keep the length of your extended leg against the floor. If you are sufficiently limber, you may be able to touch your toes and to bring your nose close to your right knee. Straighten up slowly.

Repeat the same stretch with your left leg extended and your right leg bent.

Toe raises. Stand with your hands on the back of a chair or something of similar height. Slowly rise up onto your toes, and then slowly lower yourself back down. Breathe in as you rise up, and breathe out as you return to the floor. Repeat ten times.

* * *

After you have done these or other stretches, do something aerobic. Running lightly in place, doing jumping jacks, or dancing vigorously are all effective.

EXERCISE 2. (I/G) *Moving as Your Character*

Objective: to assume your character's physical characteristics.

Instructions:

1. Choose an animal that you feel either is like your character or embodies one of his aspects. Move like that animal; imitate its sounds as you move.

2 Move as if you are a creature halfway between the animal and your character. Make noises that are sort of like the animal and sort of subtextual feeling sounds. (There is absolutely no right or wrong way to do this. Experiment.)

3. Move as your character, but retain the sense of your animal image. Sing subtextual sounds or gibberish.

4. Be your character moving in different surroundings: walking through sand, rushing in a big city, wandering through a park, trying to catch a taxicab, waiting in a grocery store line, buying clothes or jewelry, choosing a book in a library, and so on. Sing subtextual sounds as you move.

5. Walk as if you are your character at different ages: ten, twenty, forty-five, sixty, or eighty. Walk as if your character is wearing different kinds of clothes: dressed for a formal dance, for a ball game, for an African safari, as an astronaut. Sing subtextual sounds as you move.

EXERCISE 3. (I) *Psychological Warmups*

Objective: to prepare yourself to enter your character's world.

After you are warmed up, relaxed, and focused, you are ready to prepare for your character's emotional journey. Explore the following exercises to find those that work well for you. Feel free to expand, combine, or vary any of them.

Instructions:

1. Ask yourself: How do you personally feel about the issue(s) suggested by your theme statement. (If you are performing several pieces, pick one.) How does your character feel about the issue(s)? What do you do as your character to help explore or clarify the theme?

2. Look at your character's super-objective. If it were your own personal goal, how would you achieve it? How would you deal with a real person who is like the character who presents the main obstacle to your character's super-objective? How does that compare with what your character does?

3. Invent some incidents in the life of an imaginary character who has your character's super-objective but who is not your character. For instance, you could imagine a favorite television or film character with Tony's or José's super-objective. Examine how the character you created is different from the one you play. Use the differences to clarify your character.

4. Choose one scene or verse from the piece and re-examine it in light of your super-objective. How exactly do you manifest your super-objective in that scene or verse? Are you making your super-objective clear vocally and physically, both in what you do and in the way you do it?

5. Using your score, read your words from one scene or verse aloud. If other characters have text, read it silently. As you read the other characters' lines to yourself, speak or sing your internal dialogue for those lines aloud. Or, first read their lines silently and then speak or sing your internal dialogue for those lines.

If you are the only person with text in the scene or verse, imagine what the person you are addressing (or are thinking about) says between your lines that causes you to sing the next one. If you are speaking to yourself, review the internal dialogue that takes you from one sentence to the next.

6. Go through a verse or a section of a scene breath by breath. Find an impulse for each one. Go through it a second time, actually taking each breath and speaking the first words of each phrase; make sure you experience the appropriate feelings in each in-breath.

7. Choose a segment of one of your scenes, or a part of your piece. Make sure you have a motivation for every word you sing and every action you do.

8. Choose one of your character's intense feelings. (A joyous feeling is just as useful as a painful one.) Recall an experience from your life that aroused that feeling or a kindred one. Relive the experience in your mind. Let it affect your body.

9. Invent a set of circumstances that logically and emotionally lead up to your opening moment in the piece. Combine what you know from the work itself with the choices you have made in rehearsals to create a story with evocative details.

10. Choose a scene or song that you will be performing; softly sing or talk through it to freshen it in your mind. After you have finished, try to invent a question about the scene or song, your actions in it, or your character that you've never asked before.

EXERCISE 4. (I) *Preparing to Enter*

Objective: to help you get into character.

Here are three exercises that will get you "into character" and that you can do while waiting in the wings. Feel free to modify or combine them to create an approach that works for you.

Instructions:

1. Review the *where, when, who, want,* and *why* of your character's Given Circumstances (see chapter 2) for the opening piece or scene. Imagine the feelings each element arouses and the impact of each element for your character. For example, you are about to perform Carmen's first scene; explore your *where* and *when.* Ask many questions. Imagine the midday break that immediately precedes her entrance: "What would I be likely to eat for lunch, who bought the food, who prepared it, with what utensils would I eat it, where, with whom? How do I feel about: the food, the person who prepared it, where I am eating, and the person (people) with whom I am eating? In a similar fashion, go on an imaginary journey calling up your *who, want,* and *why.* Create a wealth of details.

Imagine *what* has just happened to your character that requires you to enter. Make up something that gets your emotional juices going. Include details that set up your first objective and your internal dialogue. Be sure your choices are sensitively matched to your initial music and text.

2. Practice some simple movements with your character's physical characteristics: take off your shoes and then put them back on; unbutton and button your coat; walk around while softly singing your words.

3. Sit in a quiet corner and practice controlled breathing (chapter 13, exercise 1) while remaining externally and internally still. Shortly before your entrance cue, leave this still point, assume your character's physical characteristics, remind yourself of your character's super-objective and first objectives, and use the Magical *if* to propel yourself into *what* has just happened.

APPENDIX 1

Ten Maxims of Believable Singing Acting

• Your characters believe they're real people.

They don't think of themselves as "characters." Most often they don't know that they are singing, and even if they do, they always have their own internal dialogues running constantly in their heads .

• Your music is your characters' feelings (and vice-versa).

The composer has interpreted the characters' feelings in the music. Let the music guide you to the feelings that motivate your characters' actions and to the nuances of their responses. Look to it as the primary source of your characters' internal dialogue.

• All humans have a common reservoir of feelings.

Different people may react to the same situation differently, but each of us has the same spectrum of feelings—from hatred to love, despair to ecstasy. Therefore, you have in you the potential to portray all the feelings you need for any role. By the same token, each member of your audience has the potential to empathize with all of your characters' feelings.

• You are always you.

Each of us has our own body, voice, and personal history. Don't try to deny who you are; rather, transform yourself by selecting which traits to emphasize and which to downplay.

• If you don't let it show, the audience can't know.

Audiences read actions, not minds; so you must *allow* your characters' thoughts and feelings to be manifested physically. Remember, however, that the audience will assume that every action you make is an expression of your *characters'* thoughts and feelings.

• You are making art.

Since art is created by humans to communicate feelings and ideas, you can count on the fact that every character is created for a reason. You can figure out that reason and use your understanding to interpret your roles. In addition, since you are engaged in bringing to life the artistic creations of others, everything you do in a performance at least on some level of consciousness is an interpretation. Acknowledging that you are an interpretive artist leads you away from the destructive judgments of "right" and "wrong" that bedevil most performers and toward the constructive question "Am I being clear?"

• Believable characters engage your audiences.

When audience members believe you as your character, they identify with you. Once they identify, they extend their empathy; then they are available for you to arouse their feelings and to move them. This is equally true whether your character is a person in an opera or musical or the "I" of a song or lied.

• You make your characters believable by endowing them with convincing, apparently spontaneous, re-creations of real human behavior.

The audience knows that you have rehearsed, but they don't want to feel that your characters have.

• Play the minutiae of what is really happening.

You will seem spontaneous if you respond as your character to even the smallest things your colleagues sing or do as their characters.

• Never try to repeat results.

When you focus on the details of a past success, your mind cannot be engaged in the present; you lose the sense of spontaneity, and your performances take on a mechanical unconvincing quality. Focus instead on reviving the sources of your characters' actions and feelings as developed in the rehearsal process; respond in the present, and you will achieve a new—and subtly different—success.

APPENDIX 2

How to Analyze and Prepare Vocal Material
from a Dramatic Viewpoint: An Overview

First, write out the text of the piece. Leave spaces where there are musical interludes, and also leave space under each line to write in:

• A literal, word-for-word translation directly below the text. (Idioms are
an exception and should be translated as phrases.)

Do not count on the translation printed in the music to be acurate. Most
often it is a free adaptation created to fit the words of the translated language to
the music. There are an increasing number of books and internet sites with literal translations that can be helpful, but to be safe you should always check any
printed translation with a dictionary or other reliable source.

• A sensible paraphrase below the translation.

Below your paraphrase leave space to add your character's subtext and internal thoughts later. (Naturally, if you have space, you can write your translation, paraphrase, subtext, and internal thoughts directly into the score.)

Second, define the Given Circumstances of the "I" of the piece. If the "I" is
a character in a musical or opera, you will usually be able to fashion your character's Given Circumstances from the material in the score as long as you are familiar with the entire piece. In songs, art songs, or lieder, the Given Circumstances often are less well defined, and you will have to apply your imagination
to any clues in the text and the music to figure them out. You need to clarify:

• *Where* the character is (in the world, in his surroundings)
• *When* the events are taking place (in history, in his own lifetime)
• *Who* the character is (including his relationships to the other characters)

- What he *wants:*
  - For the entire piece (his super-objective: see the next section)
  - For each scene or stanza (his objectives: see the next section)
- *Why* he wants it
- *What* has just happened in your character's life that causes him to have to break into song

Third, fashion and write out:

- The theme of the piece (what it's about)
- Your character's super-objective
  - Your character's super-objective is what she *wants* (has to have) that drives her through the entire piece.
  - Your character's super-objective is most usefully phrased in the form: "I, (your character's name), *want*. . . (followed by a verb and a short object)."
- Your character's objectives in the piece
  - Your character's objectives are the goals she pursues in each scene or verse as she attempts to fulfill her super-objective. (Sometimes in songs that are part of a cycle, a song may have a single objective.)
  - Your character's objectives are best phrased in the same form as her super-objective.

Fourth, develop a subtext for the words, and your internal thoughts for all your non-singing music. Subtext is how you (as your character) feel about what you are singing; it is what your character *really* means by what she sings and says. As you make your choices, envision each song or aria as an emotional journey. Your subtext and internal thoughts should capture your interpretation of how the "I" of the song feels at the beginning of the piece, the various feelings she goes through, and the feeling she reaches at the end. Remember that the music will provide a stream of clues.

- Develop the subtext phrase by phrase, not word by word.
- Use colloquial language that captures the feelings for you.
- If words, phrases, or entire sections are repeated, give each one a unique subtext.

Write your subtext under your paraphrase.

Develop your character's thoughts and feelings for all the music in the piece for which there are no words—including any introduction, interludes or rests longer than a few beats, and any postlude. These internal thoughts need to reflect your character's Given Circumstances and the music. As you figure them out, bear in mind that almost every song or aria is a conversation, whether with a person who is presumed to be present, a person who is somewhere else, or with yourself. If you are singing to someone else, imagining how the other person might react to what you sing will give you ideas for what you might be thinking and feeling.

When you create your internal thoughts for any introductory music or interludes, work them out so:

- they are just the right length to fill the music;
- they lead you logically to sing your first words or lead you logically from what you just finished singing to what you sing next;
- they cause you to inhale to start singing at just the right moment;
- they parallel the shape of the music.

When you develop your internal thoughts for any postlude, be sure they will keep you engaged until after the last note has died away.

Write in your internal thoughts between your subtext and under your literal translation and paraphrase. You now have a continuous internal dialogue for your character.

* * *

When you have completed these four steps, you will have a thorough understanding of your character and a strong motivation for each in-breath you take. You will not need to worry about feeling self-conscious when you perform, because you will be energized by your character's need to express himself, and you will have his internal dialogue on which to keep your mind focused.

APPENDIX 3

A Short Glossary of Stage Terms

Above Upstage of a partner(s) or object.

Acting beats The actions a character takes in a scene or a song to try to achieve each objective. For instance, "I, José, will cajole, wheedle, and threaten (acting beats) to get Carmen to tell me how she feels about Escamillo (objective)."

Below Downstage of a partner(s) or object.

Blocking Performers' movements on stage—when and where they walk, stand, sit, or kneel, which direction they face in relation to others, and any business they do.

Business Physical actions, usually involving an object.

Cross To go from one place to another onstage. It is notated with an X. For example, the standard notation to indicate a move to upstage right is XUR.

Cue A signal for something to happen. It is used in three slightly different ways. For performers, cue is used to signify the line before they speak, sing, or do some action; the cue for Carmen to sing "Take back your ring" is José asking "For the very last time will you come with me?" The conductor also gives musical cues (signals). Cue can also be used to mean the signal for a technical change such as a change in the lighting (a light cue), sets (a shift cue), a sound effect (a sound cue), or raising or lowering a curtain (a curtain cue).

To cue To give the signal for something to happen.

Downstage See *stage directions.*

Given Circumstances A character's situation, as portrayed by the librettist and composer or as extrapolated from the material in the score. A character's Given Circumstances are most usefully defined by answering the six questions "*When, where,* and *who* am I? What do I *want* and *why? What* has just happened in my character's life that causes him to have to break into song?"

Heightening A process that allows performers to give more carrying power to their gestures and more conviction to characters who express extreme feelings, which also supports their believability. As described in chapter 11, performers can heighten their gestures and the expression of their feelings by clarifying their intentions, attaching their gestures and feelings to their breath, energizing their bodies' muscular pathways, and sending their intentions through their bodies to the back of the auditorium.

Internal dialogue The internal conversation that runs continuously through your character's head; the chattering of her inner voice.

Internal Thoughts That part of your character's internal dialogue that occurs when she is not speaking or singing, her thoughts and feelings (expressed as words in her head) during musical sections in pieces she sings or when she is listening.

Magical *if* The phrase *What if* applied to any aspect of a character or her circumstances, which enables a performer to imagine her way into her character or her character's situation.

Objective The goal that drives a character through a particular scene of an opera or musical or stanza of a song as she struggles to achieve her super-objective. Objectives are most usefully phrased in the form "I, (your character's name), *want* (*need* or *must have*), followed by a brief verb clause: "I, Micaëla, *want* to take care of José."

Offstage The part of the performing area that is supposed to be out of the audience's view.

Onstage The part of the performing area that the audience is supposed to see.

Prop (An abbreviation for property) An object that a performer handles onstage. Opening a letter is a piece of business, using a letter as a prop.

Public Persona A positive public self that performers develop to emphasize their most desirable performing traits. Wearing a Public Persona allows them to present themselves in the best possible light and still be themselves; they can feel natural onstage even when they are not in a role.

Sharing a scene A technique that allows two performers to simultaneously sing to each other with both being seen and heard equally well. To share a scene, the two partners stand facing each other so the toes of their upstage feet are directly opposing, and their downstage feet are a natural distance away from their upstage feet and angled in the direction of the audience. (See chapter 13 for more details.)

Stage Directions Conventionally, the stage is thought of as divided into a grid of nine equal areas, dividing the space into thirds from side to side and from front to back. The three areas of the grid furthest from the audience consist of up(stage) right (UR), up(stage) center (UC), and up(stage) left (UL). The middle section is divided into (stage) right center (RC), center stage (CS), and (stage) left center (LC). The tier closest to the audience is divided into down(stage) right (DR), down(stage) center (DC), and down(stage) left (DL).

In the United States all stage directions are given from the point of view of the performer as he faces the audience. Therefore, stage right (abbreviated SR) is to your right as you face the audience, stage left (SL) to your left. Upstage (US) is away from the audience, downstage (DS) is toward them. (The stage directions "upstage" and "downstage" originated when stage floors were slanted toward the auditorium for better visibility and acoustics.)

Subtext The unspoken feeling and meaning behind a character's words. When your character says "I love you," her subtext could be "I want you to give me that bracelet" or "Do you love me?" or "You are the most wonderful person I've ever met," depending on her objective.

Super (short for supernumerary) A performer without lines who is usually named in the script only generically—servant, soldier, etc. (In movies and television, these performers are called "extras.")

Super-objective A character's main goal (also called a "through-line of action"). It is the need that drives him to do what he does through the entire piece. Super-objectives are most clearly phrased in the form "I, (your character's name), *want* (*need* or *must have*), followed by a short (verb) clause: "I, Escamillo, *need* to be adored."

To upstage If a performer stands upstage of (above) his partner when he is listening, he is upstaging her—that is, forcing her to turn her back to the audience in order to stay in contact with him while she is singing. A performer can also upstage himself by standing downstage of (below) the person he is addressing. The term is also used metaphorically to refer to anything a performer does that inappropriately calls attention to himself, usually when someone else is talking or singing. Upstaging a colleague is both rude and bad craft.

Transparency The quality of allowing a character's feelings to show without faking or censoring. (See chapter 13 for more details.)

Upstage See *stage directions*.

APPENDIX 4

How to Research Period Practices
in Movement, Manners, and Gesture

A period piece is one that takes place in a time not our own. Clearly, there is some gray area about when a piece becomes a period one. Is *Nixon in China* by John Adams about Nixon's historic 1972 visit, premiered in 1987, a period piece? Probably not. Is Previn's *A Streetcar Named Desire*, premiered in 1998 but set in Louisiana in the early 1950s, a period piece? Yes and no. How about Kurt Weill's *Streets Scene*, premiered in 1946 and set in New York city about the same time? Probably yes.

To prepare to act a role in a period piece, you may have to research a different country, culture, era, and acting style. For a role in a Baroque opera, the composer, the country, and year in which the piece was premiered are usually the three most critical pieces of information you need. With the exception of traveling or imported productions, Baroque operas were presented using the staging conventions of the country in which they were performed, regardless of who wrote them or the era in which they were set. For instance, although it is set in Rome during Nero's reign, to learn how to move and gesture in Monteverdi's *L' Incoronazione di Poppea* (Venice, 1642), you will be well served if you familiarize yourself with mid-seventeenth-century Italian costumes, manners, dances, and stage practices.

As part of your preparation you should explore whether your character might carry any of the accessories of the period such as a fan or a sword; and if so, learn how to use that accessory under the tutelage of an expert.

Around the 1820s, composers and librettists became more concerned with local color and authenticity and paid more attention to veristic details. Therefore, for pieces written after that time you may need to research the social mores, manners, physical postures, and gestures used both in the composer's period and country and in the era and locale in which the piece is set.

If you are preparing to perform in *Pacific Overtures* (New York, 1976) or in *Madama Butterfly* (Milan, 1904), both of which are set at least in part in nineteenth-century Japan, you will need to learn how to move and gesture in a traditional Japanese manner. You will profit by becoming familiar with traditional Japanese culture, customs, and manners, including geishas, Buddhism, hara-kiri, the tea ceremony, and flower arranging. To clarify the issues either Puccini or Sondheim explored in his piece—and their viewpoints are very different—you will find it useful to be familiar with their lives and artistic interests, as well as the social history of Puccini's Italy and Sondheim's America.

Sources

Books

There is a wealth of books on the history, culture, and philosophical thought of every major historical epoch and nation. There are books on period dances and manners and others on stage conventions of different eras that include pictures and diagrams. There are books on furniture, architecture, clothes, and shoes (all of which affect people's movements), as well as stage costumes and scenery of different epochs.

Visual Materials

In your research, seek out pictures showing the way people lived, moved, danced, and dressed in real life, as well as how they presented themselves in opera and theater productions. Look in books; explore the internet; visit museums, galleries, and appropriate antique stores to study paintings, drawings, prints, photographs, sculpture, pottery, furniture, china, clothes, shoes, make-up, hairstyles, calligraphy, and jewelry. Often you can find collections of period clothing or complete period rooms in museums.

As you look at various visual materials, exercise your imagination. Imagine handling the objects: drinking from that teacup or stein, sitting on a particular chair, or working by a particular light. Speculate on the kind of lifestyle the objects and dress suggest. Ask "Is my character of the class of people who would have those things?" Think like your character. Ask "How do I spend my day and what objects would I use to do what I do?" "What do I value?" "What do I think is beautiful?"

Imagine yourself wearing the clothes and moving about in them. (Pay particular attention to the footwear.) Think about how you would get dressed and how you would achieve the hairstyles. Would you need servants to help you?

Pay attention to the way people stood. Notice how they placed their feet and held their hands. (Sculptures from the period are particularly helpful.) You can usually safely assume that the poses the artists chose are idealized: they are how people *wanted* to look, which makes them excellent models for you to imitate. (For Baroque operas set in ancient times, study Baroque rather than classical representations of Greek and Roman gods, goddesses, and mythical characters.)

Explore videos. Don't confine your research just to your piece. You may find a video on the country, culture, or era you are researching; you may find a dramatic piece that is set in the appropriate time or place or is about an important person of the period.

If you find a video of a production of your piece, be sure to view it with a critical mindset. Since every production is an interpretation, you should *never* use a video as your sole source of information about the style of a piece. At the very least, also listen to a recording while following the score. Any action that is not in the score or libretto, any change in setting or period from those indicated there, is an interpretative choice by the conductor, director, designers, or performers. You can protect yourself from foolish imitation by looking at these choices and trying to understand the purpose they are meant to serve—do they reveal the characters and their feelings in a way suggested by the score? Do they enhance the theme of the piece? Do they conform to the performance practices or people's behavior in the period?

Experts

You can get useful insights by talking with experts from enormously diverse disciplines. Be resourceful. For example, if you are doing research on *Madama Butterfly,* or on an Italian verismo opera like *Cavalleria rusticana,* you may be able to take advantage of America's wealth of immigrants. From some older adults you could learn about traditional values in either Japan or Sicily and perhaps even some specifics of manners and customs. For specific information on traditional Japan, you could also usefully consult with a well-informed teacher of Japanese, of Japanese martial arts or an expert on oriental antiques or Japanese flower-arranging. For either country, talking with an informed art or drama teacher, costume designer, or historian could prove fruitful.

Do remember that just as with the skills you learn from a vocal coach, you will be expected to apply those you learn from other experts within the parameters the conductor and stage director suggest as they shape the production and help you to create your character.

APPENDIX 5

Notes on the Exercises for Teachers and Directors

Experienced teachers and directors may want to skip to "Discussing the Exercises" p. 228.

Make Your Classes and Rehearsals Places for the Participants to Grow

Of the many ingredients in the learning stew, an ample and vigorous stock of trust promotes the most growth. However, like me, you may have discovered that trust can't just be whipped up. I have found that for the recipe to succeed, it is necessary to establish an understanding that the "rules" in an acting class or a rehearsal are special—different from the rest of the participants' day. They include:

- We are not in competition; there is room for everyone.
- We all work together, so that everyone can grow and be her best.
- We share what happens in the class or rehearsal and maintain complete confidentiality outside of it.
- We agree that classes and rehearsals are times to experiment; they are times to risk going "too far"—although we also understand that "too far" only applies to passionate interpretive commitment and not to any form of physical violence. Indeed, we agree that the theater is a place of *play,* that in the theater we never hurt anyone or anything, and that any dramatized physical violence will always be carefully rehearsed.
- We accept that in classes and rehearsals we do not always achieve our goals, and that this is part of the learning process.
- When we fall short of our goals, we do not make punishing criticisms of ourselves or others but value our attempts to stretch as a part of growth.

In addition, there are specific ways that you, as the head chef, can add trust to the learning stew. The most effective way is to exemplify it. If you want to create trust, be trusting; if you want your students or performers to be constructive in their judgments, criticize constructively. Some other useful ingredients are:

- Be honest about your own feelings.
- Share of yourself.
- Be scrupulously even-handed.
- Listen to everyone's opinions.
- When you disagree, honor the other person's viewpoint and be generous in explaining your own.
- Don't be defensive. Willingly acknowledge your mistakes.
- Always be supportive.
- Always assume that each person is doing the best she can at that particular moment. (If you know the student or performer is capable of doing better, assume that something must be in her way.)
- Expect a student or performer to do his best, but do not expect him to do things of which he is not (yet) capable.
- Don't use sarcasm.
- Never humiliate anyone.
- Be detailed and specific in your remarks so the student or performer can use them as a basis to improve. Don't tell a student or performer that something isn't working well, unless you can help him discover how to do it better.
- Focus on what is useful—what makes the scene/character/moment clearer or more effective.
- Avoid using the words "good" and "bad"; they are not sufficiently specific to be instructive, and can easily be heard as personal judgments. Use words like "clear," or "confusing," "powerful" or "ineffective," "engaging" or "uncommited," "vivid" or "fuzzy," "compelling" or "lacking energy," "believable" or "disengaged."
- Always mix any negative remarks with positive criticism.
- Make time to address students' or performers' fears, anxieties, and insecurities.
- Give your full attention to the participants and their work.
- If you demonstrate something for a student or performer, make sure that you are doing it to make them better, not to make yourself feel better. Do your demonstration for inspiration, not for imitation.
- Always stop any exercise that seems to be headed toward physical violence.
- Avoid slipping toward the role of therapist—rather than teacher or director—by keeping all your comments focused around the issues of being a performer, and of how to use feelings in the service of a role. Help every-

one see and discuss how each individual's acting problems are problems fundamentally shared by all.
- Encourage laughter.

Discussing the Exercises

The most effective way to build trust among members of a group and optimize everyone's learning experience is to have an open, frank, and generous discussion after every exercise or improvisation. Discussions help the students and performers to integrate any feelings the exercises have aroused; they help everyone—participants and observers alike—to move from the specifics of what happened to the general issues of how to successfully sing and act at the same time. In fact, often the most important part of each exercise is the discussion.

Allow ample time for both participants and observers to talk about their experiences. (If you run out of time, make a plan with the group to have a discussion at your next meeting.) Encourage each participant to talk. Frequently the most reticent students and performers have the greatest need to talk about their experiences. Ask what they discovered. (I often ask each participant "What felt real?") Ask the group how the exercise is relevant to acting. Keep everyone alert to moments during which you feel the participants manifested feelings appropriate to their situations. You should feel free to talk about things you discovered yourself, but take care not to dominate the conversation.

Discussions can fruitfully include issues of discomfort, nervousness, and fear. It is helpful for the participants to know that everyone (including yourself) has moments when he may experience those feelings in the process of being a student, actor, singer, teacher, director, or conductor.

Encourage the participants to talk not only about what feelings have been aroused but about their feelings about having feelings. Reassure everyone that having feelings appropriate to the situation is success! Remind them that:

- Exploring oneself is a fundamental part of the work of becoming an expressive performer.
- Although it may not always be fun, there is no harm in sharing strong feelings or stirring up distressing memories.
- A student or performer who becomes appropriately emotionally engaged deserves our respect and admiration.

It is also very helpful to discuss how to "cool down" after an emotionally hot exercise or improvisation. Talk about "cooling down" as an issue that all performers face.

Discuss the fact that:

- Just as allowing appropriate feelings is a legitimate part of developing a role, so is feeling wrought up after an exercise or rehearsal.
- People are different in the way they "cool down". Some people may need several hours, or very occasionally even as long as a day, to feel completely themselves again.
- Anyone's "cooling down" needs may be different at different times, and as a performer becomes willing to go deeper into a character's feelings, "cooling down" may take longer.
- "Cooling down" is a skill that will become easier with practice.

Remember that no matter how or why they are aroused, feelings are feelings. If a student or performer needs to leave the room to pull herself together, by all means allow it.

A Note About the Instructions for the Exercises and the Issue of "Right" and "Wrong"

You will find that the instructions for most of the exercises allow considerable leeway both in the way you may want to assign them and in the way the students or performers may execute them. As long as the students or performers engage in the process of an exercise, there is no wrong way to do it.

I tell my students and performers that if they cannot remember the instructions for an exercise exactly when they get home, they should just do what they thought they were supposed to and it will be fine as long as they work at it—and it always is.

Even if a student or performer does an exercise in a superficial way, he is not doing it "wrong," he just won't get as much out of it. (When someone dodges the central issue of an exercise, it is helpful to remember that you may be dealing with someone who is finding it scary to get in touch with himself as he struggles to develop himself as the instrument of his art.)

Chapter 1

Exercise 1: Facial Transparency

You can increase the participants' ability to sustain their concentration in this exercise if, after you give the instructions, you ask them to discuss what they think will be the hardest thing about doing it. Inevitably, someone will say "Not laughing." Discuss the temptation to laugh as a function of self-consciousness and negative self-judging. Suggest that if they keep their focus on the details of their tasks (either sustaining the feeling behind the mask or exactly reproducing the mask through imitation), their concentration is less likely to be sidetracked. Help them experience their tasks as important.

Exercise 3: Inhaling the Idea

This exercise may help you detect and analyze several breathing problems. Watch for breaths that are stopped or "held." Two typical holding spots are the upper chest and throat.

Make sure that the participants really exhale all their breath, and that they have the sense of sending it out across the room. You want them to experience both the feeling of their breath moving through their bodies and out into the world and the sense of filling that moving breath with feeling.

Students and performers sometimes have difficulty developing a strong motivation for singing their first phrase. Help them to develop compelling Given Circumstances, particularly *what* just happened.

It is effective to do this exercise in pairs, with the participants standing at some distance from each other.

Chapter 2

Exercises 2 – 5: Intensifying Feelings

If a participant needs help getting into an experience, feel free to coach from the sidelines. Ask questions that will get her involved with the details. (Questions about sensory experiences—color, temperature, or smell—often help.)

If you are working with the cast of a production, consider asking them to choose experiences that are relevant to feelings that their characters may have or to the theme of the piece.

Read chapter 3 for extra background to help you lead these exercises.

Exercise 2: Exploring

The point of these setups is to get the participants to invest in the Magical *if* and thereby to transform their movements, reactions, and feelings. If you can help them focus on specific details, you are handing them the key to using the Magical *if* effectively. Similarly, often it is tiny details—the slightest twitch, shift of weight, or change of expression—that will indicate whether the performer is or isn't really experiencing feelings appropriate to the circumstances.

Exercise 4: Public Scripts

Coaching from the sidelines is often helpful in this exercise. If a participant isn't really letting the feelings implied by the words emerge, try asking him to read more slowly. When he comes to a moment of particularly strong feeling, you may need to encourage him to let the feeling happen. Sometimes getting him to expand on what he has written can help. It can also be useful to have the performer read through all or part of the experience a second (or third) time.

Exercises 5 and 6: The Outcast; Carmen as Outcast

You may have to allay the participants' concerns about creating an improvisation in which they will be using the same setup that others are using. Remind them that there is no one "right" solution and if they react to what is really happening, their improvisation will be unique in any case. Remind them also, that the point is not originality but to commit to the situation so it arouses appropriate feelings. And they don't have to worry about boring any people who are watching, because if they are really involved, they will always be interesting to watch.

You can make up other scenarios like this one for your casts or students or help them to make up their own. You can blend fact, fantasy, and elements from extant plots or characters. (See "Ideas for Improvisations" at the end of chapter 3 for detailed suggestions about how to generate ideas for improvisations.)

Chapter 3

Unless the class or cast is already conversant with improvising, before they develop their improvisations, be sure to clarify that improvisations are not like campfire skits in which the participants can ham it up without getting involved in their characters. Rather, they are small dramatic scenes in which the whole purpose is to become genuinely engaged, so they experience feelings appropriate to their characters. Point out that it is counterproductive to retreat into embarrassed self-appraisals or to indulge in feelings that their characters would not have in the situation.

As the groups are developing their improvisations, visit each one and help them as needed. Make sure they have agreed on their *when* and *where,* and have developed lots of detail about their *who*(s). It is usually most useful to discuss the participants' *wants* individually. Not only should each participant's *want* and *why* be well defined but her *want* should engage her with the others, preferably in a way that may create some conflict. Be sure that each participant has something at stake in the outcome. For instance, if the improvisation involves one person telling her best friend that the friend's lover is cheating on the relationship, it is crucial that the informant has something at stake. Is she jealous? Does she *want* her friend to break off the relationship, because she *wants* the boy for herself? Is she angry? Does she want revenge? Unbeknownst to her friend, did she have a relationship with the boy years ago that he abruptly broke off? To help the participants commit to choices, it is useful to limit the preparation time.

Before the groups begin to "perform" their improvisations, point out to any people who are watching that they should respond not like a regular audience but rather as supportive colleagues; they should enjoy the scene but they should try not to interfere with the participants' concentration. Also, since you can often save an improvisation that is in trouble by giving some additional input through "sideline coaching," warn the participants that you may "coach" them as they are working. Tell them that if you speak to them during an improvisation, they should stop and listen but should stay in character.

If you do "coach," begin by reminding the participants to stay in character, and then give them the new instructions or ideas. You can coach the whole group at once, or you can go up to an individual and talk privately.

Unless an improvisation has a predetermined ending, such as exercise 2, "Moving Sculptures," you should instruct the participants to continue until you say its over. Often the most revealing and strongest moments come after the participants would have liked to stop.

After an improvisation the participants may feel very vulnerable. Be sensitive to their needs and be sure the group is also.

In the discussion, your comments will set the level at which the participants and any onlookers consider the exercise. No matter how trivial the action of an improvisation may seem, you can use it as the basis for a serious and detailed discussion about a wide range of acting problems, from concentration and believability to clarity and conviction in gestures and vocal expression.

A useful opening question is "What felt real?" It helps everyone focus on identifying moments when the participants experienced feelings arising out of the improvisatory situation. Even if such moments lasted only milliseconds, the participants have met the main objective of improvising.

Sometimes a participant may have a hard time believing that he really experienced the feelings of his "character" and needs to have successful moments pointed out. Sometimes the reverse occurs: a participant sincerely believes he had appropriate feelings that, however, didn't convincingly come across to you or other observers. It is best not to dispute the performer's impressions unless you can point to specific moments—in a supportive and non-confrontational manner—that were not convincing and can explain why.

The more detailed your remarks, the more useful they are. A generalized comment like "Your concentration was weak" gives the participant very little to build on. On the other hand, if you point out his actual behavior and exactly when it occurred, you help him recognize something that was not effective and thereby help him improve. For instance, "You broke your concentration right after you said . . . when you glanced out at me for approval."

It is useful to discuss how the participants can use any feelings that were aroused in pieces or roles they are working on.

Try assigning each observer a particular participant to watch in detail. In the ensuing discussion, after each participant has talked about moments that felt real to her, have her observer discuss instances that he felt were real. Insist that the observations be specific. In so doing you prod the observers to be critically clear about what was believable; you help them learn what believable acting looks like; and you encourage participants and observers alike to develop standards of judgment, and to accept no less than excellence.

Use the discussion to reinforce any growth—for example, increased physical expressiveness, which often occurs in improvisations.

Singing Improvisations

You will find that it is easy to start students and performers doing singing improvisations once they are comfortable doing speaking ones. Simply choose an exercise or set up an improvisation, and after they've done it as a spoken exercise, ask them to repeat it while singing. Remind them, as you should any group that is repeating an improvisation, to think of the repetition as a new improvisation using the same characters and the same Given Circumstances. In other words, that the new improvisation will be the same, but different.

Most novice improvisers worry excessively about singing wrong notes. You can ease their preoccupation with this issue by discussing what a "wrong" note might be in a situation where they (and the accompanist if you are using one) are making up the music. Emphasize that it is not important either to match pitches or harmonies with the other participants or the accompanist or to sing in the same style.

Encourage the participants to find opportunities for little arias in which they can explore their (character's) feelings by repeating words or short phrases; you may want to suggest that they may step aside to explore their character's feelings in "private" arias. Encourage them to also seek out opportunities for duets, trios, quartets, and larger ensembles.

Often some participants are reluctant to move beyond a sort of speaking-singing (parlando). The keys to getting the participants to really sing are to get them to focus not on the plot but on the feelings that are aroused in the situation and to have them feel free to repeat words or phrases that express those feelings several times.

You can help by coaching. When a participant delivers some word or phrase with feeling, coach him to repeat it several times, exploring different colors of his feeling. Singing your instructions as a little aria helps to set an example.

Naturally, all the instructions about leading speaking improvisations also pertain to singing ones, particularly the importance of the discussion afterward.

Singing improvisations provide a wonderful jumping-off point to explore why it is hard to sing and be believable at the same time. The ideal time for such a discussion is after a singing improvisation in which some, if not all of the participants did engage their feelings, so palpable evidence that it can be done is fresh in everyone's mind.

Accompanists

Singing improvisations can be equally successful with or without accompaniment. In my experience singers are divided just about equally as to which is easier.

Anyone who is proficient on her instrument and willing to try can accompany improvisations. You can help by suggesting that the accompanist think in terms of sound textures or patterns within which the singers can work, and that the textures should be harmonically predictable and not too dense. Remind her that she doesn't have to stick with any particular style, and that the music should change and flow with the feelings in the improvisation.

Encourage the accompanist to think of herself as a member of the ensemble, sharing but not directing. Reassure her that it is not her responsibility to make the improvisation go in a particular direction or have a particular outcome.

If you want the group to repeat an improvisation, tell the accompanist that she, too, should think of it as a new situation using the same characters and the same Given Circumstances.

Exercise 2: Moving Sculptures

As the participants begin, urge them to move slowly, using all parts of their bodies. Let them continue long enough so that everyone is in an interesting position before you call "Hold." As they are holding, ask them to observe the position of each part of their bodies.

Chapter 4

When you are discussing the concentration exercises, be sure to point out moments when a participant's concentration was good, as well as places where his mind wandered. (Watch the participant's eyes and body language for clues. When his concentration is good, his gestures will reflect a natural relationship between his thoughts, breathing, and feeling, and his eyes will flicker infinitesimally whenever he has a new idea.) In this way you help the participant to feel the difference between moments when he is fully engaged and when he is only partially involved; you also palpably demonstrate that an audience member really can tell the difference.

If it turns out that a participant's concentration wandered because he was distracted by vocal or dramatic demands, discuss those demands to help him establish how much attention he needs to give them and when. Help him to associate the proper technical instructions with his subtext.

If a participant is having difficulty getting emotionally involved in a situation, help him to "turn up the heat" on his *want* and *why;* make the situation more personal and immediate. Often it is useful to help him to find a contemporary equivalent that he can relate to in his own life by exercising his imagination or recalling an actual experience.

Exercise 4: Circle of Concentration

This exercise is a very effective group warmup. If you have the students do it on a regular basis, it will improve not only their concentration but their presence.

Chapter 5

The exercises for this chapter are designed to give the participants a new perspective on the material they perform by having them assume the mind-set of the people who created it.

Many students and performers feel intimidated about trying to compose. You can help them overcome their resistance by pointing out that these exercises are really only another form of role playing: "You don't have to *become* a composer, just act like one." Make it easy: ask for only one or two phrases and let them tape their tune rather than writing it. Use a relaxed and informal approach. Emphasize that there can be no wrong solution; engage in a discussion about their feelings about composing; do an ad lib demonstration yourself.

Exercise 4: Questions

This exercise works well if you assign different members of the group to explore different aspects or different phrases of the score. Be prepared for unanswerable questions!

Exercise 5: Composing

In the discussion of this exercise, have each "composer" talk about what she was trying to capture in her composition; then encourage a discussion of the specific musical means she employed to pursue her objectives.

Feel free to tailor this exercise to the participants' musical skills.

Chapter 8

Exercise 2: Fashioning Your Super-objective

If you have your students or performers analyze their lives for their own super-objectives, offer them the option of bringing their work to class or rehearsal but not having you read it. It frees them to dig deeper, and the point of the exercise is that they engage in the process, not that they reveal themselves to you.

Chapter 10

Exercise 1: Words Without Song

For this exercise, insist that the participants read and stress for meaning. Often with less experienced students you will have to work with them on what the words really mean, even when they are singing in English. When they are singing in a foreign language, such work is essential.

It is hard for students and young performers to believe that the printed translations in their music are not accurate. After all, they are printed! Depending on your personal convictions and skills, the participants' skills, and the time available, you may refer them to the translations that come with compact disks, to any one of the increasing number of books that print literal translations for well-known lieder and arias, to dictionaries, or to the internet.

Insist that the answers to questions such as "What is the theme?" are clear. Don't allow "sort-of" or "kind-of."

Encourage a group discussion about alternative interpretations. Be sure that each reader clearly commits to one interpretation—or at least, one at a time.

Chapter 11

Be sensitive to the enormous variations in how attuned people are to their bodies and, therefore, to the differences in their abilities to get the feel of sending energy. Touching them while they gesture can be useful, but respect their dignity by asking them first if its okay. You can help a participant to improve the flow of energy through his body by putting your hand on any spot where you notice a blockage. Have him make a large arm gesture and watch to see whether the movement seems to ripple along the entire length of the movement's pathway, or have him sing a phrase while making a gesture and look for a natural connection between the words and the gesture as well as for a liquid continuity in the gesture.

You can have the participants in exercise 2, "Pathways," help each other in a similar way. Have them pair up with one person standing behind the other. While the person in front does a large arm gesture, unfolding it from the base of his spine, instruct the person standing behind to gently run his hand up his spine, across his shoulder, and along his arm.

You can also help participants to feel energy moving through their bodies by leading them through visualizations. Begin by doing a relaxation exercise in which they lie on the floor with their eyes closed. (Just have them take ten slow, easy breaths, which you can count out if you like.) Then instruct them to create a sense of heat at the base of their spine. (You can substitute "energy" or "color" for heat.) Have them imagine moving the heat slowly up their spines, and into various parts of their bodies, at your direction.

After you have finished the visualization, have the participants discuss their experiences; if some of them don't "get" it, don't be discouraged. Instead, do such visualizations on a regular basis. (Wesley Balk, in *The Complete Singer Actor* and subsequent books, has developed many exercises to help students and performers become aware of their energy and use it to advantage in performance.)

Chapter 12

Exercises 1 and 2: Perfecting Your Public Persona; Practicing Parts

It is hard for performers to strike a balance between being natural and creating a positive impression. You can perform an invaluable service by giving them feedback. Create opportunities for your singers to practice walking across the room to a piano, stopping, and announcing themselves in front of a group.

As always, the more detailed the comments (whether from you or their peers), the more useful. "You look at the floor when you walk"; "Your stride is too long, it looks awkward"; "Your facial expression looks frozen"; "You sway when you talk" are examples of specific and constructive comments.

One of the most useful approaches to helping singers be natural and positive is to encourage them to get in touch with their pleasure in singing. Arrange to get together informally when they can hang around the piano and sing for each other. Have them talk about why they love to sing.

Chapter 13

Exercise 5: Creating Gestures

This exercise is both silly and hard, and therefore is fun and helpful to do in a group. You can do it as a warmup, having each person choose a song or aria that she knows by memory (or one from a piece you are all working on); then, in rapid succession, each person stands up and sings one verse, or maybe just a couple of phrases, from her chosen piece, making a gesture on each word. If she fails to gesture on a word, the others signal by clapping once. You can have her go back until she can do a section without missing or, better yet, quickly move on to someone else. Every person should have several opportunities to try. The speed and the silliness help everyone to loosen up.

Chapter 14

Exercise 2: Moving as Your Character

This exercise makes a wonderful pre-show warmup.

Index

Exercise titles are listed in quotation marks.
Page numbers appearing in italic type refer to exercises.